D1631329

QMUL LIBRARY

71465
25-7-68

LAWRENCE DURRELL
A STUDY

LAWRENCE DURRELL

A STUDY

by

G. S. FRASER

with a bibliography by
ALAN G. THOMAS

FABER AND FABER
24 Russell Square
London

WESTFIELD UNIV. LONDON COLLEGE

First published in 1968
by Faber and Faber Limited
24 Russell Square London WC1
Printed in Great Britain by
Latimer Trend & Co Ltd Plymouth
All rights reserved

S.B.N. 571 08526 X

© *1968 by G. S. Fraser*

CONTENTS

CHAPTER ONE

A 'PERSONAL-APPEARANCE' ARTIST

I

Wyndham Lewis, painter, novelist, poet, satirist, theo-rist of art, informal polemical philosopher, became, through *Time and Western Man*, a formative influence on the young Lawrence Durrell's theory of art. In a book of cruel criticism, *Men Without Art*, Lewis has a chapter called 'Mr Wyndham Lewis ("Personal-Appearance" Artist)'. Lewis, in fact, meant merely that as a satirical artist concerned with outward appearances he concentrated on the absurd way many people look and behave, not on romantic guesses about their inner selves. Yet Lewis was a 'personal-appearance' artist in another sense; like a great music-hall comedian or popular tele-vision journalist, like Max Miller or Malcolm Muggeridge, he is always doing his act, putting on his show, intimidating or cajol-ing his audience. He *is* the show. In this respect, and perhaps in this respect alone, Lawrence Durrell, a lyrical comedian, a comedian of sympathy, resembles Lewis, a harsh corrective comedian depending on the unsympathetic 'external eye'.

Any professional writer (I have been one) must salute first of all in Durrell a Protean quality, a versatility and virtuosity that has, however, something very solid behind it. There is in Durrell an honest journeyman of letters, a craftsman who will have a shot at almost anything, and create occasionally some-thing major or spectacular but always a workmanlike job. The range is very wide. There are poems and verse plays, as large an actual bulk of these as T. S. Eliot's. There are the three books about Mediterranean islands, Corfu, Rhodes, Cyprus, in a tradition that stems from Norman Douglas's *Siren Land* and D. H. Lawrence's *Sea and Sardinia*. These books have Douglas's urbanity, learning, unshockability, combined with something that Douglas did not in a high degree possess, Lawrence's immediate sense of heat, light, local emotion, landscape. There is something also in these books of the *panache* and the Burtonian interest in odd scraps of crazy or funny information (though Douglas had this too) of Durrell's friend, Patrick Leigh-Fermor.

One can add to the catalogue. There is *A Key to Modern Poetry*, not the work of a born critic, and written rather against the grain, when Durrell was lecturing for the British Council in the Jesuit-dominated city of Cordoba, on the pampas of Argentina; a book, nevertheless, which, though no masterpiece, throws a great deal of light on the attitudes towards Groddeckian psychology ('We are lived by forces we do not understand') and the Einsteinian notion of a space-time continuum that underlie *The Alexandria Quartet*. There are two early novels, of which the first, *Pied Piper of Lovers*, was put in for a first-novel competition with Cassell's; it did not win the competition, but was published, with a dust-jacket, a stiff Picassoesque Harlequin, designed by Durrell's first wife, Nancy Myers. Some early passages, based on Durrell's childhood memories of India, have great vividness, and are to be included in Alan Thomas's forthcoming anthology of Durrell on the spirit of place. Still, it is not very good on the whole; and Durrell's second novel, *Panic Spring*, published in 1937 by Faber, under the pseudonym Charles Norden, is very professional but essentially efficient *pastiche: pastiche* of the Norman Douglas of *South Wind*, the Aldous Huxley of *Those Barren Leaves*, the topic of the honest and complicated English puritan exposed to fierce or comical Mediterranean simplicities. I must admit I have not been able to read either of these books all the way through: still, *ex pede Herculem*. . . .

In Durrell's later life, there is a bewildering intermixture of works of high ambition and what might be called honest pot-boilers. There is *White Eagles Over Serbia*, a Buchanesque thriller which was accepted by Durrell's English publishers as first-rate for 'teen-agers, though Durrell had more in mind relaxing adults. Like the Wodehousian collections of stories about the comic diplomatist, Antrobus, this work suggested how much, in his popular works, Durrell was leaning on voracious childhood reading of middlebrow or lowbrow fiction. The Antrobus stories nevertheless had another quality, the tang of inner knowledge of Embassy life, which links them not only with Wodehouse but with Sir Harold Nicolson's small masterpiece, *Some People*. The novel first called *Cefalû* and later republished, with some revisions, as *The Dark Labyrinth* is a very interesting combination of nineteen-thirtyish or even nineteen-twentyish popular fiction techniques (stock characters, stock situations) with a very ambitious allegorical intention.

There are the poems, to which I shall be devoting a separate chapter; here Durrell's gifts are notable and his intentions are wholly serious. There are the three verse plays, *Sappho*, *Acte*, and *An Irish Faustus*, all of which have had a cool reception in this country, though *Sappho* was performed at the Edinburgh Festival, in 1961, with that fine actress Margaret Rawlings in the title role. In his plays as in his novels, Durrell seems to be an important writer who is nevertheless, in Yeats's phrase in *A Vision*, 'out of phase' with his time. *Sappho* was performed on the Third Programme in 1957, but the post-war English vogue for the verse play, the vogue of Eliot and Fry and Ronald Duncan, was over, and audiences were looking either for something like *Look Back in Anger* or like *Waiting for Godot*, for the Theatre of Social Protest or the Theatre of the Absurd. *The Alexandria Quartet* of rich, baroque novels similarly had to compete (though it competed reasonably successfully) with the critical naturalism and knock-about comedy, the strong dislike of any sort of pretentiousness, of the early novels of Kingsley Amis and John Wain. Durrell is in his mid fifties, was born in India, and has spent only about seven continuous years of his life in England. The relevance to us of all his writings, socially, is not that they reflect contemporary English language, manners, and attitudes, but that they remind us of traditions which we have, perhaps too carelessly, forgotten.

Standing apart, but in the same room as the centrally important *Alexandria Quartet*, is the early wholly personal novel, *The Black Book*, which, if it could have been published in London instead of Paris, might have importantly affected the trends of contemporary English fiction in the 1930's. These are both, in the Durrellian canon, major efforts, to which the author has given everything he has got. But, as he said in a correspondence with Henry Miller, which we shall be looking at in detail later, he does not feel that he can be making major efforts, except at considerable intervals of time. Yet, as a journeyman, he has to keep his hand in. When I knew him in Cairo in the early 1940s, for instance, he was (besides writing political leaders) turning out a 'Beachcomber' column for *The Egyptian Gazette* which was quite as amusing as J. B. Morton's famous column in the English *Daily Express*. A daily stint of writing, whether ambitious and important or not, is probably for Durrell almost a physical necessity. Not only a necessity, but a pleasure. As an all-round man of letters Durrell compares, in versatility and productivity, only with Robert Graves.

2

The comparison with Graves also suggests a contrast. Graves is a man whose whole life, in joy and suffering, has been dedicated to the Muse. The purpose of his prose books has been either to earn a living for his family or to throw light, as in *The White Goddess*, on what Graves thinks the proper life-stance of a poet should be. Graves writes poetry for love, not for the love of art, and poetry for him falls outside history, especially outside the history of literature. He is the most scrupulous of living verse craftsmen, but for love's sake, not for the sake of popular or academic fame. Graves, also, though a passionate is a puritan poet; a feeling of distaste for the body and its greedy and rebellious needs is always only just conquered in him by the robustness of his physical temperament, his toughness, and also his sense that the body is the strange instrument of love. The ordeal of marriage with Nancy Nicholson and of his poetic partnership with Laura Riding was, for Graves, not unlike the ordeal of trench warfare: there is a fine short poem suggesting a rueful relief in surviving, against all odds, both ordeals.

Durrell is quite different; he has not belonged to what Graves in his essay on Kipling calls 'the highest caste', the caste of the military officer on active service. There is no real tension in him, I think, between body and soul; one would call him basically a benignly lazy man, sensuous, humorous, contemplative, certainly not austerely passionate, self-torturing, haughtily witty, like Graves. I think he has not Graves's sense of the sacredness of poetry; he is certainly pretty modest—too modest, possibly—about his own, and thinks of himself less as the poet as such than as the lyrical comedian, the comedian-sage. Communion with the Muse, the passionate fulfilment of romantic love, is not for Durrell, as for Graves, an end, but a means. The whole point of *The Alexandria Quartet* is that through the splendours and miseries of romantic love, the whole barrack-room drill of it, it is possible for the victim of this passion, like L. G. Darley, to reach detachment, clarification, serenity, a benign distancing. This state, for which perhaps there is no one adequate word, is the proper state of the artist.

Graves is a puritan, not only in a moral sense, but in the classical severity of his style both in prose and verse; in his hatred of over-emphasis, obfuscation, showing off. Durrell, as an artist or craftsman, is at the opposite pole. He is a great show-off. Both his prose and verse, as Dr George Steiner has noted, have a rococo quality: set pieces, large mobile spectacular effects, sudden violent shocks, small amusing frivolities of detail. The rococo quality of Durrell's writing recalls the now fashionable epoch of *Art Nouveau*, or the work of the Sitwell family at its best—Durrell wrote regretfully to Sir Osbert about the first volume of his autobiography: 'More pedigree than prose!'—and contrasts sharply with the deliberate dry and flat sobriety of tone and simplicity of construction which have been the mark, since about 1953 (the date of Dylan Thomas's death) of the more promising younger English writers.

If one were to select a good writer of that younger generation, about as far away in feeling from Durrell—and in taste as well as feeling—as one can get, one would pick Philip Larkin, a great poet (possibly) of sad and fastidious rejection, a poet attracted by fantasies but grimly firm in his refusal to live them out. Durrell in fact differs from all his important younger English contemporaries in having managed to live, and seen nothing basically odd about it, a 'story-book' life. He has risked and achieved so much that, to writers like Larkin, he must seem almost tastelessly unreal. Yet one should add that Durrell's admirers (we often admire what is the opposite of ourselves) include some leading members of that 'Movement' generation: John Wain, Bernard Bergonzi (who has written the best essay I know of on Durrell's poetry), Alfred Alvarez. Alvarez, I remember, in a review, said that he expected on principle to dislike Durrell's poems but found that he liked them, an experience that may be fairly common.

Durrell's taste as a prose writer—a taste never sobered by a university education—is for colour and exuberance rather than sparseness or elegance. I would guess that in revising a prose narrative his inclination, like Balzac's, is to add and enrich rather than to cut down. Baroque or rococo art has in it an element of the showy, the hasty, the *trompe-l'oeil*. Durrell worked with enormous pains and care on the texture of his first important prose work, *The Black Book*, achieving in the end a prose almost indigestibly rich. He then learned, like one of his masters, Stendhal, the over-all gain to style that comes from writing rapidly and confidently. One could not, of course, call his prose style Stendhalian. Durrell likes what Pater called 'purple panels'. He is also by nature a brilliant *improvisatore*, and in *The Alexandria Quartet* two of his characters, Pursewarden and Capodistria, make up wonderful horror stories, rather in the manner of Baroness Blixen's *Seven Gothic Tales*; but almost all the characters are brilliantly inventive in narration, and might be brilliantly inventive liars. Yet the rapid writing and the fantastic ornamentations, scrolls and swags, have a deep sense of construction behind them. Durrell had been brooding for years on the pattern of *The Alexandria Quartet* (originally thought of as *The Book of the Dead*) before, in Cyprus, in the evenings, writing rather than typing so as not to awake his baby daughter, he set, in a large, hard-bound, quarto-sized ruled exercise book, pen to paper. Frequently, on the verso pages (Durrell's close friend Alan Gradon Thomas possesses the manuscript) there are simple schoolboyish drawings, of archetypes not persons, for the faces of Melissa and Justine.

3

Whom did Durrell come out of? (In the sense that all great Russian writers of the nineteenth century 'came out of Gogol's *The Overcoat*'.) Pursewarden, a choric figure, the type of the complete artist, in *The Alexandria Quartet* is perpetually setting up D. H. Lawrence as a code-hero for all modern novelists. How far does Durrell really connect with Lawrence? As a very young man, Durrell was furious about the attitude of the Home Secretary, Lord Brentford, towards *Lady Chatterley's Lover* and towards Lawrence's suppressed exhibition of paintings. He comes so little to England that, in spite of Frank Harris and John Cleland and versions of Sade on every railway bookstall, in spite of the mini-skirt and swinging London, he still thinks of our extremely permissive England of the 1960s as the pompous and puritanical England of the late 1920s and early 1930s. He does resemble Lawrence in having found England drab and petty and constricting, and having moved to warmer climates and simpler peasant societies; yet before he started living abroad, Lawrence knew England in his bones. An Anglo-Indian (in the older sense), born abroad, and going abroad again as soon as he could, Durrell never has, perhaps, really known England. He understands, what is something very different, the roles that Englishmen play abroad and the developing oddities, in a hot climate and a foreign setting, of English national character.

Dr. F. R. Leavis has described Durrell and his friend Henry Miller, in Lawrence's phrase about James Joyce, as 'doing dirt on life'. To critics who want to emphasize Lawrence's working-class roots, his passionate moralism, his brutal (sometimes) social *ressentiment*, Durrell's admiration for Lawrence must seem odd. But it is not so odd as all that. Durrell prides himself on his Irish ancestry, thinks of himself as Irish by temperament, is a formal experimentalist in the novel like Joyce, and yet, even in *The Alexandria Quartet*, is perhaps basically more like Lawrence. Like Joyce, he has his elaborate formal scheme, his rigid experimental framework; but in the actual detailed texture of the prose, one feels something like a Lawrentian spurt and lapse of creative impulse, quickness, immediacy, concentrated impact, impatient but piercing summary. Like Lawrence, also, Durrell seems sometimes in *The Alexandria Quartet*, the initial spurt having lapsed, to have to flog himself rhetorically along.

Durrell, nevertheless, differs both from D. H. Lawrence and from his own friend and mentor, Henry Miller, in not using much in prose the device, a device springing essentially from working-class speech, of repetition, of hammering away, again and again, on a key idea or phrase. He resembles Lawrence perhaps in his feeling for landscape and for the *genius loci*, the little god of a particular place; in Corfu, in 1965, he told me that favourite and revisited landscapes had a much deeper emotional meaning for him than favourite and revisited people. In this sense of the magic of place he resembles not only Lawrence but Kipling, a writer as essentially isolated as Lawrence, and, like Lawrence, a fierce prophet, a fabulist; as I have said, the only good passages in Durrell's first novel, *Pied Piper of Lovers*, seem to be the Kiplingesque ones, India through a child's mind. . . . But where Durrell, of course, is to some admirers of Lawrence shockingly different from Lawrence is in Durrell's ironic tolerance of, humorous sympathy with, a wide range of odd kinds of sexual behaviour. Yet, even there, is one quite sure? Lawrence had his own kind of tolerance of strange behaviour, of daring sensuality, in what he felt to be fundamentally a life-giving relationship.

In the end, for Durrell, in *The Alexandria Quartet*, the nearest one can get to an ideal relationship between a man and a woman is neither the compassion-love of Darley for Melissa nor the mutually destructive 'passion-love' of Justine and Darley but the much calmer 'loving-kindness', ending in soul-friendship, of Darley and Clea. Strife between men and women, the male desire to dominate, the woman's desire to under-mine, are all central in Lawrence; he is very much a novelist of the will. The love-relationships in *The Alexandria Quartet* are usually quite detached from the will, the desire for power over others; love is an unwilled event in the history of the psyche, men and women, or men and men, or women and women, are brought together not of their own volition but through the working out of a life-pattern, Groddeck's trans-cendental It. There is a great deal of violence in *The Alexandria Quartet* but, apart from one attempted suicide of a middle-aged homosexual who has been repulsed by a worth-less young man, and apart from the kicking to death of Scobie in his woman's disguise by frustrated and furious sailors, the layers of motivation behind the violent acts have to do with political necessity or family honour not with sexual possessive-ness. Durrell's characters in this novel are immoral by conven-tional standards, but they do not treat each other as objects. The need for distance or separateness, even in the most intimate relationship, the need to respect the otherness of the other, is something which Lawrence felt, but which Durrell feels even more deeply.

One says all this. Yet one should add that Durrell's first important art-work in narrative prose—'novel' has the wrong connotations—*The Black Book*, expresses a violent revulsion against what Durrell calls 'the English disease'. The phrase 'the English disease' suggests the Elizabethan phrase for the pox, 'the French disease', and also the nineteenth-century French phrase for flagellomania, 'le vice anglais'. Durrell is not being so clinically specific. The animus behind *The Black Book*—given that Lawrence is writing about decaying aristocracy, decaying industry, hampered and frustrated love in the still half-rural, half Early Industrial Revolution Midlands, where Durrell in *The Black Book* is depicting a scabrous and obscure outer London bohemia—is not dissimilar to the animus behind *Lady Chatterley's Lover*. Both Lawrence and Durrell are concerned in these books with what Durrell calls 'the English death': they are both concerned with the question which the young Auden posed, in 1932, at the beginning of *The Orators:* 'What do you think about England, this country of ours where nobody is well?'

The animus which the young Durrell shared with Lawrence was against a failure of happy, direct, and spontaneous inter-relationships; against the deadening and sterilizing effect of intellectual or social self-conceit, and of self-protective self-enclosure. Sourness, pretence, affectation typically grow up in a community where a class system, a system of social deference, no longer corresponds with a power system or, more broadly, with the needs of the total functioning of society. It is a great pity, even today in England, that an artist has either to pretend to be a gentleman or to make too much of a defensive or offensive ploy about not being one; that it is not enough to be creative, generous, and direct, one must also try to be smooth and clever. Both Lawrence and the young Durrell were terribly aware of the corroding effect on the feelings of the malice that is bred by a pervading pretentiousness based on a pervading sense of insecurity. The feeling behind *The Black Book* is not unlike Lawrence's famous reaction, in his letter about an evening with David Garnett and Francis Birrell, against Cambridge cleverness: the endless emission of preformed and processed ideas, coming out of the mouth like black-beetles, and the distorting and sterilizing effect of the cult of condescending cleverness on the soul.

Durrell thus very much resembles Lawrence in that his standard of response, to people, situations, scenes, is very much a 'life-standard'. He responds to those aspects of life in which he finds hope, resilence, generosity, fulness of being, livingness; he recoils from occlusion. He differs from Lawrence in his far wider gift of comic sympathy (in this, at least, he does resemble Joyce rather than Lawrence). He responds with rich comic sympathy to characters like Scobie in *The Alexandria Quartet*, the aged transvestist with his 'tendencies', from whom Lawrence might have turned away in disgust (though saying this one should remember Lawrence's warm appreciation of Baron Corvo and his remark, in one of his letters, that he admired Norman Douglas as a man who was never afraid to follow his own truest impulses). The whole question is tricky, for there was in Lawrence himself a deep layer of latent homosexuality. The Lawrentian male must dominate and the woman who herself seeks equal satisfaction is a betrayer. In this sense (Stephen Marcus's recent book on Victorian pornography and official Victorian attitudes to sex might bear this out) Lawrence, born in the Victorian age, remained always a late Victorian. Latently homosexual relationships are a standard feature of Victorian fiction (Sherlock Holmes and Dr Watson, for an obvious example). In Lawrence the latency did not remain comfortably latent enough; hence Gerald and Birkin, the embarrassing business about 'blood-brothership' with Middleton Murry, the general streak of feminine spitefulness when Lawrence is referring in his letters to other male authors. . . . It is, on the other hand, because Durrell is an extraordinarily purely masculine creature, because there is no homosexual component at all, that one can feel, in his make-up that he attracts the trust and companionship of so many men of so many different kinds, is at ease in any company. Just because he is not at all drawn himself that way, he can treat a character like Scobie with humorous sympathy. And he does not, unlike Lawrence, have any personal reason for insisting on monogamous marriage as the only valid solution for the sex problem. He has had three marriages, the first two stormy, but in each case to an extremely attractive woman. He does not think that, to be valuable, a relationship must also be permanent.

Yet it could be said that, like Lawrence, Durrell reacts, especially in *The Black Book*, against the sterile, the deadening, the dead. He can present sexual scenes that are perverse and horrible but the presentation of the children in the child brothel in *The Alexandria Quartet*, for instance, has a note of compassion and horror, not of authorial complicity. Unlike the Marquis de Sade, from whom he takes his epigraphs in *The Alexandria*

Quartet, Durrell is not a didactic writer; he is not saying, 'Go thou, and do likewise.' He is simply taking in, as compared to Lawrence, a much wider range of the disturbing oddity not so much of human sexual behaviour as the layers of motivation and habituation that underlie it. Sexual behaviour is for Durrell an element in narrative composition, a source of crucial instances of human character in action. It is not an end in itself for, in Durrell's deeper philosophy of life, the sexual is something that must be transcended. And one of the chief themes of *The Alexandria Quartet* is, of course, that sexual obsession is a main source of error and illusion; it is as Darley slowly liberates himself from his obsession with Justine that he begins to see his experiences and those of the other characters for what they really have been. He has to separate even from Clea before he or she can truly understand and achieve the vocation of the artist. T. S. Eliot's *Waste Land* is all about sex and about the ways in which, used unsacramentally, it can go wrong; but it is not thought of as either an improperly exciting or an immoral poem. Durrell considers this most insistent, shocking, intense, absurd, comical and wonderful of human impulses as a signpost —towards its own transcendence and a new ordering of the self.

Deeply as Durrell admires Lawrence (and admired Lawrence in his youth, long before Dr F. R. Leavis had battled for a recognition of Lawrence's life and seriousness by the English departments of universities), one can see why Dr Leavis disapproves of Durrell, and why Lawrence might have. Sexual episodes are often broadly and coarsely funny for Durrell; Lawrence is by no means without a sense of the comedy and incongruity of sexual relationships, but he disapproves of the kind of comedy that is external and hard—he would disapprove of Pursewarden's view of seduction as a great joke, of Durrell's sympathy for a comical rake like Pombal. He might think of Durrell also as aiming ultimately at the kind of mind-intimacy which Lawrence so abhorred in Poe. And Poe comes in aptly here; there is a taste in Durrell for the grotesque, the macabre, the sinister, which might derive partly from Poe, partly from the darker side of Dickens, the uncomfortable combination of the sinister, the grotesque, and the farcical in characters like Fagin or Quilp. Like Dickens, Durrell sometimes enjoys frightening his readers; there is a 'Gothick' strain in him. This darker strain gives depth to his work without dominating it. He is a human writer of wide imaginative receptivity; not a pornographer of either lust or cruelty, and not, like Sade, a kind of marvellous monster. He does not 'do dirt on life' but is a writer sometimes obsessed by the dark underside of things, the secret, the unspeakable, the forbidden, what Jung calls the Shadow. His robust appetite for life, the sun, landscape, food and wine, companionship, fights, I would guess, against a deep and recurrent awareness of the death-wish. Benign and jovial as his personality is, he can in black moods (a very close friend of his told me) sometimes seem 'a devil incarnate'.

4

He is also a careful and conscious artist. Once in Cairo, when I was going through a dry and dead period in my attempts to write poetry, Durrell asked me to consider the example

Pale horizontal sky, dark curving valley

It seems flatly descriptive, except that it is not clear exactly what one would mean by call the sky 'horizontal': perhaps that one has the sense of the sky behind a valley spreading sideways, like a theatre backcloth, rather than descending vertically. The line of verse, anyway, is like a sketch for a painting, a dark U-shaped or V-shaped foreground, a pale flat background, a fairly simple colour and shape contrast. Take it that one finds this dull. Try out instead an apparent nonsense:

Dark curving sky, pale horizontal valley

This suggests a silvery or sandy foreground, a valley which is almost flat, with a thundery cloudy sky bulging forward above it —if, indeed, it suggests anything. Tinker about with it again, and you might get something mysterious:

The valley sky, dark curved horizon paling

What Durrell was suggesting to me was that for the poet whose feelings have gone stale a kind of manipulative magic with words used almost as coloured counters, a cold ritual, may prove spiritually refreshing; it may renew one's sense of power over words at least.

Durrell has also several times, especially when I was in Cairo and very short of money, emphasized to me the importance, if you are trying to write a novel, of writing rapidly and even carelessly. This showed acute insight into why, in various attempts over the years to write a novel, I have never got much beyond Page One Chapter One. With the exception of *The Black Book*, all Durrell's novels, even *The Alexandria Quartet* or rather each of the four members composing that, have been written like *La Chartreuse de Parme* in a space of weeks, not, like *Madame Bovary*, in a space of years. The only time I met Ian Fleming he told me that, to write each of the James Bond novels, he abandoned himself to a trance-like state and wrote rapidly and incessantly for two or three weeks, the story being the only reality for him, the outer world a pale illusion: John Buchan similarly wrote *The Thirty-Nine Steps* during a fortnight's convalescence. Durrell has been as ambitious as Stendhal and as much an entertainer as Buchan or Fleming, but his productivity like theirs depends on the ability to bracket off 'the real world', to devote all his energies, for a given short time, to the play of imagination or fantasy. Whether it is imagination or fantasy that queens it over Durrell's world—basically, how 'serious' a writer he is—is, I suppose, the key critical question about him.

One talks of bracketing off 'the real world', but of course the creatures of Durrell's imagination or fantasy are very 'real' to him and to many of his readers. In Corfu, Durrell showed me a letter to him from one of his great comic creations, Scobie. Scobie explained: the story in *The Alexandria Quartet* that he had been kicked to death by sailors and had subsequently become a Moslem saint was all a taradiddle; he had returned to England

and set up in partnership with his dear old friend, who used to manufacture earth-closets, Toby Mannering, but they were now in a bigger way of business, and in a more advanced stage of technology, manufacturing water-closets. The tone was authentic. The writer *must* have been Scobie. . . . Durrell was half willing to believe this. For part of the philosophy underlying *The Alexandria Quartet* is that there is a life-pattern inside all of us that will work itself out, comically or tragically, with certain variations, wherever we find ourselves. You take your basic character wherever you go with you, but a change of setting and circumstances can alter your fate. Durrell, I think, believes in fate, but in a fate loosely predetermined; a new setting can allow an apparently quite new aspect of character to flower. Thus, in *The Alexandria Quartet*, Johnny Keats, the comic and feeble poet-cum-journalist, goes to fight in the Western Desert and acquires an exulting Dionysian ferocity apparently quite foreign to his former self; yet, still restless, excitable, a febrile chatterer, he is the old self as well as the new self, an old self that has found room for fuller growth. The seeds of the new self were there from the beginning.

Durrell, to put this another way, is concerned in his fiction not with a growing change in character, in response to changing challenges, but with a process of self-discovery, a stripping away of layer after layer of the self of outward social habit, till a hard core is revealed, which was always there, and in a sense always half-known. In this respect, he is more like an ancient historian than a modern novelist. Collingwood, in *The Idea of History*, points out that ancient historians take it for granted that Tiberius was always very wicked but needed to become Emperor before he could show how wicked he really was, whereas the modern historian's picture of Tiberius would be that of a good soldier and public servant whose character slowly deteriorated under accumulating pressures of strain, disappointment, and fear. Durrell, in this sense if not in others, is a classical writer. A preoccupation with the mystery of self-identity lies at the core of *The Alexandria Quartet*.

People, for Durrell, are not themselves, but are layers of disguises, tricks, deceptions when one meets them day by day. True friendship, true knowledge of identity, is discovered when friends or lovers live at a great distance from each other, each on his own special psychic island, like Clea and Darley, and write each other what Auden calls 'long, marvellous letters'. For Donne, no man was an island; for Durrell, every man is. It is by long marvellous letters that Durrell and close friends of his like Henry Miller and Alfred Perlès keep in touch. Durrell described to me in Corfu how each of his friends among the Greek writers, Seferis, Katsimbalis, and the others, has his favourite island of retreat. Each despises and yet humorously appreciates the other's choice. Durrell's own Corfu, for instance, is thought by many of his mainland friends to be too soft and subtle and Venetian, too unGreek.

Every man is an island, but letters pass between islands. For Durrell, perhaps, the state of earthly beatitude is a state—for all the dances in the tavernas, for all that we must 'break the ring'—of peaceful inner solitude in communion with seascape and landscape; a state in which memories of friends take on a legendary or heraldic, a complete and symbolic quality. The actual presence of the friends, the rubs and gaps and awkward-nesses of daily communication, might shatter the image. A guest like a fish, says the Mediterranean proverb, stinks after three days. But there are the long, marvellous letters; and there are occasional short meetings, the more significant for being short.

5

In 1965 I spent a marvellous week-end in Corfu with Durrell and his third wife Claude, who died tragically in 1967. I had already been asked to write this book, and so I asked Durrell some technical questions. Were his poems, for instance, planned in advance or did they grow from a 'given' image, phrase, or cadence? Would he think of them (they are sometimes cryptic and incomplete) as the poems of a novelist, or did he prefer to think of his prose fictions as the novels of a poet? It was late at

24

night, and Durrell and I were sitting on a wooden bench fronting the dark sea: by the bay on which Odysseus may have landed when he met Nausicaa (a great crusader's castle, in its deep foundations perhaps King Alcinous's castle, lay up a windy road on the hills behind us).

I asked my questions and Durrell told me that I must know from my own experience as a poet how silly it is of the critic to ask such questions, how dangerous to the poet himself to attempt to answer them. The centipede, in fact, dare not ask itself which foot it habitually puts forward first. . . . Durrell, in fact, works by flair and intuition. When he gives interviews, he plays up, in a friendly but often also in a spoofing way, to the special interests of the people who are probing him. It is a privilege (though in working on this book I found it created a very protracted writing-block) to know an author reasonably well, as a person, when one is writing about him. But in the end one must treat him as if he were dead or a stranger or somebody known only from bald facts and dates about his life. One must work out for oneself the puzzles that arise from the words on the page.

Yet, though I think of this book as a critical rather than a biographical study, Durrell's personality has fused with his *persona*, and is very much at the core of his art. So I would like to give some personal impressions of him, followed by a very brief account of his background and history.

I was a shabby little private at G.H.Q., in Cairo, almost hysterically lonely and miserable, when I first met Durrell in 1941, but he had liked some things he had read of mine, and was beautifully kind to me. He had got out of Crete just in time, with his first wife Nancy. After some years in Cairo, Durrell went to work as Press Attaché in Alexandria. I saw him over these years briefly and occasionally, but our meetings were always memorable, at least to me (I was two or more years in Eritrea, out of his orbit). He is a short, stocky, sturdy man, what Kretschmer calls a 'pyknic type'; and he has the gift, which according to Kretschmer often goes with this physique, of creating instant sociability.

My daughter Helen, when she met Durrell in Corfu in 1965, described him as a 'jolly little satyr' in her travel diary. In Corfu, in tavernas in the evening, Durrell was always getting us up from the table to join in Greek round dances. 'We must break the ring,' he would say. Breaking the ring, making every-body join in, is his great social gift (the breaking of a ring of power, forged by black magic, is the central motif of his best verse play, *An Irish Faustus*). I forget whether he sang while he was dancing, but he has a very pleasant voice—to be heard in his poems—light in timbre, musical, a little catch or roughness in it, the voice of a musical-comedy star of the 1920s and 1930s like Jack Buchanan. (He wrote some tin-pan-alley lyrics in the 1930s, to make money, but they tended to be rejected as 'too highbrow': Alan Gradon Thomas possesses a very funny gramo-phone record in which Durrell sings a song of his own invention which is a homage to, rather than a parody on, Noel Coward.) My daughter's phrase was apt in that Durrell's appearance, his stocky vitality, does suggest a satyr, a jolly woodland demigod: in a bar in Cairo, at some time in the 1940s, Sir John Waller took a photograph of Durrell in which—no doubt because of the way in which his hair was brushed—short stubby horns seemed to be about to grow out of the corners of Durrell's forehead.

Cairo, between 1941 and 1945, was a city through which many poets passed, and in which some lingered. As poets, they were good, bad, and indifferent; as persons they were as fascina-ting as characters in *The Alexandria Quartet*. This was the time, in the title-phrase of Hazlitt's essay, of 'my first acquaintance with the poets'. There I met Durrell himself, Bernard Spencer, Terence Tiller, Hamish Henderson, Ruth Speirs, John Gaws-worth, John Waller, Hugh Gordon Porteous, Uys Krige, Dorian Cooke—who crops up in Durrell's poem *Alexandria*:

> . . . *the small, fell*
> *Figure of Dorian ringing like a muffin-bell*

I have forgotten, in that list, my friend Iain Fletcher and a poet of belated great fame, Keith Douglas. The best of these were published in the periodical of which Durrell was the main editor, *Personal Landscape*. He was very busy, I think, but found time to be kind. He could also be cross. Scribbling-mad in those years, I wrote an impression of my first long conversation with him, called, on the model of Laurence Housman's impression of Oscar Wilde's conversation in Paris, *Echo de Paris*, *Echo du Caire*. I left it with Reggie Smith and Olivia Manning, Durrell found it, and furiously tore it into shreds. He cornered me about it and told me that I could be a poet but seemed more interested in becoming a snotty little journalist, interested only in whether the poet picks his nose.

I saw Durrell briefly in London in late 1946 or early 1947, one evening in The Hog in the Pound in Oxford Street, a pub in which Tambimuttu, the editor of *Poetry London*, used to hold court among the poets. Durrell was polite, but obviously bored with all the company, except David Gascoyne, whose poetry he much admired; but he told even David to speak up and stop mumbling. I felt in that particular evening of Crippsian twilight that Durrell had moved away from that London bohemian world, still exciting to me, of near-poets and weak-beer pubs; indeed, he left us early, to dine with some diplomatist friends. People like myself had described Durrell vividly to our London friends, from our Middle East experiences of him, and I think many of them were a little disappointed: a close woman friend of mine said to me: 'He is a nice, bouncy, comical little man, but you all talked as if he were the tops!' The rationing, the drabness, the weak bitter beer, the generally rather slugged air of immediately post-war London must have been uncongenial to Durrell. My closest friends and I didn't feel this; we were simply relieved that the war was over and we were out of the Forces.

After that meeting in late 1946 or early 1947, Durrell and I corresponded a little, for I reviewed many of his volumes of poems as they came out, and always appreciatively. The success, the world success, of *Justine*, *Balthazar*, *Mountolive* and *Clea* delighted but, I must confess, at first slightly piqued me: there is always a mixture of feelings when a writer whom one knew and admired in one's struggling youth achieves the triumph that still eludes one in one's struggling middle age. . . . But we did continue to write to each other. Durrell's letters were sometimes sharp. I had edited an anthology, *Poetry Now*, into which out of a democratic sense of fairness, the worst possible quality in an anthologist, I had put far too many poets. The poets I included attacked me for putting in the other poets I had included, and the very few I had left out were crosser still. Durrell thought the whole thing a spoof, a solemn piece of irony, and reproached me for 'looking down a long nose' at contemporary poetry and trying to make the poetic effort in our world today appear futile. There was another letter in which Durrell tried to arouse my interest in a peculiarly bogus new religion or philosophy invented by some retired American businessman. A spoof, a solemn piece of irony on Durrell's part (I was the sort of person likely to swallow anything)? Or an odd revelation of a streak of gullibility of his own? I do not know.

6

At last, after agreeing (with queerly mixed feelings) to write this book, I saw Durrell in the summer of 1965 in Corfu after a lapse of nearly twenty years. I was spending a camping holiday in Italy and Greece with my wife and three children. Scrambling up from his cottage by the sea to meet us, bulging muscularly out of khaki shorts and a short-sleeved sweatshirt, Durrell, biscuit-brown with the sun, seemed hardly changed physically. We spent two or three days camping under his oleanders, visiting King Alcinous's castle, swimming a lot— Durrell is bouncily at home in the sea like a dolphin—and eating and drinking and dancing in taverns in the evening. He enchanted my children by his hearty profanity and schoolboyish swearwords: 'Don't worry about washing your clothes too much,' he would say. 'Sweat into your shirts and cross yourselves backwards.' As always before, I felt what a life-giver he is, making everyone around him jolly and relaxed, making them feel more amusing than they are: and yet ultimately how very rum, how very mysterious! Late on one long night of talk he suggested that he and I should grab the one remaining bottle (they were old gin bottles which he had filled with retsina from a cask), swim out with it so far to sea as we could, swig it down between us, and sink: 'Think what a service that would be, George, to English literature!' He swam out far, but I went to bed: the next morning he had swum a mile before I was up, and was fresh as a daisy . . . though saying that, but for the weather, but for the sea, we had drunk enough the night before to kill ourselves.

We dined, I remember, one night with a very distinguished thinker, Denis de Rougemont. This stern Swiss Calvinist, famous for his denuciation of romantic love as the most dangerous of Western heresies, was the last person I would have imagined a possible close friend of Durrell's, but they were obviously *vieux copains*, who took a delight in teasing each other. In this vein, Rougemont asked me why on earth I wanted to write a book about Durrell. Catching the mocking tone, I said, though in clumsy and stammering French, no doubt it was a bit of a let-down after writing about Eliot and Pound and Yeats, but wasn't Durrell unique in some sort of way?—in his gift, both in prose and verse, of giving personality to landscape, of making it the embodiment, almost the definition of a particular mood? And (I added) in his lyrical comedy, in his gift for blending the comic, the fantastic, and the macabre? Had he not after all, which is the central thing one asks of any real writer, found his own voice, created his own world? The subject of this discourse sat smiling enigmatically, like a small Buddha, and soon had us all 'breaking the ring', dancing.

Leaving Corfu very early one morning, to get the car ferry to Igoumenitsa on the Greek mainland, when Durrell and his wife Claude and her son by her first marriage Barry were still fast asleep after our wild last night, I had a vague sense of the whole visit as slightly unreal, like something in a story, but at the same time exhilarating. I was left with the old sense of Durrell's gift for immediate intimacy. In his unbounded social and physical energy I saw, more clearly than before, the roots of his gifts as a writer. I had noticed also a reserve, a sense of proportion which suggest that much is hidden under what, in *The Black Book*, he calls his 'ingenuous mask'. We had talked of a dear friend of both of us, a fine poet, who had recently been killed in an accident: 'Silly old thing to fall off a train like that,' Durrell said. We talked of a woman we both knew and liked: 'Not *beautiful*,' he said in the slightly irritated tone a tutor uses to correct a student with a tendency to gush or exaggerate, 'just very, very *pretty*!' Behind the solid physical and social presence, there was something Protean, elusive, unpredictable. The gaiety perhaps had something latently menacing in it, like the gaiety of a Greek satyr-play. Odd contradictory images floated into my mind. A jolly suburban businessman standing double whiskies at the nineteenth hole: and a smilingly in-scrutable Taoist hermit. I thought also of Aldous Huxley's famous description of D. H. Lawrence, in his introduction to his edition of Lawrence's letters, as differing from all the other very gifted men Huxley had known not in degree but in kind.

It would be wrong to call Durrell inhuman, subhuman, or superhuman. He has as much touchiness and vanity as most other writers, he gets worried about what the critics will say; and as a man, he likes to be liked, a very human and endearing weakness. (Some of the very greatest writers are free from it.) There are plenty of people, like my perceptive woman friend in London, like non-literary colleagues of his whom I had known in Cairo, to whom Durrell is merely 'a jolly little man'. This elusiveness of the inner core is a main key to Durrell's achieve-ment as a writer. Voluble and explicit, Durrell yet leaves very much unsaid; and in particular he may deliberately stress very lightly things that are of very deep importance to him.

7

If one were wanting to define Durrell's central gift as a writer, one would find oneself thinking in terms of theatrical performance rather than of strictly literary achievement: what one is most aware of is a fluent and fluid, light and easy mastery of the audience, an actor's sense of timing, never lagging, always belting it along. There is nothing of that sharp and severe separation, which Eliot admired in Flaubert, and perhaps exemplified himself, between the man who suffers and the artist who creates. The charm, the vivacity, and the unpredictability of the man are at the core of the artist's achievement. 'Love me, love my dog': one cannot like Durrell's writing without liking, or thinking that one likes, Durrell. He belongs with those writers like Byron, like Oscar Wilde, like Yeats, whose artwork is essentially a kind of life-commentary, and who do not make full sense till we read their poems or novels alongside their letters or journals (for instance, Durrell's letters to Henry Miller or the intimacies of his island books). The art is what the *persona*, the actor of the literary role, has made out of the often troubling and untidy adventures of the personality. Durrell's art is what Durrell has made out of Durrell; transforming Durrell into the playing parts of Lawrence Lucifer or Lawrence George Darley (L.G.D., 'Lineaments of Gratified Desire').

Something, then, about Durrell's family background and literary formation. Social class, the great obsession of so much English fiction, has never mattered much to Durrell. He was not at a major public school or at Oxford or Cambridge and told me, in Corfu, that I would be wasting my time trying to track down the Durrells in Burke or Debrett. He was born in India, in 1912, his father an English civil engineer, his mother an Irishwoman. He likes to think of himself as Irish rather than English by temperament (I do not think that he has ever visited Ireland). The Indian childhood, the heat, the colour, the still Kiplingesque social atmosphere deeply affected his childish imagination, though he has never gone back to India. The family, which included two brothers and a sister (one brother, Gerald, is also famous as a writer) came back to England when Durrell was at the prep-school stage, settling for a time in Bournemouth. Durrell was at various private schools, but though the hero of his second novel, *Panic Spring*, is a school-master, his school years did not have the emotional importance for him that they have for many English writers. His gift for learning languages and his enormous and accurate English vocabulary suggest, however, that at some stage he was well taught; though these gifts may owe more to an early passion for reading and a quickness of social response in foreign milieux. Very early, Durrell wanted to be a writer. He hated the English climate, the small pretences and snobberies of the pre-war English class system—the atmosphere of Bournemouth, the genteel seaside town, full of retired people, may have sharpened this hatred. One dreary winter he suggested that his mother and brothers and sister should move to Corfu, where the climate and the people would be a pleasanter, and where it would be cheaper to live.

Gerald Durrell, Lawrence Durrell's younger brother, in describing this move in *My Family and Other Animals*, says:

> Larry was designed by Providence to go through life like a small, blond firework, exploding ideas into other people's minds, and then curling up with catlike unctuousness and refusing to take any blame for the consequences.

Lawrence Durrell figures throughout this book as a delightful figure out of a James Thurber story or a Brian Rix farce: lying in bed in his burning bedroom, for instance, which he has set on fire himself out of sheer carelessness, swigging brandy, and ordering other members of his family to fetch buckets of water. Gerald Durrell notes a trait which was one of the first I myself noted in Lawrence Durrell: a tendency to give people brief authoritative lectures on subjects about which they might claim to possess as much expertise as, or more than, himself. Yet one should not take the comic character in Gerald Durrell's book as drawn wholly in the round. These Corfu years coincided with the very painful years of literary apprenticeship, recorded in Lawrence Durrell's own *Black Book* and in his correspondence about this with Henry Miller.

Like many young writers, Durrell discovered his purely verbal talent, his fluency and skill in handling words, before he discovered who he was, what his own real voice was like, what was the original and personal and new thing he had to say. His first two novels are in a conventional mode. His early poems had much more individuality than his early prose, but lacked any very definite stance. The leading or the most discussed younger poets when Durrell began to write and publish poems in the 1930s were Auden, MacNeice, Day Lewis, and Spender. Rather in reaction against these, or at least doing contrasting things, were Dylan Thomas, George Barker, and David Gascoyne. The young Durrell admired Auden very much and shared Auden's early interest in Groddeck, the psychologist who believed that all illnesses express some falsity or obstruction in the will, and that our life-patterns work out an unconscious drive (not at all the same thing as Freud's Id, but rather a nucleus of growth-possibilities) which Groddeck called the It. Durrell's poetry, however, has never the latently Christian attitude which is present even in Auden's early poems: nor did he share Auden's interest in Marx, though his attitude to established society was, in the old slang sense of the word, very 'Bolshie'. His admiration for Auden did not lead, either, to the obvious imitation of Auden's verbal mannerisms to be found in Day Lewis, in Ruthven Todd, in Rex Warner, and in a poet who was later to be one of Durrell's closest friends, Bernard Spencer. It was through Durrell's poems in *Seven* in 1938 and 1939 that I 'discovered' him. But he had been publishing poems even more obscurely, in small pamphlets of limited circulation, since about 1931. He never published any verse in the 1930s in the periodicals that could make a big reputation, Geoffrey Grigson's *New Verse* or *The Listener* under Janet Adam Smith's literary editorship.

He must have put more faith in his prose. His first novel, *Pied Piper of Lovers*, came out in 1935, under his own name. It had no critical or financial success. In the same year he discovered Henry Miller's *Tropic of Cancer*, saw in it the hope of a break-away from dead convention in fiction, and got in touch with Miller. *Panic Spring*, his first book to be brought out by Faber, was published under the pseudonym Charles Norden, partly because *Pied Piper of Lovers* had been such a flop. It is a more skilful piece of work, but, as has been already suggested, was still very much a work of *pastiche*. It was not terribly successful, but Faber were interested in Durrell's promise, though they would not yet publish his poems.

Faber had taken a writer of talent, whose first novel had flopped, and whose second novel was accomplished rather than exciting, without quite knowing what to expect in his third novel. From some of his letters, it became clear that this was not going to be a further novel more or less in the manner of *Panic Spring*. Instead, Durrell wrote a huge meditative narrative, intimately close as his previous fiction had not been to his personal life and his creative and emotional problems. He cut this down very drastically, and also elaborately revised parts of it, and sent the result to Henry Miller. Miller was enthusiastic.

To Durrell's great surprise, T. S. Eliot, who, with three or four other readers, read *The Black Book* for Faber, was also enthusiastic. But there could be no question in 1937 of publishing the book in England except in an expurgated edition. . . . Today, after the *Lady Chatterley* trial, *The Black Book* is not likely to shock a balanced and mature reader though there is a late adolescent rawness about it that might still be found distressing. Durrell has always been a writer centrally concerned with the erotic impulse, but his eroticism is a total response to nature, not something narrowly sexual. He is sometimes Rabelaisianly obscene, he is not squeamish or easily shockable, but I think is never, properly speaking, pornographic. His eroticism is lyrical, like that of his friend Henry Miller, a kind of cosmic excitement; and he sees, as I have already suggested, the erotic experience as what Kierkegaard would call one of the 'stages on life's way', a stage towards the serenity of the sage who is also the artist.

Durrell was, of course, tempted by the possibility that a publisher of Faber's reputation might, by bringing out even an expurgated version of *The Black Book*, bring him instant renown. And he was reluctant to risk the break with Faber that he imagined might result from his choosing to publish *The Black Book* elsewhere. For the time being, however, he allowed Miller to persuade him that it is impossible to aim at being a popular writer most of the time, bringing out one's 'real' books only at rare intervals (though in a qualified sense, given the craftsmanship that Durrell puts into a thriller or a book of humorous short stories, this is what Durrell has since actually done). Durrell, then, decided to burn his boats. And *The Black Book* came out, unexpurgated, in Paris, with the Obelisk Press.

In 1937, in September, Durrell visited Henry Miller in Paris. They immediately became the closest of friends, and have remained so since. They had a jolly time in Paris editing four numbers of a magazine called *The Booster*, the house organ, ironically, of a very respectable institution, the American Country Club in Paris. When the American Country Club turned sour, *The Booster* was continued, in a rather fugitive way, as *Delta*. In Paris, Durrell met other writers who were to become close friends of his, including Alfred Perlès and Anaïs Nin. Back in London, Durrell met T. S. Eliot for the first time, and Eliot's then secretary, the poet and Shakespearian scholar Anne Ridler. Durrell and Mrs Ridler, though seeing each other seldom, were to remain friends, each sending the other draft poems for craftsmanlike comment.

In London, the young Durrell had earlier made friends with some of the more bohemian members of London's literary Right. He greatly admired the poetry of Roy Campbell, though Campbell's name was almost taboo in poetic London of the 1930s because of his stand on the Spanish Civil War. Durrell knew John Gawsworth, the author of *Apes, Japes, and Hitlerism*, a study of Wyndham Lewis, whom Durrell greatly admired; and Count Potocki of Montalk, a wild Polish reactionary, the author of a number of polemical pamphlets about the London literary world. I think such people attracted Durrell by their talent or their personal eccentricity rather than by their views. It was Campbell's vivid force as a poet that he admired rather than his politics though, in a French volume of tributes to Campbell published after his death, Durrell defended Campbell's right to extravagant views which he was willing to fight for. Durrell thinks of himself as a 'colonial' rather than an Englishman, his politics are very conservative by home standards, but I think he was pulling my leg in Corfu when he asked me whether Mr Wilson was a tool of Moscow. Politics are not centrally important to him, and I suppose he described his own accurately when he said that they are those of the Conservative who reads *The Daily Telegraph* rather than *The Times*. He differs from many Conservatives in being anti-insular and all for the Common Market; though his Europeanism contrasts oddly with a wistful feeling for the Empire, springing from his Indian boyhood.

There were other visits to Paris and London but in 1939 Durrell and his first wife, Nancy, were in Corfu, where Henry Miller briefly joined them, as the first step on a never-achieved pilgrimage to Tibet. The war, however, soon broke out. For a time, Durrell taught in the British Institute in Athens. Later, as the Greek situation worsened, he went to Kalamata in the south, escaped with his wife by caique to Crete, and finally came to Egypt. There he was Foreign Press Service Officer in Cairo for some time, but later became Press Attaché in Alexandria. In his Cairo days, he was the centre of an interesting group of poets, which included Bernard Spencer, Terence Tiller, and Keith Douglas, and helped to edit a magazine, *Personal Landscape*, which differed from most war-time poetry magazines in that its contributions were chosen with fastidious care. These were the years in which he absorbed some of the impressions that were much later to be woven into *The Alexandria Quartet*. His marriage with his first wife, Nancy Myers, broke up in these years. I met her once in Durrell's flat in Cairo and remember her as slim, fair-haired, blue-eyed, a painter who talked well about painting: she had a certain cool flavour of English pastoral landscape. She and their daughter Penelope Berengaria went to Palestine.

In 1945, Durrell was transferred from Alexandria to Rhodes, and found leisure to bring various books to completion: *Cities, Plains and People*, his very impressive first volume of poems; *Prospero's Cell*, the first of the island books, about Corfu in 1938; and *Cefalû*, a hastily written mixture of psychological thriller and allegory, later retitled *The Dark Labyrinth*. He also began to gather material for another island book, about Rhodes itself,

Reflections on a Marine Venus. Towards the end of his service there as Director of Public Relations, he married his second wife, an Alexandrian, Yves or Eve ('Gypsy') Cohen. I remember meeting Eve briefly a year or two later, perhaps at a London pub gathering with Tambimuttu, who edited *Poetry London*. She was as dark as Nancy had been fair, and I was struck particularly by her large and strong and beautiful white teeth: I had an image of her fiercely stripping a bunch of grapes with them. After Rhodes, Durrell went to Argentina to lecture for the British Council in Cordoba and then became Press Attaché at the British Embassy in Belgrade.

I have sometimes wondered at the ease with which Durrell, in these difficult post-war years from 1945 to about 1953, when many writers who had begun to make a name during the Second World War were marking time, both wrote and published so much and slipped into one responsible post in the public services after another. It was partly, of course, availability. Most writers who had been abroad during the war wanted to come home, but England was never 'home' to Durrell in that sense. He did not equate a literary career with life in literary London. But he differs also from many writers in his quick, extravert temperament, his social adaptability, his practical resource. There is a stereotype of the poet as awkward, slightly neurotic, touchy, in social groups either embarrassingly withdrawn or embarrassingly self-important. Durrell has none of these characteristics, except perhaps an occasional tetchiness rather than touchiness, a humorous impatience.

I imagine he did all these jobs very well, but that the life of public service never appealed to him as a vocation competing with his literary vocation. It provided him with very interesting raw material for the comic Antrobus stories and for *Mountolive*, but it must often have been socially constricting. Durrell's basic conservatism has nothing to do with a taste for Embassy splendours; it is based rather on his feeling for the peasantry and for traditional face-to-face relationships. He likes village life in Corfu or Provence, with news of the great world reaching him from visitors or in letters.

37

Not all these tours of duty can have been happy. He disliked Latin America. He positively hated Jugoslav Communism and in Belgrade his second wife, Eve, had a break-down, and their relations became strained. In 1952, Durrell went to Cyprus, bought a small house, and determined to settle down at last to really serious writing. He had already completed his first verse play, *Sappho*, and was anxious to embark on others; the pattern of *Justine* and its successors was already simmering in his head. In Cyprus, he hoped mainly to write, supplementing his still not large income by teaching English in a Cypriot grammar school. But it was not long before the troubles broke out; and Durrell, with his command of modern Greek, his love of and easy intimacy with the Cypriot people, once more had to be made official use of. At once a philhellene and a robust and simple British patriot, of an old-fashioned sort, he went through a period of considerable emotional distress. Yet he managed almost to the last both to do his official duty and to keep on decent terms with his village neighbours. He managed to write, too.

He was now separated from Eve, who had settled in England. He met in Cyprus and fell in love with a married woman, herself a writer, Claude. She was not able to obtain a divorce and become Durrell's third wife till 1961. I met Claude, as I met Nancy and Eve, only once, but over a longer period. In 1965, she was a perfect hostess, trim, elegant, and gay; though French by origins, she shared with Durrell, I remember, a learned enthusiasm for P. G. Wodehouse. Durrell told me proudly that she kept his papers and multifarious correspondence in perfect order. It was she who would drive back from the taverna, late at night, by a rough and winding road, when Durrell and I were high. There was that sense of ease between the two which speaks of a solid and lasting marital companionship. Suddenly, tragically and unexpectedly, she fell ill in the winter of the following year and died on New Year's Day, 1967.

Justine was nearly finished by the summer of 1956. In the autumn of that year, Durrell left Corfu for England, where he borrowed a cottage in Dorset, and worked on a book about his

Cyprus experiences, *Bitter Lemons*. This is the most penetrating and saddest of his island books: it is also the book that reveals the strain of strenuous, pragmatic common sense in Durrell, shows the worried, conscientious and efficient public servant.

Justine was Durrell's first great popular as well as critical success, though the success of *Bitter Lemons*, partly because of its topical urgency, was even more immediate. Durrell was now freed of the need to do anything for a living but write. He and Claude settled in Provence, where the succeeding three novels of *The Alexandria Quartet* were written with incredible rapid energy. *Justine* had been in Durrell's mind for years and its gestation in Cyprus was long and troubled. In Provence, with Durrell sometimes toiling for fourteen hours a day at his work table, *Balthazar* was written in six weeks; *Mountolive*, which has a different technique and is more like a 'traditional' novel, in twelve weeks; and *Clea*, the coda, which some people think the weakest and others the finest member of the Quartet, in four.

Durrell, after the success of *Justine*, was able to devote more time to his verse plays, whose failure with English critics and on the British stage has been as striking as the success of his novels. Durrell had the misfortune to begin his serious career as a verse dramatist just at the time when the post-war taste for verse drama, created by T. S. Eliot and Christopher Fry, was fading, and when Samuel Beckett in his own translations from his own French, Brecht and Ionesco in translations by other people, John Osborne and Arnold Wesker in doggedly earnest native English harangues, were setting a series of new fashions: the drama of the Absurd, or of Negation; Epic Theatre; the Drama of Non-Identification or Audience Alienation; the Drama of Protest, the tirades of the oppressed and mediocre, the 'insulted and obscure'. Critics like Kenneth Tynan could have little patience with Durrell's exercises, as they would see them, in an outworn, fadedly literary, and reactionary mode.

Royalties from *The Alexandria Quartet* kept pouring in. But Durrell is neither a very rich man, nor a writer who wants to rest, even if he can afford to, on his laurels. The Wodehousian humours of the Antrobus stories, the Buchanesque thrills of

White Eagles Over Serbia, have helped to keep the pot boiling. Durrell, with typical versatility, was working when I visited him in Corfu on the script and general advice for an American film, a documentary one, about the voyages of Odysseus. A year or two ago, also, in a French woman's magazine, *Elle*, I found the first instalment of a serial, *Judith*, about Israel in the early and bloody days of its establishment as a state; this was obviously a hastily novelized filmscript and one wondered even whether Durrell, who had written the script, had himself done the novelizing. But these other writings (apart from the plays) are not all highly professional hackwork, for there is a fairly recent new volume of poems, *The Ikons*. Knowing Durrell's temperament one suspects that over a number of years he has been incubating a new novel of major ambition. In fact the proof copy of an important new serious novel, *Tunc*, has reached me just in time to be considered in the final chapter of this book.

The success of *The Alexandria Quartet* in England, America, and, in translation, in Europe, is legendary. Durrell has the kind of European renown that has belonged in the past only to Shakespeare, to Byron, to Oscar Wilde, to the T. S. Eliot of *The Waste Land* and the Joyce of *Ulysses*; that, among classic American writers, has belonged only to Poe; one might add to this list the fame of Graham Greene, at least in Roman Catholic countries, and the disturbingly high French reputation of Charles Morgan. That list suggests that European critics may sometimes mistake the intrinsic literary quality of a writer in English. There is a vulgar streak, something flashy and meretricious, in the early Byron, in much of Oscar Wilde, in all of Poe; but it is possible also that this can disguise from English readers Poe's purity of imagination, Byron's power, the authenticity of Wilde's life and art as a total performance in the vein of tragical farce. There is a traditional fastidiousness in conventional English literary criticism, partly properly a fastidiousness about language, but partly a deep-rooted national horror of people who do not know their place, who overstep the mark, who show off. The dismissive judgements of English literary criticism are partly judgements about somebody who was not, in the end,

really 'one of us'. It is wrong in fact to write off European esti-
mates completely simply because even the finest European critic
cannot have our own sense of the niceties, the stridencies and
false notes, of our own language. They may catch at originality
at a deeper level, that of myth, symbol, the creation of archetypal roles. And if European critics are oddly blind to what we
find a 'vulgar streak', traditional English fastidiousness, in its
in-group complacency, its feline condescensions, can have its
own vulgarity, of an unconscious and therefore more deeply
corrupting sort. Better, at any time, the rash enthusiast than
the cautious snob!

In so far as one can think of the typical great novelist, the
novelist in the classic sense, one thinks of somebody like Jane
Austen or Tolstoy, who, working from within a society to which
she or he firmly belongs, describes it with great sympathy and
accuracy. In reading Jane Austen or Tolstoy also (though their
minds pervade their fictions) one is primarily aware of the
author's world, not of the author. In Charles du Bos's famous
phrase about Tolstoy: 'If life could speak, life would speak thus.'
Making even the highest possible claims for Durrell, one would
describe him as a great writer of subjective romances, not a great
novelist in the classical sense. Durrell knows what the 'traditional'
English novel is and in *Mountolive* he has shown that he has the
talent to write in this *genre* if he wants to; the passages about the
routine of Embassy life there have the accuracy and sympathy of
that fine forgotten novelist, Maurice Baring. But even in *Mountolive* there are other passages that are more like *The Arabian
Nights*. There is something in Durrell of the tale-teller of an
Eastern bazaar. The incredible, the extravagant, surprise, shock,
coincidence, indecency; Durrell is as much interested in exploit-
ing such ancient devices of the tale-teller's art as in depicting
actuality. His Alexandria, in *The Alexandria Quartet*, like T. S.
Eliot's London in *The Waste Land*, is an actuality, one can trace it
on a map; but more importantly it is a phantasmagoria, a symbol. It is a screen on to which Durrell projects the vicissitudes of
his psyche.

Durrell's self-chosen exile from England has exiled him then from that tradition of sobriety of observation, of loving acceptance of continuity, which is perhaps the central tradition of the English novel. But if one thinks of him as primarily a poet, his isolation from the squabbles, the gangings up, the reconciliations of the London literary world, has been fortunate. Like Lawrence, in his later years, or like Graves, by living among strangers he has found space to breathe. It leaves a black mark on one throughout one's life as a poet if in youth, seeking safety in numbers, one has allowed oneself to become a member of the New Apocalypse, the New Romantics, the Movement, The Group, the Beats, the Black Mountain school, and so on. Arguments about a recipe for poetry, cook-book arguments, take the place of the effort to create poetry, to respond to it, to judge it. The whole scene becomes hot, vociferous, crowded, smelly. The poets become the puppets of the fashion-mongers, the public-relations men. We get Muggeridge standing on a platform to introduce Graves or Ungaretti. The life of literature becomes a kind of gang warfare.

Durrell, as a poet, has escaped all this. Though starting, as I say, with a certain hesitancy about stance and direction, he has remained true all along to his own voice and vision. He does not think his poetry his most important achievement, he is modest about it. Yet the poetry seems to me to give the best lead-in to his general achievement. Therefore my next chapter will be devoted to Durrell the poet. Durrell the man, I realize, for all the various angles from which I have tried in this long first chapter to look at him, must still remain for me—as for my readers—elusive. The words on the page of poetry will prove a better clue to his labyrinth than one's scattered personal memories, or a bald and brief chronology of dates and facts.

CHAPTER TWO

THE POET'S VOICE AND VISION

I

A poet's primal instrument, Professor Francis Berry has suggested, is his physical voice, a voice of a certain timbre, capable of certain modulations, variations of pitch and pause and pace, which is a pleasure for himself as for us to listen to, even before he or we have given much thought to what he is saying.

Durrell's natural voice is a pleasant light tenor; it has a certain fur or burr upon it, little harsh catches here and there. Its range of tone and pitch is limited but flexible. Its qualities are a musical amenity, a kind of shallow ripple, an occasional hypnotic lulling, a little chuckle. For deep effects, it uses a certain formal withdrawal, but never so stiff as Graves's; one seems to hear the poet not muttering to himself, as Yeats and Frost sometimes mutter, but speaking in a fine ghostly tone to his own ingenuous mask. It is not a wilfully or dramatically dominating voice. Durrell never plays speech stress against sound. He surrenders himself to a chosen pattern; rhythmical patterns, riddle patterns, refrain patterns, command the physical instrument.

If one were to bring in here Eliot's three voices of poetry, the poet talking to himself, the poet talking to others, the poet assuming and imitating the voices of others, Durrell's voice is all three, but without drastic or harsh changes of modulation in passing from one voice to the others: the self, the anti-self, the multiplicity of possible selves are all three contained within a very suave but fairly narrow range of modulation.

There is no poem of Durrell's, for instance, really brutally in the first voice, the voice of raw, harsh, and painful self-confession: the poem almost 'bloody-minded' in its directness, impatient with its own structure and emotion, like some of the poems of D. H. Lawrence. The first voice is already public, informed with a certain social and aesthetic suavity. There are quite a number of poems in the second voice, the poems for instance about Horace or about Byron, which are broadly in the tradition of Browning's and Tennyson's dramatic monologues, *My Last Duchess* or *Ulysses*. But these are not pure impersonations. It is Durrell's view of Horace or Byron that is presented in monologue rather than Horace or Byron themselves. Durrell is making a commenting, critical, intrusively authorial, once-removed half-imitation of the styles, the modes, the life-spirits of such poets. The poems of the third voice are mainly the verse dramas, which will be considered in another chapter. Here it may be said that landscape is more important to Durrell than people; in his poems, he makes landscapes more interesting, more dramatic, than he makes people, and yet the landscape is not there for its own sake but for its complex expressiveness, its meaning for Durrell as something on to which he can project, and by means of which he can define, moods, elusive and obsessive recurrences of human feeling.

There are other kinds of poems, more or less frivolous ones, poems of the sort which Graves defined in a preface to one of the editions of his *Collected Poems* as 'satires and grotesques'. 'The Ballad of the Good Lord Nelson' is a good example. Unlike Graves, Durrell, nevertheless, could not be described in either his prose or verse as a very witty writer. Freud, in his important and neglected short book on wit, took wit—in a wide sense, which included the pointed popular joke—as essentially a condensation of painful and shameful feelings that effects an emotional economy. One of his best examples is the exchange between the aged lecher and the ballet dancer: 'I can never give you my heart': 'My dear, I never aimed so high.' Durrell has all his life been so free of our usual need to suppress or repress the painful and shameful feelings, so frank, open-hearted

44

and ingenuous, that this bitter kind of wit has never been a very
important instrument for him. What he has instead is a splendid
sense of humour. One should remember the semantic history of
the word 'humour'. For Ben Jonson, who in his comedy of
humours gave the word its central place in the English language, a humour meant a disbalance of temperament, a
monomania. This disbalance struck Elizabethan and Jacobean
audiences, less humane in this respect than ourselves, as very
funny—a visit to Bedlam, in these days, was a week-end treat,
like a visit to the Zoo. The semantic shift was from 'humorous' = 'crazy' to 'humorous' = 'funny'. The word 'funny' has
undergone a similar semantic shift in the opposite direction.
One should note in this connection that Durrell's humour, as in
The Black Book, is sometimes 'black humour,' that his sense of
comedy, as in the character and fate of Scobie, often verges on
the comic-macabre. Yet one should think of the wild and sometimes crazy humour of Tourneur, Webster, Middleton, Marston
(like Eliot, Durrell has has a passion for the darker Jacobean
dramatists) rather than 'sick' humour in the narrower contemporary sense. Durrell's humour is the expression of a temperament.

The poems themselves are the expression of a temperament,
rather than the history of a soul, and to say this is perhaps to
define Durrell as a minor poet, though of a very distinguished
sort. Both Yeats and Eliot provide us with what could be called
the history of a soul, and it matters very much that, in their
collected volumes, the poems are arranged in the order of composition. In his selected and collected volumes of poetry,
Durrell, on the other hand, arranges his poems by affinity of
tone and topic, ignoring the order of composition, and for him
this kind of arrangement seems right. Again, though the quality
of his writing in verse is remarkably even there is no poem which
marks a watershed, like *The Waste Land* or like *Easter 1916*, or
marks a climax like *The Four Quartets* or, let us say, Yeats's
Byzantium poems or his *Among School Children*. Looking for the
watershed and the climax, one looks instead to *The Black Book*,
and to *The Alexandria Quartet*, a work hinging on the metaphy-

sics of space-time. As a writer in verse, Durrell is in a sense
timeless. When an individual poem was written does not matter
much, either in relation to Durrell's biography or the development of his art. This timeless quality is, paradoxically, more
often a mark of the very good minor poet than of the major one;
one thinks, for instance, of Thomas Campion or A. E. Housman.

If there is not wit in the Gravesian sense in Durrell's poems,
there is often an inspired frivolity, a delightful dancing light-
ness; a swing like ballads or pop songs or lovely nursery nonsense,
a fondness for the kind of raven-and-writing-desk riddle to which
the answer, as at the Mad Hatter's tea-party, does not matter.
There is this purely lyrical quality, and there is the central importance of landscape, or more broadly of the scenic. Yet, compared with his close friend, that fine neglected poet, Bernard
Spencer, Durrell does not give us the naked Mediterranean scene.
Spencer was, in a real sense, a classical poet: he had the gift,
while never losing the high, thin, almost hysterical music of his
voice—a kind of polar opposite to Durrell's mellifluous crunchi-
ness—of presenting something nakedly, the movement of the sea,
the white glare of waves and cliffs, an Egyptian ox with bound eyes
turning a water-wheel, 'the dour look of olive trees', with absolute
and uncommenting visual exactness. Durrell is not a *visuel* in that
sense, he mixes his moods with his pigments, his poems, like his
prose works, are perhaps all in the end essays in oblique self-
portraiture. I have written elsewhere that Durrell's poems recall
a rich blended wine, port or sherry, while Spencer's have the
taste of a pure even if sometimes thin or bitter unblended vint-
age. Spencer tastes sometimes of pure rock, herb, water; Durrell
tastes of these things too, but always also of Durrell.

2

Such generalizations, however much they mean to oneself,
must convey comparatively little to the reader not intimately
acquainted with Durrell's poems. I shall choose, not quite at
random, a number of poems for closer examination, trying to

bring out the flavour, the essence, something for which the words and rhythms are only a signal, which can be intuitively recognized, but which eludes paraphrase. Let me start with a perfect short lyric, 'Water Music':

> *Wrap your sulky beauty up,*
> *From sea-fever, from winterfall*
> *Out of the swing of the*
> *Swing of the sea.*
>
> *Keep safe from noonfall,*
> *Starlight and smokefall where*
> *Waves roll, waves toll but feel*
> *None of our roving fever.*
>
> *From dayfever and nightsadness*
> *Keep, bless, hold: from cold*
> *Wrap your sulky beauty into sleep*
> *Out of the swing of the*
> *Swing of sea.*

The quality is incantation, magic: tired and loose words, which can here be used in their literal sense. The poem is a lullaby, a magic or incantatory device for soothing someone to sleep. The sleep into which the words soothe the sulky beauty is sleep literally but also sleep metaphorically, sleep as the opposite of sulkiness, 'our roving fever', 'dayfever and nightsadness'. The device of

> *Out of the swing of the*
> *Swing of the sea,*

borrowed from Hopkins's 'Heaven-Haven', has the suggestion, as Durrell's simplest lyrics often have, of profound blurred metaphysical implications: the smaller rhythm of the breaking waves, as it were, within the larger rhythm of the changing tides, rhythms of motion on different scales eliding each other, and reaching stillness. The poem is too short to include the whole cyclical movement of nature, but it reduces that to the swinging of two pendulums, each blurring the other. 'Winter-fall' is the descent of winter on the year, 'noonfall' the falling of noon sun in the water, but in a nursery rhyme the sun might literally fall into the sea or one's lap: 'smokefall' is the drifting of smoke from the funnels of a steamer down into the water. 'Starlight' contrasts with these sleepy, moving, falling things, a bright, clear, still, scattered light that might keep one awake. But broadly the very things that the sulky beauty is to escape from, the rolling and tolling of the waves like the swing of the swing of the sea, are the very things with which this love-magic is lulling her to sleep. The 'dayfever and nightsadness', the restless activity and retrospective remorse of mankind, though they are what the sulky beauty has to protect herself against, to 'keep, bless, hold' from, are what hers like any life must be made out of.

And one should notice an interesting syntactical or idiomatic point here. One can hold from something, keep from something, but can one, in ordinary English, bless from something? So there is an underlying possible meaning: 'From (the experience of) dayfever and nightsadness (learn to) keep, bless, hold (what is positively valuable).' All that one has to keep and bless and hold in the end is, perhaps, the dayfever and the nightsadness, or what one has learned from them. The adjective 'sulky' in the first line and the third-last line suggests a refusal of the conditions of life: yet it is a word of gentle reproach, used to children or attractive, unreasonable women, quite different in emotional tone, for instance, from the word 'sullen'. It is worth noting that a *boudoir* or bower, the ballad word for a woman's apartment in a castle or a cottage, is, quite literally, in its French form, a place where women can *bouder* or sulk: shut themselves away from the noise and trouble caused by men.

I have been trying to bring out the sense of this poem in what Robert Graves and Laura Riding insist is the only proper fashion, that is, at greater length, in the poem's own words. But the tone and feeling and intention of the poem come across especially in the intricate verbal music. Using this poem in practical criticism classes, I have found that hardly any student

notices that it has no end-rhymes. A musical effect richer than
that of end-rhyme is got from internal rhyme, consonantal
patterning, and word repetition. Here are two lines marked
for vowel echo in syllables of main stress:

> *Waves roll, waves toll, but feel*
> *None of our roving, fever.*

One can see that 'roving fever' echoes expansively the long-
vowel sequence of 'toll, but feel'. When we mark consonantal
patterning in the same two lines (not marking initial allitera-
tion on syllables of minor stress) we get:

> *Waves roll, waves toll, but feel*
> *None of our roving fever.*

There are other little felicities one could notice. If Durrell
had written, in a line which he later varies,

> *Wrap up your sulky beauty*

instead of

> *Wrap your sulky beauty up,*

he would have missed the sharp enclosing echo of the beginning
and ending words, 'wrap' and 'up', each with its short vowel
ending on an unvoiced plosive (that 'wrap' is a near-homonym
of 'rap'—I find it possible, and I dare say Durrell does, to half-
sound the *w*—is not unimportant). The words 'wrap' and 'up' do
wrap up, or rap down, the line at its beginning and end, and
their abrupt, cross sound does, like the word 'sulky', suggest an
original mood of exasperation or tiredness on the poet's part,
out of which, as a curative measure, the poem's total gesture of
incantatory tenderness has grown. We have mixed feelings
about the sulky beauty to whom the poem is addressed. The
word 'cold' in the fourth-last line, given resonance by the internal rhyme with 'hold', suggests the main peril—coldness of
heart, sulky retreat from life—that besets this about-to-be-sleep-
ing beauty.

There are other points almost too delicate to make, without
appearing to break a butterfly on a wheel. That 'Swing of the

sea' at the end of the first stanza becomes 'Swing of sea' at the end of the last avoids an effect of mechanical repetition, and keeps up the general feeling of a wave-motion, a lapping, running through the poem—the effect of rhythmical motions lullingly similar, but never quite the same. I would scan the second line, for instance, as having four almost equal main stresses,

From sea-fe*ver*, *from* win*terf*all,

even though the stress on the last syllable of 'winterfall' is not so strong as the stress on the first, but my scansion of the fifth line would be

$$\text{I} \quad 2 \qquad \text{I} \quad 2$$
*K*eep *s*afe *from n*oon*f*all,

where the numbers above the syllables indicate primary and secondary degrees of stress (there is a more usual system where a higher numeral indicates a higher degree of stress, but I am not using it here). The rocking, lulling, but never mechanical movement of this perfect small poem is, of course, only coarsely indicated by such devices. They are worth using merely because, as every university teacher of English soon discovers, many otherwise sensitive and intelligent lovers of literature are incapable of making a piece of verse sound and move properly in their heads.

That was a perfect short poem; some of Durrell's longer and more ambitious poems are far from perfect, and obviously not all of his short poems are as good as 'Water Music'. I present it as a sort of diploma piece, which establishes Durrell as a verse technician as skilful, say, as an American who is roughly his contemporary, Richard Wilbur. And I must recognize, of course, that Durrell's and Wilbur's kind of accomplishment is now out of fashion, at least temporarily. Poets so different as Robert Lowell, Robert Creeley, Ted Hughes, Philip Hobsbaum all share a taste for a kind of rough and struggling poetry, a poetry forcefully and painfully working its way through emotional and linguistic obstructions, a poetry with what Donald Davie, contrasting a poem of Pound's with one of Wordsworth's, to

Wordsworth's technical dispraise but to his moral advantage, once called 'the reek of the human'. Durrell's poems are sometimes rough, smacking of improvisation, full of references which only a madly well-informed reader can validate, family jokes:

> . . . *the small, fell*
> *Figure of Dorian ringing like a muffin-bell*

but his theoretical approach to poetry is not based on the assumption that all poems *must* be like this. There is not enough pain, fear, and resentment, enough explicit horror at the contemporary social and political scene, at the mess that most lives make, in his poetry to keep him abreast of immediately contemporary taste. In a strange sense he is too well and happily integrated as a writer and a man, too complete an individual, to appear widely humanly representative when a recurrent deep poetic theme is what Gabriel Marcel calls 'the broken world', the individualities smashed, the bitter Beckett-like recognitions on the scrap heap. He is too happy.

A poem like 'Water Music' does at least very firmly establish Durrell's skill. It would be tedious to examine the workmanship of other poems in similar detail and I shall now be dealing, more briefly, with topics, themes, recurrent moods, devices of presentation. But one other short poem, excellent in a different way, is worth quoting in full because it illustrates in a very concentrated way Durrell's attitude (a main topic, also, as we shall see in the next chapter, of *The Black Book*) to English landscape and history. Durrell's general attitude to landscape one might describe as that of a connoisseur, an anthologist. He collects landscapes of all kinds, but where the English landscape is concerned one might say that, like Coleridge in 'Dejection: an Ode', he 'sees, not feels, how beautiful it is'. Yet there is a wistfulness that may imply a held-back wish to surrender. Wordsworth and Jane Austen can neither of them be favourite authors of Durrell's, but he has too catholic a taste and too open a sensibility to be totally unaware of the special sort of beauty that goes with restraint and sobriety. Here, anyway, is the poem I am talking about, 'Bere Regis':

The colonial, the expatriate walking here
Awkwardly enclosing the commonwealth of his love
Stoops to this lovely expurgated prose-land
Where winter with its holly locks the schools
And spring with nature improvises
With the thrush on ploughland, with the scarecrow.

Moss walls, woollen forests, Shakespear, desuetude:
Roots of his language as familiar as salt
Inhaling cattle lick in this mnemonic valley
Where the gnats assort, the thrush familiarises,
And over his cottage a colloquial moon.

Durrell's sense of himself as not an insular Englishman, yet his half-regret in this sense, comes out in 'colonial', 'expatriate', 'the commonwealth of his love'. Not more than seven of his fifty-six years have been spent continuously in England. I would take it that this poem was written in the borrowed Dorset cottage where he worked on *Bitter Lemons*, or when staying in Bournemouth just before. The poem, however, is not a specifically local one, the mild climate of Dorset, the crumbly chalky cliffs full of fossils between Lyme Regis and Charmouth, the associations with Jane Austen, with Hardy, with King George III, these are not brought in. There is a general sense, rather, of a countryside still unspoiled but in a sense tamed, 'this lovely expurgated prose-land'. The big houses have become expensive private schools, the dark prickly holly tree seems to protect them from the poet's intrusion, and he sees spring as strumming on the landscape, improvising a little poem, as he is doing himself. The moss on the walls, the woollen forests—do sheep graze in the clearings, or does 'woollen', like 'moss', suggest the decay that creeps over still things, crumbling soft grey twigs of dead conifers?—mingle in Durrell's mind with Shakespeare; this lost pastoral world was Shakespeare's world, but it has run to seed. And yet the agonizing sense of what the old England was is there, as nourishing to the poet as a salt-lick to cattle, near the roots of his memory; the gnats, the thrush, the moon over the

poet's cottage all make a composition, but in a familiar, colloquial style, too near prose. In a sense the poem might be a
critical comment on Georgian poetry, on the failure of the
Georgian poets even at their best to recreate old England, now a
kind of ghost, except with a low-toned wistfulness. The poem, if
one likes to put it that way, is about a birthright renounced.

Durrell spoke to me in Corfu about his sense that modern
England constricts the sensibilities where the Eastern Mediterranean opens them out. One could contrast that poem with an
exultant stanza from 'Summer in Corfu':

> *State me no theme for misery. The season*
> *Like a woman lies open, is folding,*
> *Secret, growth upon growth. The black fig*
> *Desire is torn again from the belly of reason.*
> *Our summer is gravid at last, is big.*

Or one could contrast it again with the wind-swept exultant
violence of the first stanza of one of his most finely modulated
poems, 'Alexandria', written in Egypt in wartime:

> *To the lucky now who have lovers or friends,*
> *Who move to their sweet undiscovered ends,*
> *Or whom the great conspiracy deceives,*
> *I wish these whirling autumn leaves:*
> *Promontories splashed by the salty sea,*
> *Groaned on in darkness by the tram*
> *To horizons of love or good luck or more love——*
> *As for me I now move*
> *Through many negatives to what I am.*

The sense of motion and openness there contrasts very obviously
with the deliberately flat and slightly limping metrical movement of 'Bere Regis'. The poet is possessed by a kind of exalta-
tion which will whip his immediate circumstances, like the
whirling autumn leaves, into a desired dancing pattern. The
world is at war. But the lovers and friends whom he names or
alludes to in the poem will not yield to desuetude or disaster.
The wind is a purifier:

So we, learning to suffer and not condemn
Can only wish you this great pure wind
Condemned by Greece, and turning like a helm
Inland where it smokes the fires of men,
Spins weathercocks on farms or catches
The lovers at their quarrel in the sheets;
Or like a walker in the darkness might,
Knocks and disturbs the artist at his papers
Up there alone, upon the alps of night.

I used to worry about the colloquial and indeed sub-literately colloquial grammar of the line

Or like a walker in the darkness might,

where there is no euphonic reason, that I can see, for substituting 'like' for 'as'; I think now that it works towards an impression of casual and insolent ease. The slangy carelessness of 'like a walker in the darkness might' buys, as it were, the right to compose a final line in the grand style:

Up there alone, upon the alps of night.

One notices there the phrase 'this great pure wind' as in 'Bere Regis' one had noticed 'this lovely expurgated prose-land': 'expurgated' in 'Bere Regis' had a joky flavour, suggesting bowdlerized Shakespeare in the expensive girls' private schools, protected by winter and the hollies. But another beautiful short lyric ends with a different use of the idea: 'Lesbos':

The Pleiades are sinking calm as paint,
The earth's huge camber follows out,
Turning in sleep, the oceanic curve.

Defined in concave like a human eye
Or a cheek pressed warm on the dark's cheek,
Like dancers to a music they deserve.

This balcony, a moon-anointed shelf
Above a silent garden holds my bed.
I slept. But the dispiriting autumn moon,

In her slow expurgation of the sky
Needs company: is brooding on the dead,
And so am I now, so am I.

The idea of the process of the growth of the artist's consciousness
as a 'slow expurgation', a movement

Through many negatives to what I am,

is a clue to a fundamental stance in Durrell's poetry, perhaps
also in his best prose. Symptomatic also is that the first two
terzets of 'Lesbos' are about cosmic harmony, the turning earth
pressed against the darkness, like two lovers dancing cheek to
cheek; but the image of harmony is immediately counterpointed, though not annulled, by the image of the loneliness of
the moon and the poet, the lonely task of purification, the
inescapable obsession with death, with the dead, which can allow
no harmony to be whole-hearted. We must be exultant in the
world but the world is always much sadder than it seems.
Durrell is not an inventor of new poetic concepts, a 'creator of
concepts' as Eliot in *Four Quartets* is described, by D. W. Harding, as being. He is content, like an Elizabethan poet, like
Shakespeare in his sonnets, with perennial topics, the beauty of
the world, its transience, its danger, the triumph of time, the
battle of love and art against time. For him, as for the Elizabethans whom he loves, the originality of the poet lies not in the
discovery of new topics, new moods, but in ingenuity, in invention, in what the Elizabethans called 'device', in handling
the old ones.

3

One of Durrell's favourite poets is Browning and he is interested like Browning in anecdotal poems, poems about characters. The characters are, some of them, possible versions of
Durrell, and the character-poems are also efforts at expurgation,
revealing the element of falsity, the playing of a part which
both hides and reveals a wound, a central weakness: this

Durrell sees, as Freud saw it, as lying at the core of the artist's vocation. Thus Horace is a man

> *Disguising a sense of failure in a hatred for the young,*
> *Who built in the Sabine hills this forgery*
> *Of completeness, an orchard with a view of Rome;*
> *Who studiously developed his sense of death*
> *Till it was all around him. . . .*

and the friend who has lent Durrell a copy of the Loeb Horace writes on a flyleaf the final critical comment:

> *'Fat, human and unloved,*
> *And held from loving by a sort of wall,*
> *Laid down his books and lovers one by one,*
> *Indifference and success had crowned them all.'*

Rochefoucauld is another great man who has built a wall between himself and love, and whose art therefore is also a forgery of completeness, 'somehow faked':

> *Yet in reason I mastered appetite,*
> *And taught myself at last the tragic sense;*
> *Then through appetite and its many ambushes*
> *I uncovered the politics of feeling, dense*
> *Groves for the flocks of sin to feed in.*
> *Yet in the end the portrait always seemed*
> *Somehow faked, or somehow still in need*
> *Of gender, form and the present tense.*
> *I could not get beyond this wall.*
>
> *No. The bait of feeling was left untasted:*
> *Deep inside like ruins lay the desires*
> *To give, to trust, to be my subjects' equal,*
> *All wasted, wasted.*
> *Though love is not the word I want*
> *Yet it will have to do. There is no other.*

Reading through Durrell's poetry, I notice that the little weak word 'love', so rubbed and so ambiguous, is, indeed, for him as for Auden—in this at least a definite influence—the word that 'will have to do'. The wall between Rochefoucauld and love, and the sense of human need, darkness and loneliness that goes with love, means that the *Maxims* are mainly important for what they leave out:

> *So the great Lack grew and grew.*
> *Of the real Darkness not one grain I lifted.*
> *Yet the whole story is here like the part*
> *Of some great man's body,*
> *Veins, organs, nerves,*
> *Unhappily illustrating neither death nor art.*

There is a more vivid, less distanced poem about Byron, to whom Durrell is perhaps more temperamentally akin than to Horace, certainly than to Rochefoucauld: an imaginary monologue at Missolonghi:

> *Picture to yourself*
> *A lord who encircled his life*
> *With women's arms; or another*
> *Who rode through the wide world howling*
> *And searching for his mother.*
>
> *Picture to yourself a third: a cynic.*
> *This weeping published rock——*
> *The biscuits and the glass of soda-water:*
> *Under Sunium's white cliffs*
> *Where I laboured with my knife*
> *To cut a 'Byron' there——*
> *I was thinking softly of my daughter.*

Thinking softly, perhaps, of the dead Allegra. The Biblical inscription which the English clergyman, who would not bury her, would not put up: 'I shall go to her, but she will not come to me.'

There is a crude question, but it is a necessary question, to ask about all good poets, major or minor: what is the message? Or, as this is sometimes put, what is the 'philosophy of life' that emerges from Durrell's poems? It seems to me to be a message of acceptance of life, an acceptance tinged with a very deep sadness, but in the end reverent and joyous, and yet delicate rather than gross, quite free of religious dogma or religious cant, but in the end seeing the world and human life as a grand, though fragmented and ironically riddling, sacramental symbol. Durrell is not a Christian, though he very deeply admires T. S. Eliot and though the finest, the longest, the most intricately ornate of his early poems, 'A Soliloquy of Hamlet', a kind of exercise in wild verbal felicity, in baroque improvization, is addressed to one of the best Christian poets of our time, Anne Ridler. But his hatred of 'the wall', his insistence that there is 'no other' word than love, have profound affinities with the Christian sensibility, where it is most open, honest, and vulnerable. He hates the flat and abstract, the using of words that once sprang from a profound and new intuition as mere stale rhetoric or as dead counters. But he feels the power of the words that have held power.

I remember once saying to Arthur Waley, at a time when I was revising for Unesco a selection of translations from the Sikh sacred book, the *Adi Granth*, that I thought I found true poetry in the ragas of the early Gurus, but after that it tended to become a shuffling around of tired counters: every Guru had to write some poems, and not all were poets. Waley told me that in the same way early Buddhist texts are magnificent, but then there is dilution, expansion, mechanical shuffling around. Durrell has a profound sense of the numinous, but he is not going to go beyond his immediate experience, to make words empty and hollow. He worships the *deus loci*, because that is the god he has met: the sense of miracle and immanence in places, Hopkins's 'inscape', Wordsworth's 'spots of time'. The *deus loci* is an earth-god and a hearth god:

> Deus loci *your provinces extend*
> *throughout the domains of logic,*
> *beyond the eyes watching from dusty murals,*
> *or the philosopher's critical impatience*
> *to understand, to be done with life:*
> *beyond beyond even the mind's dark spools*

in a vine-wreath or an old wax cross
you can become the nurse and wife of fools,
their actions and their nakedness——
all the heart's profit or the loss.

So today, after many years, we meet
at this high window overlooking
the best of Italy, smiling under rain,
that rattles down the leaves like sparrow-shot,
scatters the reapers, the sunburnt girls,
rises in the sour dust of this table,
these books, unfinished letters—all
refreshed again in you O spirit of place,
Presence long since divined, delayed, and waited for,
And here met face to face.

He *tells* us that he has met the *deus loci* face to face; he does
not quite confront us with it, as in different ways Pound and
Graves can. I never quite feel, reading Durrell's poems, that
little shiver up the back of the spine, that sense of being possessed, that, say, Graves and Eliot and Yeats can at moments
give me: 'something above a mortal mouth'. He is not a poet
whom I must, compulsively at intervals of years, re-read—as, in
the novel, compulsively, at growing intervals of years, one re-
reads all Jane Austen. Perhaps there is something that one
misses. *Hysterica passio*, the really wild dance, the throwing it all
away; perhaps there is often a contrast between the measured
exactness of the cadence, and the too literate violence of the
images: in 'A Soliloquy of Hamlet':

Then suckle the weather if the winter will not,
Seal down a message in a dream of spring,

More than this painful meditation of feet,
The frigid autist pacing out his rope.

The candle and the lexicon have picked your bones.
The tallow spills upon my endless bible.

It is interesting that the young Durrell, with his passion for books about medicine and psychology, knew the precise meaning of the word 'autist', which we all now know from articles about autistic children in the top newspapers or the highbrow weeklies. To be autistic is to work something out for oneself, in oneself, refusing the assistance of parents or teachers. It is a central paradox about Durrell that this Kretschmerian pyknic, short, jolly, plump, muscular, 'breaking the ring' in folk dances, should, in poetical composition, convey often the sense of what he calls 'the wall', the solitary dancer in a self-walled enclosure.

CHAPTER THREE

A WATERSHED: *THE BLACK BOOK*

I

In his preface to the 1959 Olympia Press reprint of *The Black Book*,[1] Lawrence Durrell explains why this work—his third novel, but his first really original and personal piece of sustained composition in prose—still matters so much to him:

> With all its imperfections lying heavy on its head, I can't help feeling attached to it because in the writing of it I first heard the sound of my own voice, lame and halting perhaps, but nevertheless my very own.

He goes on:

> This is an experience no artist ever forgets—the birth-cry of a newly born baby of genius, the genuine article. . . . It built itself out of a long period of despair and frustration during which I knew that my work, though well-contrived, was derivative. It seemed to me that I would never discover myself, my private voice and vision. At the age of twenty-four things usually look black to one!

The Black Book gives rise to what to me are the most interesting passages in the published correspondence of Durrell and Henry Miller. By the terms of the contract for the 'well-contrived but derivative' *Panic Spring*, Faber and Faber had an option on Durrell's next two novels, unless they should refuse the first of the two. He told Faber's that he was writing a book that, in the late 1930s, would be unpublishable in England; the reply was

---

[1] It has not yet been published in England, but was published in the United States by Durrell's American publishers, E. P. Dutton, in 1960.

that Durrell could publish it where he liked if Faber's turned it down, but that they must have the first refusal.

Writing from Corfu in February 1937, Durrell gives Miller a modestly jaunty account of the new book:

> I like it, frankly. It's a good little chronicle of the English death, done in a sort of hamstrung tempo, with bursts of applause here and there. I think it's a book Huxley could have written if he were a mixture of Lawrence and Shakespeare. It dates from that insomniac day when I felt a sort of malaise, and began to wonder if I could really be content as a best-selling novelist (once my ideal). Very little is censorable in the ego of the book. Nothing in fact. I had to go easy on the ego because a twenty-four-year-old ego is a dull thing to contemplate.

Durrell goes on to say that though the 'I' passages in *The Black Book*, the passages written by a stand-in for Durrell called Lawrence Lucifer, are not very censorable, passages about other characters, notably 'the irrepressible dying diarist called Gregory and a quite unprintable person called Tarquin' are not only censorable but 'slightly libellous'. I have made no attempt at all to find out who the originals, or part-originals, of these or other characters may have been. Many important first novels—and *The Black Book* is Durrell's first 'real' novel—do, of course, have the air of coming more directly and painfully out of raw experience than a novelist's later, more mature and distanced work.

The immediacy of personal emotion is, in any case, much more critically interesting than any elements in *The Black Book* of the *roman à clef*. The novel includes for instance a long letter by Lawrence Lucifer to a close friend, a valediction to the traditional beauties of England, particularly Gothic and medieval England as that flowers in Shakespeare. The 'I' of the novel asserts that by destroying the traditional beauties of medieval England, typified by crusader's tombs and country graveyards, a beauty built over corpses, he will somehow recreate them. This letter, addressed to 'Alan', has Durrell's close friend Alan Thomas in mind but its interest is not the interest of autobiography, but that of a virtuoso piece of prose, an at once lyrical and macabre fantasia on medieval themes. Again, the cool, beautiful, pastoral girl, an *anima*-figure rather than a person, who does not appear as an active character in the book but who touches off in Lawrence Lucifer passages of elegy and lyricism, alternating with expostulations of stifling fury, may have some relation to Durrell's first wife, Nancy. Durrell says in one of his letters to Miller that he made Nancy miserable when he was writing the book. But the literary interest is in how Lawrence Lucifer projects his feelings, not in the person they are projected on.

The girl in the book exists, in fact, mainly as part of a sequence of pastoral imagery, bringing in loam and hawthorn and country cottages. The handling of characters, like the large range of grotesque, comic, or pitiable characters in the book, with whom the narrator's emotions are not deeply engaged—except, sometimes, the emotion of comic disgust—is more objective, though where he is not exhibiting his gift for lyrical prose, Durrell is often exhibiting his gift for humorous distortion, for fantastic caricature. No doubt the large shabby hotel and the grotesque combination of a crammer's establishment and a business-training college, between which two places much of the exterior action of the book takes place, come off, at least at a tangent, from actual experience. One has a sense in fact quite often in *The Black Book*, as hardly ever in *The Alexandria Quartet*, of the really raw grotesque 'life' incident or character which feels as if it needs some cooking, before it can become 'literature'. Though never pornographic, *The Black Book* is, because of this rawness at moments, genuinely obscene, sometimes in a slightly embarrassing way. Very young writers often do not quite realize, overestimating the tolerance, underestimating the squeamishness, of their elders, how shocking they can seem. An admirer of Durrell's, Gerald Sykes, has perceptively remarked that when Durrell wrote *The Black Book* he was too young to know how to be 'naughty with style'.

Durrell, however, throughout the book, is very expertly 'naughty with style' in quite a different sense. He has wicked, often parodic fun with the ranging possibilities of English prose style. The prose, throughout, is so deliberately mannered, so richly and consciously cadenced, so packed with exotic but apt words, that at times *The Black Book* seems primarily a new *Euphues*, an exercise in virtuosity in the handling of rhythm and diction. The prose lends itself often, as very little contemporary prose does, to the kind of quantitative scansion which, in his *History of English Prose Rhythm*, George Saintsbury applies so revealingly to deliberately ornate and artificial writers like De Quincey, Landor, and Pater.

The prose, in fact, often asks, if not to be read aloud, at least to be murmured, to be slowly cadenced in the inner ear. Here is a typical passage, scanned as Saintsbury might have scanned it:

> Ăs fŏr thĕ whāle / thē ĕxtĕriŏr / ūnĭvērse / whĭch wās /
> Hīldă / (thĕ nāme / nŏw lĭch / ĕnīsed, / spōnged, / scūrfed,
> / dīmmed), Gōd knōws / whēre shĕ / spĭns, / ĭn whāt / lōgă-
> rĭthmĭc / wātĕr / ōvĕr thĕ / Pōles, hĕr / grēat / flūkes / flāsh-
> ĭng / blūe, rēachĭng / ūp / ālmōst / tŏ thĕ mōon.

It is not only the cadencing here but the manner of indirect and fantastic evocation that recalls some of Pater's most effective 'purple panels' from his essay on Leonardo da Vinci. There is a revealing sentence a little higher up the page on which this passage occurs: 'I am so happy in my weakness. I do not even regret Pater.' ('Pater' in this sentence just could, of course, but I think doesn't, mean 'Daddy'.) Durrell's diction in his more deliberately rhythmed passages goes, however, much further in the direction of what Saintsbury called catachresis, a deliberately disturbing conjunction or association of phrases, than Pater himself. The Paterian cadences are often counterpointed by a deliberate choice of harsh or ugly words and images:

> Thĕ pĭanŏ / wăs fūll / ŏf galvānĭc / bāllĕrīnăs / , fālling ĭn
> / splāshĕs ŏf / flūffy ĕx / tīnctĭŏn ă / rōund hĭm.

The rhythm there beautifully evokes a run-up, a hastening, before an elegiac, dying-fall slow-down; but the words 'galvanic' and 'fluffy' mock the stale romanticism of the ballet fan. In the

passage which immediately follows this sentence, I underline
the violent catachreses but bother to scan only the second
sentence:

> The swan with the *goitre* singing Wagner, its *arse* keeping
> time, its mouth full of *toothpaste*. But the real / —death, if
> you like / (these abstractions / bore me); the doom / which
> he   saw / settling / down / over / England, / which   we /
> smelled out / and report / ed true / for him / —that he / has
> missed.

In the scanned sentence there, the long four-syllable feet at the
beginning give an effect of rapid understatement (in prose as in
verse a long foot quickens tempo, and reduces emphasis, a short
foot slows tempo, and heightens emphasis). Then there is a
slow gravity of movement in the shorter, heavier feet, a signal
that we are, after all, to take the statement as wholly serious.

Yet the young Durrell, so much tempted by 'poetic' prose,
and with such a dangerous facility for the 'poetic', perhaps a
facility, as in Pater himself sometimes, for the cloying, the pretty,
the sickly, will pull himself sharply up: with a word or a phrase
wilfully harsh, perhaps wilfully disgusting. The harshness, the
disgustingness, like the cadenzas and the bravura, must have for
Durrell himself today, as for other readers, a slightly touching
flavour of prolonged adolescence. Here is another example of
this counterpointing:

> Sheerly / punctilio, / as it were, / dedicated / to a *rape* /
> under a / cherry tree / and the smell / of *sperm*: and that
> / incom / prehens / ion in / your eyes. / Magic, / you say, /
> it was magical? / The past / is al / ways mag / ical. / Store
> me / the images / in a velv / et casket / among the / letters
> with rib / bon round them. / If I began / would you hold /
> the *bucket* / under my head / for the *vomit* / of Englishry /
> —the images?

The words *rape*, *sperm*, *bucket* and *vomit* are there to counteract
the too sweet, too stale effect of *cherry tree, your eyes, velvet casket,
ribbon round them,* as also of the triple run of *magic, magical,*

magical and the twice-repeated and climactic *images*. The coarse words also help to prevent the Elizabethanly contrived triple final cadence,

> *for the vomit*
> *of Englishry*——
> *the images. . . .*

from seeming too much mere contrivance. But at the same time the trills, roulades, cadenzas stop the angrier, coarser, nastier passages from being taken *au pied de la lettre*.

I have noticed, I may say in passing, a similar complexity of effect in Durrell's conversation: there often seems to be a contradiction between things he is saying, perhaps sharp, harsh, malicious, more often rumbustiously buffoonish, and the light, rippling or chuckling music of his voice. Durrell's voice, in prose as well as conversation, invites one to take timbre and rhythm as subtly modulating sense, as introducing a note of compunction or tenderness perhaps where one least expects it.

A voice like Durrell's, which one listens to for its own sake, perhaps at first only half attending to what is being said, is a great advantage to a poet. It might be thought a handicap, rather than otherwise, for a novelist. Henry Miller, at first rejoicing in the richness of language in *The Black Book*, quite soon began to be worried by it. He thought that a lot of the Durrellian verbal novelties, which sprang very largely from Durrell's wide reading in psychology and in medical books, were splendid nonsense words. He had not a good dictionary and so Durrell's fancy words were often to Miller (to use a Durrellianism) mere cryptic glyphs. He wrote to Durrell:

> *Aboulia, magma, floccus.* . . . When you finally left the Ark grounding on Mt. Ararat what a consolation it must have been to find that all your marvellous words were also rescued from the Flood! The Picassos on the wall! Yes, and with it, floccus, magma, aboulia, alexia, aphasia, amusia, anoi and Miss Smith's red coon slit, her conk, her poll, her carnivorous ant-eating laughter, her Chaucerian Africa with Freudian fauna and flora, with Chamberlain's agraphia. . . .

66

Slightly anxiously, if not exactly touchily, Durrell wrote to Miller explaining that he was not a nonsense writer, that all the out-of-the-way words in *The Black Book* both have a dictionary meaning and make precise sense in the contexts in which they are used. Magma, for instance, is a geological term for the hot, sticky, porridgy substance at the earth's centre which spouts up to form volcanoes or crystallizes into igneous rock. Words like aboulia, alexia, aphasia, agraphia and so on reflect Durrell's medical reading but also remind us that he knows Greek, ancient and modern, so well that words with Greek roots are as transparent to him as words with Anglo-Saxon and Latin roots to the ordinary educated reader. Durrell was rightly proud of the range of a vocabulary which rivals Joyce's without resorting to word-coinage and wrote to Miller:

> One thing I've hammered home is that there is no word-coining in it. The vocabulary may be Elizabethan, Middle-English, Dutch etc. but EVERYTHING MEANS SOMETHING. That is why Laughlin's dream-writing contributors bore me stiff with their 'wingle wangle obfuscating inspissate hunger-marching shitshat.' Come, we demand more than chewing-gum. WE ARE HUNGRY.

2

If Miller could not understand all the words in *The Black Book*, he at once grasped its thematic pattern. The reason why *The Black Book* may still leave many young readers, as it left the young Dylan Thomas, 'sickened and excited' is its dizzying emotional swing. The book appears to express now total rejection, now total acceptance; now frenetic disgust, now manic celebration. Miller put this very clearly, in one of his letters to Durrell:

> The theme is death and rebirth, the Dionysian theme which I predicted in the Lawrence book must be the theme for the writers to come—the only theme permissible or possible. Your rebirth is the most violent act of destruction.

More subtly, Miller put his finger on the recurrent symbolic motif of the book, the motif of a sense of stifling enclosure in the womb, a violent emergence from it, and the danger of the regressive wish to get back. Durrell, or Lawrence Lucifer, himself defines this in a footnote about Hilda, the ever-open whore. Hilda, though whorish, contradicts Freud by also being a mother-figure: cramming the sturdy infant, the baby Pantagruel, Lawrence Lucifer, back into her cosy and claustrophobic peace.

Hilda has become sterile at the end of the novel, her ovaries have been removed, possibly she is dying of venereal disease (she warns Lawrence Lucifer that she is terribly ill, and that he ought to have a blood-test). Hilda, with her immense red bush of pubic hair, is a figure of grotesque, pathetic, and obscene comedy. Yet she is the only female character or image in *The Black Book* with whom Lawrence and the other male characters (at least, those who are sexually normal) are completely at ease. Hilda represents, under the mask of farcical pathos, an equation of peace and death. Farce cannot rob her of her grand scale. Like the quite opposite virginal mother figure, Madame About, the impoverished teacher of French, dying of cancer, Hilda is a figure of heroic generosity and dignity. She is, even when dying and sterile, a personification of the womb. She *is* the womb. And the womb for Durrell in *The Black Book* is the symbol of all creativity, of all constriction and release, giving birth with awful pain, immortal as a principle, terribly vulnerable as an object. About to take the risk of making love to the sterilized and perhaps diseased Hilda, Lawrence Lucifer writes:

> Forgive my imprecision, but it is as if I were packing for a long journey. Hilda lies open like a trunk in the corner of the room. There is room for everything, the gramophone, the records, the cottage-piano, the microscope, the hair-restorer, seven sets of clean clothes, manuscripts, a typewriter, a dictionary, a pair of jack-boots, skates, an ice-pick, a crash-helmet, a sheath-knife, a fishing-rod, and the latest book-society choice.

He adds, in the elucidatory footnote to which I alluded in the last paragraph: 'This is the recurrent regression-motif with which everything seems to end: another back-to-the-womber's allegory.'

That passage about Hilda as a travelling trunk, with its use of asyndeton and catalogues, recalls some of the prose passages in Auden's *The Orators*, a book which the young Durrell must certainly have read and admired. A dominant motif in *The Orators* is the deadly power of the Mothers, a motif which recurs at the end of Auden's and Isherwood's *The Ascent of F6*. Auden and some of the poets closely influenced by him, like Cecil Day Lewis, reacted against insidious maternal power with a kind of romantic male tribalism, a glorification of the airman, the climber, the Arctic explorer, 'men without women'. Freudians believe, putting it broadly and too simply, that over-domination of the son by the Mother can lead to homosexuality. The taboo upon the Mother is so strong that *any* kind of normal sexual intercourse is a ritual profanation of her image. The English public-school system, with its segregation and tribal disciplining of young males, its insistence on 'hardness', can channel this horror of thinking of the Mother, and therefore of woman as such, as a sexual object into lifelong latent or openly admitted homosexuality. Many of the male characters in *The Black Book* do seem in fact to be consciously or unconsciously homosexual, emotionally if not physically.

Death Gregory, whose journey forms the one completed inner story, in *The Black Book*, within the womb of Lawrence Lucifer's outer commentary, is a typical victim of the dominating mother and of a genteel education. He is a lonely middle-aged rentier, with literary tastes, with minor and precious literary talents, a self-punisher, full of proud self-disgust. He picks up a half-educated girl off the streets. She is sick, she is simple, she is pathetically ignorant and grateful, and he is able to feel tenderness for her, real love, because she reminds him neither of his mother nor of the prostitute, Fanny, who initiated him sickeningly into sexual experience. But Gregory has become too twisted, too withdrawn, to express properly the tenderness he really feels. He thinks he owes it to himself to be bitter, cynical, self-betraying. Thus he almost encourages the girl to betray him with a flashy gigolo, Clare, though in her heart she wants to be loyal to Gregory.

Finally Gregory marries the girl. This is a gesture of love again, though he conceals the love from her. Soon he comes almost to hate, partly for snobbish reasons—his friends, who accepted her as his mistress, jib at her as his wife—and partly because the poor girl develops an irritating *petit bourgeois* possessiveness. The girl dies, without Gregory's ever having made it clear to her that he desperately loves her. He writes his story in green ink, exposing himself, as he puts it, to a firing squad of green bullet-like self-reproaching words. Later he marries another woman, older, coarse and common, who feels no emotion for him, who is mean and undemanding (mean in thinking first about security, undemanding of love) as Gregory will be with her. The new life will enclose Gregory in a grim womb-substitute, an over-furnished, stuffy, lower-middle-class interior. His end will be a completely sterile relationship with a nanny-substitute rather than a mother-substitute.

3

Gregory is the figure in *The Black Book* for whom Durrell arouses most human pity. The most sinister figure in the book but yet, like the much more likeable Scobie in *The Alexandria Quartet*, grotesquely comic, is Tarquin. It is difficult to feel much pity for Tarquin (he is the one character in the book whom at one moment Lawrence Lucifer wants to hit) but he is not in the end hateful, perhaps because he is not fully human enough to be hateful; in the end, he is what Lawrence Lucifer, in a Jonsonian sense, calls 'a humour'. We see Tarquin first as an overt but sublimated homosexual, obsessed with the gigolo, Clare, but insisting that his obsession is 'platonic'. While Clare is away from the large shabby hotel, where many of the characters live and where most of them foregather, Tarquin makes an expedition to Brighton where, for the first time in his life, he possesses a woman: an experience which disgusts and appals him, and so unsettles him that he begins to act, for the first time, on his hitherto rigidly controlled homosexual impulses. He even seduces Clare, but out of this experience, also, there comes nothing but disgust and self-contempt. It is too late for Tarquin to be open, to surrender, to feel tenderness for anything or anybody, as Gregory felt his pathetic unexpressed tenderness for the sick young girl who died. He is shut in his 'horrible tower'.

This kind of emotional sterility, or occlusion of the soul, Durrell in *The Black Book* seems to see as particularly the illness of the failed artist. Tarquin is a composer of some talent, as Gregory was a writer; and, since Tarquin is a more forceful and ruthless person, we are made to feel that the potential talent was perhaps greater. But Tarquin, too, collapses, like Gregory, in a sterile but in his case solitary womb-world. He lies in bed more and more, rarely getting up, sitting in the end in a state of semi-paralysis, listening over and over again to the same comic jazz record, chosen just because it insults and desecrates his naturally fine and fastidious taste in music. He is another slow self-destroyer. In the end, they will come to take him away to a hospital or an asylum. Two other grotesque minor characters, Lobo and Perez, are both perhaps also on the verge of a homosexual state: one tormented by a memory of rejection, the memory of a woman, the *anima*-figure who always haunts him, but, to repulse him, she once crammed her vagina full of sand: the other a compulsive and casual womanizer. Clare, the gigolo, represents another kind of dehumanization of sex; man or woman, it does not matter to him, as long as the transaction brings material profit.

4

The normality of all the characters is perhaps to some degree under question. Lawrence Lucifer is aware of the regressive element in his own attachment to Hilda: for his *anima*-figure, to whom much of his more bravura writing is addressed, his feelings are a fusion of love and hate, utter tenderness and destructive resentment. When he describes the vibrant primitive

sexuality of the negro girl to whom he is teaching Chaucer (a
sexuality felt merely as a vibration, for he makes no advances
to her), there is a certain horror mingled with his comic lyricism;
a certain guilt, also, for in teaching her English literature, he
feels that he is draining the healthy African blood out of her
veins and filling them, instead, with poisonous ink.

In this ornate book, there are certain passages of straight
traditional narrative, and one of these describes a visit which
Lawrence Lucifer pays to his friend, the boisterous, progressive
life-worshipper—but a life-worshipper maimed by inner un-
belief—Chamberlain. Chamberlain is out, only Chamberlain's
wife is at home. Out of the sullen compulsion of mere propin-
quity, they make love to each other, without physical eagerness,
without personal liking. The theme of hidden homosexuality
comes out here also. Stifled by the atmosphere of Chamberlain's
books and furniture, Chamberlain's psychic atmosphere around
him, Lawrence Lucifer feels, disgustedly, that he is making love
to Chamberlain himself. And the sullenness, the rancour of
Chamberlain's wife reveals how hollow all Chamberlain's talk
about life-worship is; he has entrapped his wife in a kind of
greyness, a deadness. Later, Chamberlain's social façade, his
cheerful bouncy idealism, slowly collapses under the strain of
this sterile relationship with his wife. Then she becomes pregnant (perhaps because of this single encounter with Lawrence
Lucifer, who, in this sterile world, is a kind of fertility-god) and
Chamberlain becomes happy again.

The result of his happiness is interesting. Chamberlain
decides to throw away all ideologies:

    'What do you think?' he says, throwing his hat on the
rack with the air of a matador. 'She's pregnant!' We sit
down on the sofa, and he collapses with laughter, showing
every tooth in his head. Then he sits awhile sniffing hysterically, stroking my knee and talking about morning sickness, evening sickness, and midnight belly-bumping. He is
all unnerved, but filled with a kind of fanatical happiness.
'So everything seems settled! God! what fools we make of
ourselves. All the agony I've been through, over a damn

ten-centimetre foetus. By the way, I've got a marvellous job, two hundred a year more. I'm through with the body mystical and all that stuff from now, I can tell you. . . .' He is planning a beautiful suburban existence, complete with lawn-mower and green house. I can see that. I have not the will to mutter anything but compliments to him. The child will be still-born, I know, but I am not allowed to tell him that.

Lawrence Lucifer knows, I think, that the child will be still-born because he feels that his own cold contact with Chamberlain's wife has not altered her essential emotional deadness, the deadness of the Chamberlains' relation with each other. Yet though Chamberlain here is a figure of great pathos, strangely, Durrell, in his letter welcoming Henry Miller's first enthusiasm about *The Black Book*, almost verbally echoes Chamberlain:

As soon as the boat's ready we go. No more books, no more writers, no more anything. I WANT A GOOD STEADY JOB WITH A LITTLE HOME LOTS OF CHILDREN A LAWN MOWER A BANK ACCOUNT A LITTLE CAR AND THE RESPECT OF THE MAN NEXT DOOR.

I have quoted the passage about Chamberlain at length for several reasons. It is, as I say, one of a number of passages in *The Black Book* which exhibit the 'straight' novelist's gift rather than the virtuosity of the stylist. When he wants to, Durrell can present a scene, an incident, a character without trimmings. What mannerism there is in the Chamberlain passage—'with the air of a matador', 'showing every tooth in his head', 'midnight belly-bumping', 'damn ten-centimetre foetus'—suggests the bluffness of a writer like Richard Aldington or like Wyndham Lewis in the vein of *Tarr*. The idea that it is better to be a plain and decent businessman rather than a pseudo-artist or pseudo-intellectual was one which both Aldington and Wyndham Lewis strongly held. Durrell himself is not being superior or sarcastic about the lawn-mower and the greenhouse, or the good steady job and the respect of the man next door. Better to be a healthy, happy, uncomplicated, and moderately useful social animal than to be Gregory or Tarquin.

Yet even in such straight narrative passages the central theme of *The Black Book* is not lost sight of. That Lawrence Lucifer should be *certain* that Chamberlain's baby will be still-born is very implausible as straight realistic narrative, but it is something necessary to underline the theme of *The Black Book*, which is more or less the theme of *The Waste Land:* death and rebirth, certainly, as Miller saw; but, more specifically, in its working out, social sterility as exemplified in the sterility of most of the exhibited sexual relationships. The sterility, the death, breeds the awful hunger for mere life. Durrell himself states this very clearly:

> *But the hunger, the ravening at the*
> *bottom of all this I recognize at last.*
> *It is not a thirst for love, or money,*
> *or sex; but a thirst for living.*

5

What Henry Miller had to say about *The Black Book* is still the most perceptive criticism of this very important and still somewhat neglected work, and has much bearing also on Durrell's future development. Miller complimented Durrell on having 'expanded the womb feeling until it includes the whole universe', but, after his first stunned admiration for the range of Durrell's vocabulary, his subsequent feeling was that the style drew too much attention to itself, was 'too rich and savoury to gulp down quickly', and that the book would be improved by pruning: 'there are passages of minor importance where you elaborate for no good reason—perhaps because the machine was geared up and you couldn't apply the brakes.' He quoted some friends of his:

> They complain of fatigue, of preciosity, while admitting to the power and beauty of your language. But *language*, a little too much of it? . . . This is a common enough phenomenon, so don't let it worry you. You have simply overshot your wad. Hitting the right stride is always a matter of

getting beyond language, don't you think? Of being immediate.

In fact, greatly as they admire each other, no two writers could contrast more in their essential gifts than Lawrence Durrell and Henry Miller. Miller is both an extraordinarily uneven and an extraordinarily unselfconscious writer. He belongs to the tradition of American writers like Mark Twain, Theodore Dreiser, and William Faulkner. We put up with a great deal that is rambling, clumsy, or tedious, for the sake of that gift of 'getting beyond language', of 'being immediate'. It is experience which turns such writers in one great American tradition towards creation; though they may seem, when they start out, not to possess any of the writer's ordinary tools. Durrell is the opposite type of writer who is forced to enlarge his experience to find material for his verbal skills to work on. The most profound womb-image in *The Black Book* is, probably, the enclosing, almost plushy richness of the verbal texture. Durrell replied to Miller with exemplary humility:

> And of course language is my problem. Why I am your most ardent admirer is because of the way you use everything and are used by nothing—in writing, I mean. I set out on a voyage to find myself—and find language. A vicious thing good writing is. I wish I wrote worse—in the good sense.

Durrell certainly never worked over the surface of any subsequent book as laboriously, or over such a long period of time, as over *The Black Book*. He learned perhaps from this correspondence with Miller to write rapidly, to take risks. *The Alexandria Quartet* is, of course, full of bravura passages but there is not the sense of indigestibility, of congestion, which worried Miller in *The Black Book*. But a certain delicacy in the handling of language was part of Durrell's formation; Miller's blunt directness was something Durrell never really aimed at, nor, had he aimed at it, could he have achieved it. A man from the first of oblique attitudes and sophisticated verbal talent, he could never, by willing it, become a magnificent *naïf*.

6

Miller was useful to the young Durrell, over *The Black Book*, not only critically, but in helping Durrell to be a man. Durrell, by the terms of his contract with Faber's, had to give them the first refusal of *The Black Book*. He expected them to hate it, but on the contrary they were enthusiastic. 'Enthusiastic letters from Morley and Pringle and a typical "kind letter" from Eliot,' Durrell wrote to Miller. But the only form in which they could publish it was an expurgated edition. Durrell was sorely tempted. Faber's then as now was a firm of very high reputation and, if Durrell was hoping ultimately to get his poetry published by them, they were the firm that published Eliot and Pound, and that had made the reputations of Durrell's slightly older contemporaries, Auden, MacNeice, and Spender. Their novels and their general prose books were advertised generously, were widely reviewed, and sold widely. To become established as a Faber author was, for an author in his mid-twenties in the late 1930s, something not to be scorned. Durrell must have felt that he was being offered all the kingdoms of the world for a little self-castration. And, after all, if Faber's published a bowdlerized *Black Book*, might not Jack Kahane in Paris still bring out an unexpurgated edition?

Miller has a streak in him of granitic American puritanism. You do not compromise. In a letter to Durrell he drives home this point in prose of muscular, unliterary plainness, like the prose of Lincoln or Ulysses S. Grant:

Frankly, I am not in accord with you about accepting Faber's plan, just because it is a pis aller. No, with that logic, that attitude, you'll always be fucked good and proper. Don't you see, according to *their* logic, you *must* conform—because they control the situation. But the moment you say to hell with that and decide to do as you damn please *you find the man* to sponsor you. But, anyway, whether you lose out permanently with Faber or not, all that is beside the point—that is *their* affair. Yours is with your own conscience. On that grain of faith out of which you built your book you must rest. You stand firm and let the world come round. . . . In other words, forgive my advice, but I would say you can't look two ways. You've got to accept the responsibility for your actions.

The trouble was that the young Durrell was a little attracted by the role of Mr Facing-Both-Ways. His answer to Miller was almost a wail:

You see, I CAN'T WRITE REAL BOOKS ALL THE TIME. It's like an electric current: increase the dose very gradually. . . . Once every three years or more I shall try to compose for full orchestra. The rest of the time I shall do essays, travel-books, perhaps one more novel under Charles Norden. I shall naturally not try to write badly or things I don't want to : but a lot of things I want to write don't come into the same class as *The Black Book* at all. I consider that resting. Travel essays, about Greece, literary essays, Hamletry, and all that. This kind of literary gardening will soothe me and stop me fretting myself.

Miller's reply was stern and realistic:

Don't, my good Durrell, take the schizophrenic route. If there are just half-a-dozen people in the world, like myself, who believe in you, that should more than outweigh the other considerations. The danger is in the psyche—believe it or not. You are young, happily married, full of encouragement, praised to the skies, healthy, not hungry, not penniless, befriended, surrounded with congratulations, with what not, a boat to boot, be Jesus! the Ionian skies, isolation (which I would give my shirt to have) and so on. Now don't, my dear good Durrell, ask me to weep with you because you are *alone*. You ought to be proud of that. That's in your favour. You can't be alone and with the herd too. You can't write good *and* bad books. Not for long. Show me examples, if you know any. You must stand or fall either as Charles Norden or as Lawrence Durrell. I would choose Lawrence Durrell, if I were you.

Durrell took Miller's advice and refused to expurgate *The Black Book* to make it acceptable to Faber's.

This did not lead to a break with Faber's, and, in fact, Durrell's subsequent career has been much more like the one he envisaged for himself than the one foreseen by Miller. It is not that he has chosen to write 'good books *and* bad books' but that he knows both that he must constantly keep his hand in and also that he cannot write at the fullest pressure all the time. Charles Norden, as an alias for books Lawrence Durrell was slightly ashamed of, was dropped; but, for instance, the Antrobus books, *White Eagles Over Serbia*, *Key to Modern Poetry* (which Faber's rightly did not publish, for it is not up to the standard of their best criticism), perhaps *The Dark Labyrinth* and at a higher level the island books are work by a good professional. It is, in fact, only at intervals of a number of years that Durrell can bring out a very ambitious work: 'It's like an electric current: increase the dose very gradually. . . .' What mattered was not so much his future as, in Miller's phrase, the 'danger . . . in the psyche'. Durrell took a risk, a bold decision to risk a break with the possibility of conventional success. He was to have his conventional success, as well as the other kind of success, after all; but Miller had given him the courage to stand on his own feet.

7

The great spirit that broods over *The Black Book* is not, however, that of Henry Miller but that of T. S. Eliot. Essentially, *The Black Book* is a set of variations on *The Waste Land*. *The Waste Land* is a poem about sterility, about the late autumn or early winter (in the Spenglerian sense) of a culture. This sterility is poetically reflected in the sterility of the most potentially creative and potentially destructive of all human relationships, that of sexual love. Yet the drive of the poem is a desperate, perhaps impossible quest to get beyond sterility. Its setting is a phantasmagoric London, modulated in a dream-like fashion, though vividly physically present. There is a perpetual juxtaposition of that which is sordid, the carbuncular bank clerk, the girl opening tinned food and drying her combinations on the window sill, with all the echoes of ancientness and splendour in London's memory, Spenser's Thames, the pleasant whining of a mandoline in a Lower Thames Street pub, St Magnus Martyr with its inexplicable splendour of Ionian white and gold. In the language, Elizabethan allusion or pastiche juxtaposes with cockney slang. The horror, the boredom, the disgust, which *The Waste Land* embodies so vividly, are pierced from above and below with sudden glory and compassion. A profound death-wish transforms itself into an agonizing pilgrimage towards the sources of life.

The Black Book is *Waste Land*-like in its setting, but I mean that in a moral, not in a topographical sense. I have in mind a much broader resemblance, the sense of a contrast between the magic of an older England, a past magic that comes alive to Lawrence Lucifer in the pastoral presence, nymph or shepherdess, of his *anima*-figure, suddenly alive in a world of rough stone cottages and apple blossom—the contrast between that lost pastoral world and the comic-macabre or comic-grotesque hell, the city detritus of a once organic culture, that Lawrence Lucifer is more often exploring. The rich past chokes him; he feels he is treading on corpses. He is caught, as Tarquin and Gregory are caught, between a rich cultural inheritance, which has gone dead, and a world of brute impulse. The inherited culture breeds a fastidiousness, which in the end is *fastidium*, disgust with life.

In characters like Clare, Lobo, and Perez (the names suggest *Gerontion*, the Sweeney poems, and *Sweeney Agonistes*) mere brute impulse reveals itself with a sterile disgustingness that might seem to justify a cultural disgust. A way out is suggested only indirectly, in the rebelliousness and disgust of the hero, and in Death Gregory's perpetual verging, in his relationship with his pitiable wife and mistress Grace (her name is not unsymptomatic), on 'the awful daring of a moment's surrender', which never in the end takes place. There is no way out, either, for any of the characters except Lawrence Lucifer, through art.

Death Gregory's writing builds the walls of isolation closer round him, Eliot's 'prison', Dante's *'orribile torre'*. Lawrence Lucifer's own role, like his name, is ambiguous: is he a bearer of light into dark places, or a rebel angel, relishing the torment of all these damned souls? Or for all the energy of his protests, is he himself among them? 'Give, sympathize, control': the final impact of *The Black Book* is as ambiguous as the final impact of *The Waste Land*. We ought to give, sympathize, and control, but can we? What real serenity and wisdom has Lawrence Lucifer reached at the end? Is the whole book not a projection of his youthful unresolved turbulence? And has the *anima*-figure not a point when she writes to Lucifer: 'Your poetry is wild and unformed. Concentrate on style. And I don't understand how you can both love and hate the same woman at the same time.'

This girl's voice expresses the feeling for a just measure, in life and art, for the 'nothing too much', a feeling which, often natural to young women, is acquired only with great effort by young men. Her words will have infuriated Lawrence Lucifer because of their cool indifference to the sense of 'suppurating hatred', of Gothic suffering, which is his obsession and his subject-matter. And her advice was not advice which, except in his poems, sometimes, and in his books about islands, Lawrence Durrell would ever be able easily to take. In love with the naked burning impact of white light on Greek marble, with rocky bareness, sparse elegance, Durrell was nevertheless to remain a Gothic spirit: Rabelaisian in his taste for gaminess, stuffing, verbal copiousness: Hamletian in his taste for 'wild and whirling words'. *The Black Book* in its lardedness, unctuousness, morbidity, black farce, belching lyricism, hopeless pity, and in its occasional passages of undoctored French naturalism, records the birth-pangs of this unclassical, even anti-classical talent.

Lawrence Lucifer's name, as I have said, is ambiguously symbolic. In one of the set pieces in *The Black Book*, the young Lawrence Lucifer—perhaps also the young Lawrence Durrell—admits and displays the combination in him of self-enclosure, self-obsession, and fundamental opacity of the self to the self:

In this theatre it is all or nothing. Oneself is the hero, the

clown, the chorus; there are no extras, and no doubles to
accept the dangers. But more terrible still, in the incessant
whine of the chorale, the words, words, words spraying
from the stiff mouths of the masks, one becomes at last
aware of the identity of the audience. It is my own face in
its incessant reduplications which blazes back at me from
the stone amphitheatre. . . . In the mirror, there is no
symptom whatever: take me, I am to be accepted or denied:
not to be understood, but experienced: not to be touched,
but a funnel of virtue: not a Christian, but an admirer of
God in men. Do not enquire of the ingenuous mask, I say, it
can tell you nothing.

8

Professor Graham Hough, in his excellent recent work, *An
Essay on Criticism*, classifies a number of kinds of literary work
whose unity is doubtful. They include indefinitely expansible
work like Pound's *Cantos*; works which solve the problem by
'frankly remaining unfinished, like Byron's *Don Juan*'; works
which have had inorganic sequels tacked on to them like *Pamela*
and *Robinson Crusoe* (some critics, notably George Steiner, have
had this sort of worry about Durrell's *Clea*; for me, as for Henry
Miller, this is a book doing in 200 pages what most novelists
would have done in 500, and, unlike Miller, I do not consider
this a fault). Finally, Professor Hough lists 'works of great beauty
and insight that yet remain imperfect because they pose a
situation or a problem and then fade out without resolving it, or
give a resolution that is inorganic or contrived (*Wahlverwandt-
schaften, Le Grand Meaulnes*)'. From what he has written about it
elsewhere, I think Graham Hough would put *The Waste Land*
in this last class; so the young Durrell remains in congenial and
distinguished company.

The Black Book, in fact, *is* messy, as so many powerful books
by very young men are. The novelists whom the young Durrell
drew on, Pater, Norman Douglas, Richard Aldington, D. H.

Lawrence, Wyndham Lewis, Aldous Huxley, can all teach a young writer lessons about keeping a page of narrative prose alive, lessons about texture, but not one of them is a great structural inventor. Kenneth Young introduced Durrell to one of the few modern English structural masterpieces, Ford Madox Ford's *The Good Soldier*, after Durrell had written *Justine*, and Durrell was grateful he saw it so late. Ford's sheer neatness might have discouraged him from a more ambitious but more open-ended structural experiment. *The Alexandria Quartet* has an organic unity that *The Black Book* has not, since its broad *charpente* is controlled throughout by an elaborate theory of the discovery of the actual as a series of unveilings of partial misrepresentations, a theory which commands the order of presentation of both reflections and events. More briefly, thoughts about structure and presentation give *The Alexandria Quartet* its trellis shape, and the roses of rhetoric must be trained over the right part of the trellis. *The Black Book* is, by comparison, structurally loose. Gregory's tight monologue within Lawrence Lucifer's loose commenting monologue gives a certain general shape: a framework into which the young Durrell can fit, almost at random, his set pieces of powerful writing, his 'blocks', as Henry Miller called them. But the book has not within itself the reasons why it should not be a great deal longer, as in its first draft it was, or considerably shorter, as Henry Miller thought with advantage it might be, than it is. Many of the 'blocks' could be shifted around to different positions, some could be dropped altogether, without a great deal of difference in the total effect.

Messy, often painful, sometimes embarrassing to read, as it is—embarrassing for poor young Durrell's sake—*The Black Book* does squeeze out its author, a new voice in a new time, a sturdy bawling baby, an infant Pantagruel, alive and kicking from its womb. In his preface to the 1959 edition, Durrell quotes the wise words of an older friend, a doctor of medicine, a Greek:

> The crudities match and belong. I have never understood why writers should not be regarded by the reader as enjoying much the same rights as doctors. You do not

suspect indecency in a doctor who makes you strip in order to examine you. Why shouldn't you give the writer the same benefit of the doubt? As for your novel—you can't have a birth without a great deal of mess and blood. The labour pains, the groans, sounded quite genuine to me; I suppose because I regard art as a serious business, and spiritual birth as something like the analogy of the physical. No, you are not pretending! Hence the impact of the book, I think.

I have given *The Black Book* a more extended critical treatment than it has ever received before. It has been comparatively neglected. I hope I have suggested both how interesting it is in itself and what a crucial role the book, and the decision to publish it, unexpurgated, in Paris played in Durrell's development.

CHAPTER FOUR

THE LOVER OF ISLANDS

I

Lawrence Durrell's three island books, *Prospero's Cell* (1945), *Reflections on a Marine Venus* (1953) and *Bitter Lemons* (1957), both record the trajectory of a love affair with Greece and show growth in Durrell over a period of nearly twenty years. (Though *Prospero's Cell* was published in 1945, it incorporates much material written in 1937 and 1938, and its setting is the life of Lawrence and Nancy Durrell in Corfu in the years just before the Second World War and just after the completion of *The Black Book*.) *Prospero's Cell* is, to me, the most charming of the three, the most unflawed as a minor work of art, and its mood might be described as that of pastoral comedy. *Reflections on a Marine Venus* reflects Durrell's experiences as an Information Officer in Rhodes in 1945 and 1946, just after the war, and it is a darker and deeper book. There is still much brilliant comic writing, much loving appreciation of the humours and eccentricities of close friends, much vivid scenic description, but the underlying note is a sense of the violence and poverty which, throughout their history, the Greek people have endured, and of their stoical courage. The great set piece in *Prospero's Cell* is a chapter on the Karaghiosis puppet play; the great set piece in *Reflections on a Marine Venus* is a masterly evocation, recalling in its graphic sweep the historical writings of Sir Steven Runciman, of the siege of Rhodes by Demetrius Poliorcetes. This description has its humours and ironies, but they are of a grim sort. The

84

humour, everywhere, in *Reflections on a Marine Venus* is linked
with a sense of the sadness and precariousness of life, a new kind
of compassion.

Lawrence Durrell was able to allow himself time to mature
these two books. In 1945 he published an account of experiences
of 1937 and 1938, in 1953 he cut down, with the help and advice
of his friend Anne Ridler, his overgrown manuscript about his
experiences of 1945 and 1946. The third book, *Bitter Lemons*,
was written more hastily. Beginning to be estranged from his
second wife, Eve, and leaving Jugoslavia, which he detested,
Durrell came in 1952 to Cyprus. His intention was to buy a
small house, in a Cypriot village, with his savings, and to settle
down to serious writing, supplementing his income by some work
in a Greek grammar school or Gymnasium. Already, when Durrell arrived in Cyprus, there was a great deal of talk about
Enosis, and at first Durrell met with some churlishness and
hostility, but he was soon accepted—because of his courage, his
open friendliness, his fluent modern Greek, his fondness for
wine and gossip, his lack of 'side'—as a good neighbour and
friend. He did not find any real communal strife: a Greek schoolmaster recommended him to a Turkish house-agent, and the
Turkish house-agent recommended him, again, to a Greek
carpenter and builder to put the picturesque old Turkish house
which Durrell had bought into order.

He did not take Enosis very seriously; obviously, the Cypriot
Greek liked to talk about it, but Durrell felt that the traditional
Greek love for England, for an England represented to them by
Byron and Churchill and the brave young Englishmen who
had fought with the Cretan resistance, would be much stronger
than a mere pan-Hellenic sentiment. He did feel that the
English administration was too paternalistic, too colonial, that
there should be wider local self-government. The educational
system, originally modelled on the German system, seemed to
him, from his experiences as a schoolmaster, absurd and in-
efficient. He regretted the lack of a good book-shop, a theatre,
even a swimming-bath in the capital, the lack of outlet for
Cypriot energy and talent. But he took the common view of

mainland Greeks that the Cypriots were an indolent and patient people who would go on submitting, as they had under the Lusignans, the Venetians, and the Turks, and for nearly eighty years under the English, to being governed by a minority of foreigners more energetic and determined than themselves.

His life in the village of Bellapaix remained for a time idyllic, variegated by visits from travellers like Rose Macaulay, Freya Stark, his brother Gerald, and Sir Harry Luke, but during the years between 1952 and 1956 the situation steadily deteriorated, and ended in open revolutionary violence. Durrell was once again caught up in official work in Nicosia as a press officer. He felt at first, and a Greek diplomat friend, visiting Cyprus, confirmed this, that the Athens government was being pushed only reluctantly into supporting Enosis by pressure at home, and that timely concessions would ease this pressure—the offer of a constitution, say, which would permit a local parliament to vote for Enosis in principle, but after a lapse of fifteen or twenty years. Meanwhile, the rather old-fashioned, Indian colonial style of administration and police organization in Cyprus could be brought up to date. The violence when it came sickened him, and he felt in the end that there was no answer to it, for the moment, but counter-violence, represented by the new governor, the efficient soldier, Sir John Harding. England somehow had to hang on to Cyprus because of its commitments in the Near East. The friendliness of the villagers, though it never turned into open hostility, muted into silence, and when Durrell finally went to collect a few papers from his house in Bellapaix, before going away for ever, no one in the village street greeted him. They were full of grief and rage because of the execution of the young terrorist, Karaolis. A few days before, Durrell's best Cypriot friend, the schoolmaster Panos, had been shot, perhaps for being too friendly with the Englishman. Yet Panos himself had said to Durrell at their last meeting: 'But it is not Karaolis only who will be hanged; the deep bond between us will have been broken finally.'

As he left Bellapaix, Andreas, who had worked so hard on Durrell's house, had the courage to say farewell to him. And the taxi-driver who took Durrell to the airport tried in a clumsy way to say something comforting: 'Even Dighenis . . . they say he himself is very pro-British. . . . Yes . . . yes, even Dighenis, though he fights the British, really loves them. But he will have to go on killing them—with regret, even affection.' But the taxi-driver's remarks seemed to Durrell surrealistically absurd. He was never again to wish to live in Greece permanently and he had discovered also that, lover of Greece though he was, he was more fundamentally a British patriot. He saw that Harding's operational measures for restoring order were, militarily, the only thing to do and yet that they shut the door on an emotional reconciliation between Cyprus and England; similarly Arch-bishop Makarios's deportation was operationally right, and in terms of long-range politics disastrous. Durrell went back to England, having put all political solutions aside. All England could now do was to try to restore order, cling to her bases, give up any pretence of caring for Cypriot wishes or rights.

In the chapters on the violence, Durrell is fierce against Athens radio and its wild rhetoric, in what itself is often a fiercely rhetorical way. Like many writers on politics who profess to be coolly realistic, he is moved by emotions too deep and painful for cool definition. He rages at sixth-formers he taught, whom he finds in a detention camp; but he is disturbed to find that among the detainees are the men of culture, the men who read the kind of modern Greek poetry he reads himself. What hurts members of an ousted colonial administration, of an ousted privileged minority, and what especially hurts the liberal and sensitive among them is not the loss of power and privilege (Durrell had lived as simply as a peasant, found many of the administrators dull, tasteless bores). It is the galling sense of no longer being loved, looked up to, depended on, needed. It is like the rejection of a stern but fundamentally kindly father by a group of backward sons. After all, it seems they can stand on their own feet. Perhaps they never really loved him. A relationship with Greece that had began in Corfu as Shakespearian golden comedy, that had taken on in Rhodes the graver notes of the dark comedies, ended, perhaps, for Durrell in Cyprus with the rending severance of tragedy. He would never forget his last visit to Bellapaix:

> The eyes avoided mine, flickering shyly away from my glance 'like vernal butterflies'—I cannot say that they were full of hate. No. It was simply that the sight of me pained them. The sight of an Englishman had become an obscenity on that clear honey-gold spring air.

Things, between Durrell and Greece, it might seem, could never be quite the same again. Yet one of Durrell's closest friends, Alan Gradon Thomas, who saw this chapter in typescript, felt that I was overstressing, in my first draft, Durrell's disillusionment with Greece. His great love for Greece and the Greeks has flared up again in visits to Corfu and Athens in recent years. Another friend of Durrell's, Alan Pringle, thinks that in my detailed account of *Bitter Lemons* (which the reader will find a few pages farther on) I play down too much the happiness that keeps breaking in, even in *Bitter Lemons*, as in the vivid account of a swim towards the end of the book:

> Despite the high sea running the lagoon itself was calm save for a slight swell. The wind was north which meant that the western headland took the full force of the sea and sent down the smooth lolling aftertow into the bay. The Spring water was cold and pained one—as a drink of iced wine will hurt the back of the throat—but it was delicious. I abandoned myself to the running tide, not swimming, but simply keeping afloat, to be drawn smoothly out into the bay from where the whole screen of luminous mountain was visible. The sun had cleared them now and they were taking on that throbbing dark mauve which inhabits the heart of a violet. The trees had turned silver and the slices of corn-land to the east glittered king-cup yellow and shone like bugles. . . .

Certainly, whatever temporary disillusionment his Cyprus experiences may have brought upon Durrell, it was not a disillusionment with the Greek landscape.

2

Prospero's Cell is worked up, in many of its passages, from notes taken or a journal kept in Corfu in 1937 and 1938, just after the bloody throes of *The Black Book*, just before the Second World War. This strangely serene book is a mosaic portrait of an island, its geography, history, characters, and folklore. It is in the key of sympathetic comedy; but even more it is an evocation of pure happiness, the happiness that has no history. It is a poetic definition of what is meant by *dolce far niente*.

The prose sings. The very first sentence comes spinning, singingly spinning, off the page: the only opening sentence of any of Durrell's prose books, that one finds one has immediately by heart, like a line of verse:

> Somewhere between Calabria and Corfu the blue really begins.

That light, trilling note—birdsong!—is sustained without effort throughout the rest of the book. It is a book by a man who, for a blessed interval, has dropped all his burdens. Perhaps in 1937 and 1938, never wholly before and never wholly after, Durrell enjoyed a simple fulfilled love, a sense of being in the right place, with the right people; not pleasure that cloys, or ecstasy that exhausts, or enjoyment, which is a rewarding but fatiguing atmosphere of the discriminating will: but simple happiness, the sun, the sea, health and activity and loving fulfilment of the body, sound dreamless sleep, trusted companionship, the taste of spring water. To call this experience, and its presentation, pastoral is not to dismiss. That this kind of experience very rarely occurs is the exact reason why, as the persistence of the pastoral mode in poetry and comedy shows, men always hanker after it.

The book has its comedy as well as its lyricism, the comedy of the innocent enthusiasm of learning. There is Durrell's great friend from his early residence in Corfu, Dr Theodore Stephanides, a doctor of medicine, but also an expert on the geology,

the geography, the fauna and flora, the folklore and history of
Corfu. A great scholar, too modest to think of himself as a writer,[1]
Stephanides provides Durrell with more manuscript material
than he can use or control. There is Zarian, the Armenian poet,
master of five or six languages, who every week writes a long
newsletter to an Armenian paper in New York, taking notes of
every idea he hears discussed about Corfu, digesting Corfu
into his own poetry, his own fantasy. There is the Count D.,
the aristocrat who lived retired upon his country estate, who
appears to have attained a metaphysical wisdom which he is
wise enough never to express in words, and who works out the
theory, from which the book gets its title, that the island in
Shakespeare's *The Tempest* must have been Corfu. Another
literary layer is the traditional connection of Corfu with the
story of Odysseus and Nausicaa, and the problem of where
Odysseus will have landed. Every pleasant excursion and wine-
drinking becomes part of a great joint investigation of Corfu;
nothing is not relevant, yet everything smacks of fantasy, and
one of the best chapters, that on the Karaghiosis puppet play,
a beautiful accurate account of a popular audience and a comic
folk hero, has nevertheless the feeling of a dream. The speeches
of Count D., again, are like the speeches of a character in Norman Douglas, and the Count himself draws our attention to
this: 'Let us have a glass of wine, shall we? It's thirsty work talking like a Norman Douglas character.' The war is looming
over all these characters, and in a sense each is playing his part
in a *commedia dell'arte* improvization, delighting in the absurdi-
ties of his mask. Nothing disastrous, and indeed nothing painful
in the sense of satirical or corrective comedy, is going to happen
within the confines of the book; the comedy is to be wholly
sympathetic. The lyrical elements, like the glimpses of N.
(Nancy) with her fair beauty, her nereid quality, her doe-like
ears, more water-nymph than human being, hardly with a
speaking part, enhance the sense of the green or golden world,

[1] Though he had collaborated with George Katsimbalis in two volumes of
verse translations from the Greek; and was to publish his own account of a
campaign, *Climax in Crete*, two monographs, on the Microscope and on the
Freshwater Biology of Corfu, and a volume of verse, *The Golden Face*.

of Shakespearian romantic magic. The book is perfect in its small completeness, but the kind of perfection depends on the bracketing off of a good deal of reality.

3

At the end of the brief introductory section of the first chapter of *Prospero's Cell*, Durrell writes:

> Other countries may offer you discoveries in manners or lore or landscape; Greece offers you something harder— the discovery of yourself.

Paradoxically, it is part of the charm of the book that the young Durrell of *Prospero's Cell*, contrasted with the young Durrell of *The Black Book*, seems healthily incurious about his self; he has learned to leave his self alone. But the Durrell of *Reflections on a Marine Venus* is present throughout as a mature and rather bitter self. He approaches Rhodes from Egypt, in stormy weather, wondering whether he is going to be bitterly disappointed; will the Greece that he remembers so lucidly prove to be an illusion, a literary invention, built up from youthful high spirits, leisure, a favourable rate of exchange for the pound sterling? *Reflections on a Marine Venus* gets off the page, at the beginning, not spinningly, but with a certain trudging determination:

> Somewhere among the notebooks of Gideon I once found a list of diseases as yet unclassified by medical science, and among them there occurred the word *Islomania* which was described as a rare but by no means unknown affliction of the spirit.

Like 'Somewhere between Calabria and Corfu the blue really begins', this is a topic sentence; but where the first catches us into a dance, the second makes us feel: 'Oh, well, this is a rather ponderous opening, but let us read on, the man may have something to say.' Durrell, in fact, has almost too much to say and compared with *Prospero's Cell* its successor seems not exactly a 'made' book but a book bursting at the seams. The

central image of the marine Venus—'A statue of a woman:
period uncertain: found at the bottom of Rhodes harbour:
damaged by sea-water'—is a more profound image than that of
Corfu as Prospero's island. The statue is that of a matronly
figure worn by the sea so that she seems restored by magic to
adolescence. She 'has surrendered her original maturity for a
rediscovered youth'. She is a proper image, though Durrell does
not make this crudely explicit, for a beautiful island whose
history has been one of piracy, sea-war, sieges, a beauty perpetually assailed from the sea. And she fits in with the anecdote,
a poignant one, in a letter addressed to a friend of Durrell's,
at the end of the third chapter:

'. . . She stood before me without speaking. "Who is it?"
I said. She did not answer but softly placed a hand upon
my arm and I understood. We stood thus for a moment by
the harbour wall.

'I fumbled for a box of matches and struck one, saying
as I did so: "All right, if you are beautiful," The match-
flame copied itself into two dark eyes: a face much older
than itself—serious, beguiling, and most world-weary. We
climbed the slopes of Monte Smith and lay down together
in one of those rock-tombs, still warm.

'She was lean and half-starved and her clothes tasted of
sea-salt. Her poverty was poignant in a way that nobody
who has not experienced the Mediterranean can understand. In her I tasted the whole of Greece, its sunburnt airs,
dazzling bony islands, the chaste and honourable poverty
which the people has converted into a golden generosity.
Her name was Aphrodite—I know! I know! . . . She had a
rock-rose fastened to her shawl with a pin. When we parted
she detached it and handed it to me with a magnificent
friendliness. I had an inkling then that the Greeks were still
the natural poets of the Levant. They understand, you
know, that hunger is not proud and that the Tenth Muse is
really Poverty.'

The Durrell of *Prospero's Cell* is a young man with no cares and
no responsibilities: the Durrell of *Reflections on a Marine Venus* is

caught up in the 'awesome mass of wreckage' (E. E. Stoll's phrase about *Hamlet*) which is the aftermath of war: poverty, misery, destruction, the brutish violence of history are never far away. Durrell's companions, the agricultural officer, Gideon, the aged ex-counsul, Hoyle, the medical officer, Mills, are in a sense humours characters like Zarian, Stephanides, and Count D., but they are not sheltered from the impact of reality. Hoyle is old and frail, has to pause while he walks, ought to have an operation; there is something touching about him, and about the 'old rogue' Gideon, whose splendid military façade conceals perhaps a jaunty desperation. Gideon's heavy drinking is perhaps part of the comedy, but Durrell does not now think that heavy drinking is necessarily a symptom of inner happiness. Mills, the medical officer, has his cheerfulness tried everywhere by malnutrition and consumption and, when Gideon appropriates a consignment of powdered milk to fatten up some pigs he is responsible for, Mills does not really find it funny. Hoyle, bed-ridden, can find Gideon and his visits irritating. E. (Eve), the female figure, corresponding to N. (Nancy) in *Prospero's Cell*, has more of a speaking and acting part, is not a nymph merely, but somebody who has suffered. The fine descriptions of scenery, at their best perhaps in the chapter called 'The Three Lost Cities', have less of a bravura quality than the descriptions of Corfu, but perhaps more depth and more love. Durrell has a gift for sane sadness; in *Reflections on a Marine Venus* it perhaps finds its first proper expression.

4

Bitter Lemons was written much more rapidly than the other two island books, to gear in with the political crisis in Cyprus, and it is therefore a more uneven piece of writing than either of them. The pages on Durrell's English visitors at Bellapaix, John Lehmann, Sir Harry Luke, Freya Stark, his brother Gerald, and others, offer us—though Durrell does catch the dry, scratchy quality of Rose Macaulay's voice—mainly what used to be called 'politing', benign reflections in a visitors' book. We have, as Martin Green has noted, to take the brilliance of the conversation on trust. Durrell tells us that peasants are not enough for him, he needs the subtle and complex minds of the great capitals also, but in fact his peasants, or a friend who is not a peasant, the schoolmaster Panos, come out far more real and solid than the English visitors. The evocative writing, also, in the book is sometimes perfunctory:

> The village comes down to the road for the last hundred yards or so with its grey old-fashioned houses with arched vaults and carved doors set in old-fashioned mouldings. . . . The four tall double doors were splendid with their old-fashioned panels and the two windows which gave internally on to the hall were fretted with wooden slats of a faintly Turkish design.

These two sentences are not on the same page but the second comes near enough to the first to make us aware that 'old-fashioned' is trying to do work, of making us see just what the house is like, that ought to be done by Pevsnerian precision. And in what way were the arches vaulted, and just how were the doors carved, and how Turkish is faintly Turkish? This slight vagueness about precise architectural detail is over-compensated by occasional atmospheric over-writing:

> Thunder clamoured and rolled, and the grape-blue semi-darkness of the sea was bitten out in magnesium flashes as the lightning clawed at us from Turkey like a family of dragons.

Political excitement seems also, occasionally, to bring a rush of blood to the head (as of course it does with most of us), so that Durrell writes Blimpishly of 'wobbling electorates at home unable to stand bloodshed and terrified of force', or talks of 'the usual rhetorical flourishes which I had heard in every coffee-house of the capital during the past year'—a remark which reminds one of Disraeli's unfortunate dismissal of the news of the Bulgarian massacres as 'coffee-house babble'. There is also a touch, in the political passages, of the device of rhetorically rebuking rhetoric, or pedantically rebuking pedantry:

To all the opposing tensions there was only one answer—inaction—until such time as the reforms we considered necessary should be 'implemented', to use the delicious phraseology of the schoolmen.

'Implemented' is no doubt a rather pompous word, but so is Durrell's own 'phraseology' in that sentence. Durrell was, obviously, during the latter part of his stay in Cyprus, rather *exalté*. Though in one sense he knew the Cypriots more intimately than any other Englishman on the island, in another sense his emotions, including his patriotic emotions, were too closely tied up with the Cypriots to let him realize that he was exaggerating their love for England. The Governor, in an interview with Durrell, described caches of home-made arms that were being discovered everywhere, and said, with exquisite courtesy and kindness, 'It rather makes nonsense of your theory about innocent old rustics with straw in their hair toasting the Queen.' Yet these are all minor criticisms of an exciting and remarkably honest book; if Durrell had taken more time to polish and perfect *Bitter Lemons* perhaps the sense of a good man living for a time in a fool's paradise, the sense of Durrell's final pain and confusion, would not have come over so clearly.

I compared the first sentences of the earlier two island books. The first paragraph of *Bitter Lemons* could be compared with the last sentence of the first brief section of *Prospero's Cell*, which I have already quoted:

> Other countries may offer you discoveries in manners or lore or landscape; Greece offers you something harder—the discovery of yourself.

The opening of *Bitter Lemons* is an aphoristic variation on that, more generalized, more mature and hesitant:

> Journeys, like artists, are born and not made. A thousand differing circumstances contribute to them, few of them willed or determined by the will—whatever we may think. They flower spontaneously out of the demands of our natures—and the best of them lead us not only outwards in space, but inwards as well. Travel can be one of the most rewarding forms of introspection. . . .

All journeys are fated, but Durrell now knows that some fated journeys, like his to Argentina and Belgrade, can be sterile. And he knows now that introspection can, however acute, never offer one a final discovery of the self: only insight into a passing state of it.

5

As a pendant to this chapter one should say something about Durrell's one novel set on an island, *Cefalû*, later *The Dark Labyrinth*. Durrell wrote to Miller in the spring of 1945, explaining that he was disguising a morality play as a thriller, writing with deliberate artlessness, and that he had 'deliberately chosen that most exasperating of forms, the situation novel. . .'. The situation is that about half a dozen people, for different reasons, are in 1947 (the Second World War being over) companions on a Mediterranean cruise. Two intend to stop off at Crete, the others to take the round trip home, but during the stay-over at Crete the whole half-dozen, though warned by the captain of the ship that the trip is dangerous, decide to go on a guided tour of a network of underground caves, locally known as the Labyrinth. This is generally believed to be a wholly natural formation, nothing to do with the Labyrinth of Knossos, but Lord Graecen, a major art expert and a minor poet, has come to investigate the reported discovery of statues in one of the larger caves of the network. He suspects that they may have been forged, by his eccentric friend, the Levantine millionaire Sir Juan Axelos, with whom he is going to stay in Crete. Axelos has a house near the Labyrinth. The other motive for Lord Graecen's journey is that his doctor has told him he has only a few months to live. He has some chemicals, lent him by an expert at the British Museum, which will help him to detect whether the underground carvings are ancient or recently made.

Graecen is a bad poet but a kindly and sympathetic man. The most interesting of the other passengers is Baird who, after an

amateur and sterile flirtation with the artistic life, became a
traveller and a soldier. He is going to Crete to visit the grave of a
German prisoner whom he reluctantly shot during his fighting
with the Cretan Resistance. In Italy, the ship is joined by
Campion, a brilliant painter with a bitter chip on his shoulder,
caddish to women, once the lover of Baird's wife. Other passengers include Fearmax, the medium, who is miserable because he has lost the spirit guide of whom he was enamoured,
'French Marie', but who has made a good thing out of organiz-
ing various groups of occultists in one body. He wants to visit
Egypt, so that the society of which he is president will be able
to lure in the devotees of the Great Pyramid and the prophecies
deducible from its measurements. Bookish, sincere in his beliefs,
once gifted with genuine odd powers, Fearmax is neither a
fraud (though he once faked a *séance* for profit, and was found
out) nor mad, though his interests are morbid and unhealthy.
Then there is Miss Dombey (her name suggests rightly that, like
little Paul Dombey, she will have a pathetic end), a father-
fixated Evangelical missionary; Miss Virginia Dale, a pretty
but washed out London girl clerk, struggling to read for the
examinations which will get her a permanent job in the lower
ranks of the Civil Service, and grieving for a young man lost in
the war; and the Trumans, a jolly, lower-middle-class couple,
who represent earthy humour and frankness about sex. The
characters, in fact, are all pretty much out of nineteen-thirtyish
or even nineteen-twentyish Lending Library stock.

In Crete or in the Labyrinth, each of these stock or archetypal
characters confronts, fatally or helpfully, his or her own Minotaur. Fearmax, when there is a rock-fall blocking passages and
the guide is killed, follows down an evil-smelling corridor to
find the real Minotaur, which he thinks may be 'French Marie'
luring him in some astral disguise. There is a smell of rotting
flesh and a great beast carries Fearmax away in its mouth, but
the only beast that the Trumans meet is a frightened cow, which
leads them up to a shut-in fertile plateau, where, with an American lady, Ruth Adams, they settle down happily to an Edenic
life, learning the wisdom of habit and repose. Ruth Adams her-

self is so calm, so accepting, that she no longer needs even to sleep. Miss Dombey, alone and terrified, takes sleeping tablets which she always carries with her, apologizes as her mind drifts away from the Christian God she has never really believed in, but is carried back in a happy death-reverie to the China where she had her few years of happiness as a child, to her father, the big white-haired missionary, who had been her real and only Father Figure. Virginia Dale and Campion climb up to a rock ledge high above the sea; they sleep, and in the morning they jump, though Campion knows that he cannot swim (symbol of his success as an artist, his crippled state as a man). Virginia is rescued, though with a broken leg, and nursed at the Monastery, where Baird is staying with his old friend, the Abbot.

Lord Graecen's fate is typically unadventurous. He discovers in the cave that the carvings are perfectly genuine (he does not need to use his chemicals, his taste and knowledge are enough for him) and he finds his way up easily to an exit that leads to his friend Axelos's house. Just before the accident, he had both felt like proposing to young Virginia Dale, and felt that this was foolish of him. (Perhaps, though Durrell does not say so, she will marry Baird.) Baird has had a more exciting time; he finds the grave of the German he has killed, Bocklin, and finds that it is empty. He takes this as a sort of miracle, an atonement, and his wise friend the Abbot does not tell Baird that he himself has given Bocklin, as a gallant enemy, Christian burial in the Monastery; the Abbot even carefully paints out the inscription on Bocklin's memorial stone.

The names of these characters underline the morality element in the story. Lord Graecen, to whom nothing happens, except that he decides his doctor is wrong, he feels quite well, and he is not going to die just yet, is a man with *grace in* him. Baird is a man who has set out in life with a layer of pretences but to whom experience and suffering have finally *bared* his own nature. The Trumans, who find Eden, are *true man* and the name of their Lilith-figure, Ruth Adams, suggests both primordial man and infinite compassion. Campion, whose whole life has been a bitter but gallant struggle, and who sacrifices himself in the end to give Virginia Dale courage to jump, is a champion (*campion*, the Middle Scots form of the word, to be found in Dunbar's *Lament for the Makaris*). Fearmax is almost transparent: the lonely bookish figure who through books has discovered the magic of the unknown, and whose most intense and transforming experience is *maximum fear*. Virginia Dale is an unploughed field, her name speaks for itself. Miss Dombey's name is literary rather than archetypal; one remembers Dickens's great novel about the loving and rejected daughter, Florence Dombey. Axelos, the god-figure in the novel, is the axle on which the world turns, the ambiguous source of power. The great religious question is, as Auden puts it, whether 'the Goodness we have dreaded is not good.' Axelos is good, pretending to be evil; the carvings which he wishes to be taken for forgeries are genuine; his housekeeper, Katina, whom he introduces lewdly, as if she were his mistress, is in fact his wife. The only name that a little puzzled me was that of Hogarth, the psychoanalyst. Hogarth the painter did not seem relevant, nor Hogarth the expert on the Near East nor Hocart the anthropologist who wrote about Divine Kings, though the latter two are a little nearer Durrell's interests. I finally thought that Hogarth was a hogward or swineherd, perhaps magically transforming, as on Circe's island, animal shapes into fully human ones. His function, the function of any psychoanalyst, was to draw up to full consciousness or to the human level that which in most men is blind and repetitive, and therefore animal. . . .

This type of archetypal analysis can make any work of fiction, of course, look portentous; but, without listing *The Dark Labyrinth* very high in the Durrellian canon, one can admire the skill with which Durrell tells a plain story (his prose is less ornate here, I think, than anywhere else) and uses a popular mode without parodying it. But every popular mode has its pitfalls. Because the characters are *clichés*, it is hard not to take the ideas as *clichés*, too. The artist who is a cad (Campion), the rather silly gentleman (Graecen), who escapes all disaster because he is not only silly but good, the soldier tortured by remorse, the unawakened girl, the spinster whose bitter religiosity is an illness, we have met these, and the plain, decent, simple couple from the lower classes, so often before. Durrell deserves credit at least for brushing them up and trotting them out briskly; but one can see why *Cefalû*, as the book was first called, did not make a great sensation when brought out by Editions Poetry London in 1947; why it was a paperback publisher, Ace Books, which brought it out with a new title and some slight revisions in 1958, in the wake of the early renown of *Justine*; and why Faber's did not include it on their list till 1961, when the fame of the Alexandria books was firmly established. It is a thoroughly professional job, which does not disgrace Durrell; but if one had approached Durrell through it, in 1947, one would have been surprised to hear either that the author was a notable poet or that he had written, in the 1930s, another novel which was unprintable in England, richly experimental in language and structure, and darkly obscure.

CHAPTER FIVE

VERSE DRAMAS: LETTERS: ENTERTAINMENTS

Durrell has written three verse plays, in order of composition though not of publication *Sappho*, *Acte*, and *An Irish Faustus*. The first is set in Lesbos, about 650 B.C., the second in Scythia and Neronian Rome, the third in a Yeatsian medieval Ireland. The language of the first is ornate and lyrical and the play is too long for performance except in a cut version. *Acte* is a much shorter play and its language, by contrast, seems deliberately harsh and abrupt, as if someone had told Durrell that plot and character are what matter in a play and that *Sappho* is too much taken up with the lyrical expression of mood. The plot, about a Scythian captive princess and her love for a Roman general, is a grimmer one, and verges often on melodrama. The third play, *An Irish Faustus*, is, by contrast, though it pursues a dark theme as well as a comic one, serene. There is plenty of folk humour. Faustus, in the end, is playing cards in a log hut in the mountains with an old hermit, who is going to die and pass on to Faustus his final wisdom, with a rascally Pardoner, and with Mephisto, whom Faustus has earlier thwarted and tamed, destroying a gold ring created by black magic rather than use it. This Faustus is a white magician, who seeks not power but a kind of Taoist harmony with the rhythms of the universe, a harmony which is finally achieved when one learns to do nothing.

A preoccupation with a kind of repose, or quietism, as the

culmination of human wisdom is central to Durrell's philosophy
of life: 'calm of mind, all passion spent'. And some critics might
feel that this is an unfortunate preoccupation for a dramatist.
Drama depends on tension, and all Durrell's impulses work
towards the loosening rather than the heightening of tension.
Lionel Trilling notes that as a novelist Durrell seems, unlike
D. H. Lawrence, for instance, whom he so much admires, not
to be anxious to impose his own moral will on the reader, and in
fact direct clashes of will in his fiction are rather rare. He is more
interested in what people are than in what they do, and, in
Sappho, for instance, human choice plays a very small part in
working out the catastrophe, and what we remember is less the
action than the penetrating discussions of why action is both
inevitable and a mistake. *Acte* is a play full of violence and
cruelty, with a vivid picture of the at once horrible and pathetically childlike Nero, but again what one remembers is the philosophical Petronius and his calm ruminations on his own death,
and the need to accept death. *Acte* was written for the stage, and
was performed in Hamburg in German translation. Working in
with the actors, and bearing the needs of a translator in mind,
Durrell sacrificed the richness of language that characterizes
Sappho, achieving bareness and directness and concision at the
cost of a certain abruptness and baldness. The verse of this play,
indeed, seems sometimes verse only by courtesy of the type-
setter, as in this flat scene-ending:

    FLAVIA   I do not understand you, Uncle.

  PETRONIUS No. It is badly expressed. Kiss me and go to
                  bed, now.

            It is late and I am weary.

I find in these lines no scannable metre, and no rhythm other
than that of very limp prose; I suppose it could be claimed that
the limpness of the language mirrors that of Flavia's and
Petronius's feelings.

    I like *Acte* least of Durrell's three plays, and *An Irish Faustus*
most. Durrell manages to create a new type of Faustus, not
proud and damned like Marlowe's, not a restless, bustling
modern like Goethe's, but simple, wise, affectionate, childlike

and benign. He turns traditionally terrifying characters to woodcut figures in a chapbook, eternally and harmlessly playing cards. The rhythm of the play moves towards unfrightening us, to turning diabolical revelation into a winter's tale. It achieves homeliness.

2

Sappho was completed in Rhodes in 1947, published in 1950, but though broadcast on the Third Programme, and in 1959 staged in Hamburg in German, was not publicly produced in English till 1961, at the Edinburgh Festival. The post-war vogue for the verse play had by that time died down and like other Edinburgh Festival verse dramatists, Jonathan Griffin and Sidney Goodsir Smith, Durrell got a cool reception. He had written the play, he notes in a postscript, with the object of 'marrying up pace, plot and poetry'. He had not realized that the play was too long for practical acting purposes, and he recommends the excision of one rather interesting character, the drunken humorous poet Diomedes, in an early scene in the play and of a whole later scene in which Diomedes is consoled by Sappho as he dies, wretched because his son has been killed as a coward in mainland fighting, and because he lusts after the girl whom his son wished to marry. Durrell is wrong, simply by page-count, in assuming that these excisions alone would cut the script by a third.

Sappho, in this play, is the wife of an older man, Kreon, who rescued her from the earthquake which flooded the part of the town in which he was a merchant, and had her educated by a tutor called Minos. She is already famous as a poet, but bored, discontented, at a loose end. Her husband condones her occasional love affairs. She plays an important part in the religious life of Lesbos, wearing a golden mask, and, under the influence of drugs, speaking for the local oracle; but on one occasion she has omitted to take the drugs, and has herself invented an oracular message, advising the local hero, Pittakos, to go to war on the mainland, against Athens, largely because Pittakos is boring her and she wants him out of the way. In the war against Athens, he is being victorious, and will come home determined to abolish democracy and set himself up as the tyrant of a new Empire. Pittakos has a brother, Phaon, who for seven years has lived alone on a small island and who has taken a job as a diver for Kreon, who is anxious to recover from his sunken counting-house tablets that will give him title to much of the land of Lesbos.

Phaon appears at first churlish and abrupt, but is persuaded to attend one of Sappho's poetry evenings, in which poets compete in impromptu composition and recitation (Sappho herself is handicapped in these competitions by her slight stammer). As often happens, at poetry evenings, one poet, Diomedes, is very drunk and therefore the evening is rather a shambles but, left alone together, Sappho and Phaon talk about the peace and withdrawal which Sappho seeks and Phaon has found and become lovers, though both protesting that love is not the reality they are seeking for. The aged Kreon finds them together, but is tolerant.

Pittakos comes back on the evening of a night in which Sappho must act the oracle. He is pleased with his military success, but, aware that he is no politician, asks his brother Phaon to act as his political agent on the mainland. Phaon, however, is determined to return to the peace of his small island. He has managed to retrieve, while diving, a bundle of tablets from Kreon's counting house; one of these suggested to Kreon the awful possibility that Sappho, the young girl he rescued from the earthquake, brought up, and later married, may be his own daughter by a wife he had left behind him in Egypt. Kreon consults the oracle which tells him that by law he is condemned, his property forfeited, and he is to be either killed or exiled, with his family, according to popular vote. Pittakos, now chosen tyrant, sends the now sick and dying Kreon into exile, but sends Sappho, as he had wished to send Phaon, to be his political agent in Corinth, a great mainland power whose alliance he needs.

Pittakos keeps Sappho's children as hostages. Many years pass and Pittakos's empire, his circle of alliances, increases in strength; but one of Sappho's children is killed in a hunting accident, while riding with Pittakos, and Sappho uses all her skill and cunning to join Corinth and the other mainland powers in an alliance against him. Finally he is tracked down and killed on his brother Phaon's lonely island, where he has sought refuge: betrayed by the last soldier he thought loyal to him. Back on Lesbos, Sappho, old and bitter, finds the news of this revenge dust and ashes. She embraces her surviving child, the daughter Kleis:

Weep, little Kleis. You shall weep for both of us,
For the whole world if you have tears enough,
And for yourself long after you imagine
There are no tears in the world to weep with.

The perhaps you may be blessed, only perhaps.
Out of its murderous armament time
May select a single grace for you to live by:
But that we dare not hope for yet: weep, child,
Weep, Weep, Weep.

These lines, with their fluid eloquence, suggest the general quality of the diction of the play, lyrical and asking to be spoken with a certain heightening of intonation and rhythmical sweep. In quieter passages the characters can explain their moods and attitudes, often with a certain humour or irony. They are all extremely explicit and Pittakos, in some ways the least plausible of all the characters, is extraordinarily articulate in explaining that he is a plain blunt soldier who, knowing that he is not a master of words or contemplation, must use action to create an imperfect work of art.

All the characters are in a sense self-enclosed, acting or speaking out their own ideas of themselves. There are little ironies and reversals that make a comparatively minor effect in the ripple and suavity of the verse movement. Sappho was not Kreon's daughter: the tablets when more thoroughly inspected made this clear, but it was to Pittakos's advantage that the story should be believed. Did Pittakos love Sappho? If so, why was he so eager to send her away to Corinth? Both Sappho and Phaon are extraordinarily voluble about the beauty of silence, the knowledge of reality that lies beyond conscious thought or speech. It seems strange that Pittakos, the ruthless soldier, should grieve so much because he has had to kill one soldier, Diomedes' son, for showing funk. Diomedes himself is an odd character, drunkard, buffoon, good poet of his kind, dying in a heartbreak of self-disgust. The oracle is half believed and half not.

But the play as a whole does create an atmosphere of a lost civilization, at once primitive and lucid, of the volatile Greek temperament that combines egoism with generosity, clear-sightedness with reckless impulsivenesss. The fate and actions of the characters seem to be controlled by a power that might be called Luck or Accident. They act that they may brood upon the nature of their actions; they are not so much strongly emotional as creatures of mood, discussing any new mood that comes upon them, questioning their attitudes with irony. All are introspectives, even kind old Kreon, even warlike Pittakos. Each is in a sense his own island (the very small island where Phaon has chosen to live alone is a key symbol) and the distance of all the characters, from the audience, from each other, the stances which they never relinquish, the roles which they never let go, have a cooling effect, so that we are moved by this play, but not as we are moved by Shakespearian tragedy. The cool language suggests that everything is important and trivial, monotonous and momentous, trite and ever fresh, that everything is both foreordained and arbitrary. We feel a sense of the distinguished pathos of the human situation in a certain culture, not our own, a culture partly created by Durrell's imagination, but based on his knowledge of ancient Greek history and modern Greek character.

One might say that to a northern reader, brought up on Ibsen and Strindberg, the characters of Durrell's *Sappho* would seem to be endlessly loquacious, like grasshoppers, and like

grasshoppers strongly lacking in weight. They might seem to be
all surface, to have no insides. The cool polish of the diction of
Sappho reminds me, more than anything else, of some of the
dialogues, in verse as well as in prose, of Landor. The characters
have individuality and vivacity, each stands also for a universal
or recurrent human role; but they seem to have rehearsed
everything they say a hundred times, so that the laborious felicity of the expression moves us, and not the emotion expressed:
the characters seem other than quite human, are art-works conversing, belong on Keats's Grecian urn.

3

Sappho is a play about a period in human history when the
simple, the primitive, the perennial seem to have existed in a
wonderful poise with the most civilized manners and art. Nobody in *Sappho*, not even Pittakos, is really unhappy or wicked,
and that is why the effect of the play is lyrical rather than tragic.
Durrell wrote *Sappho* as a poet, without the stage directly in
mind. He wrote *Acte* for the stage and chose a period, that of the
Roman Empire under Nero, when a corrupt civilization was
confronting a raw barbarism on its frontiers. If in *Sappho*
everything is fundamentally at one, in *Acte* everything is divided,
including the human heart. Fabius, the hero of this play, has
spent his youth in Scythia, loves the Scythian language and its
poetry. As a general, he suppresses a Scythian revolt and brings
as a hostage to Rome the Scythian princess Acte. She has been
blinded in retaliation for Scythian atrocities, and as a girl she
was raped by her brother-in-law. She tries to stab Fabius on the
way to Rome, but fails, and they become lovers. In Rome, she
hopes to work for Scythian independence, and makes the
acquaintance of Nero, for whom she cooks Scythian broths at
night in his great kitchen. But Nero is suspicious of Fabius, and
Fabius's cold wife, Flavia, confronts Acte, demanding the
destruction of love letters that might convict Fabius of treason.
Flavia does not love Fabius (though her very coldness excites

him) but she wants to preserve her social position and the future of her son, whom Nero may torture to get evidence against his father.

Petronius Arbiter persuades Nero not to kill Fabius and Acte but to leave them free to work out their own destinies. Petronius will then write their story for Nero. The two lovers do not take any obvious course, neither a suicide pact, nor a flight to Egypt. Acte goes back to Scythia to help the rebels; Fabius easily suppresses the rebellion, cuts off Acte's head and sends it back to Rome. He is now high in Imperial favour, but has become a hopeless drunkard, and his son has gone mad. Flavia relates all this in a last scene in which Petronius, at Nero's orders, is opening his veins. Petronius discusses other ways in which he might have ended the story and advises Flavia to work at living, to say yes to life, so that she may not merely die in the end but achieve death. 'To become an adept of reality' is all that matters. As he is being led away to the hot bath in which he will bleed his life away, Petronius promises to tell Flavia 'one story I have never told a living soul'.

Acte is a play obviously influenced by Corneille, by the idea of the conflict of love and honour, of fear and courage, of passion and will. It lacks, however, the structure of a neo-classical play. Durrell becomes more interested in Petronius, the artist, and in Nero, the would-be artist, the haunted child criminal, than in his hero and heroine; Flavia in her hardness and toughness becomes, also, more alive and sympathetic to him than Acte, whose sufferings have been cruder, whose character is more simple. The tendency of the novelist to complicate, to include the frame in the picture, to suggest, like Petronius in the last scene, possibilities that are not fulfilled, a perpetual ambiguity between fact and fiction, usurps the duty of the dramatist to push a single plot through, with clarity of line.

I think that in this play Durrell was obviously restraining his taste for verbal embroidery, but without really achieving a plain classical style. The language, without being prose, is often pro-saic. There are few lyrical passages. At its best, the language has eloquence, as in Petronius's last advice to Flavia:

And you, Flavia? You have lived so much, yes,
But you have never worked at life, never once.
Said 'Yes' to life, 'Yes' and again 'Yes.'
Like all of us you have connived with time. . . .

This, like the rest of the speech from which it comes, is excellent didactic rhetoric, probably very speakable on the stage but not poetry, in the sense in which *Sappho* shimmers with poetry all through. The language, in fact, all through, gives me an odd sense of Durrell *willing* himself to write. For once, he is without the grace and facility which are his usual triumphs and temptations. The grey, heavy, nasty world of ancient Rome, which so much suits Robert Graves's 'comedies of evil', the *Claudius* books, is really alien to Durrell's lighter and sunnier temperament.

4

Durrell's third play, in order of composition, *An Irish Faustus*, was published in 1963. It was written at the request of a German actor who wished to play a new Faustian role. In the winter of 1966, the play became part of the repertory of Luigi Malipiero's Torturmtheater in Sommerhausen near Wurzburg, was performed over a hundred times during the season, and was critically very well received: Malipiero, who is producer, actor, and stage designer for his theatre, had already produced seven versions of the Faust legend (by Marlowe, Calderón, Goethe, Grabbe, Lenau, Vischer, and Valéry) before putting on Durrell's. The play has also, with Malipiero's company, been given a very successful performance at the small private theatre, the 'House Under the Hill', at Heilbronn, where Dr Rudolf Fuchs regularly has interesting modern plays staged, with an invited audience. Writing to Durrell about this production, Dr Fuchs says: 'The actors were under the direction of a brilliant stage-manager and the intimacy of a private house contributed to the success, which makes me very happy.' *An Irish Faustus* does, in fact, seem to me a complete success both poetically and dramatically, and it also reveals Durrell's inner nature in an intimate, simple, and homely way. He *is* the Dr Faustus of this play, at least to the degree in which Shakespeare is Prospero.

The setting is a vaguely medieval Yeatsian Ireland. The play is in nine scenes (and nine, of course, is one of the magical numbers). In the first scene, Dr Faustus is instructing the young Princess Margaret of Galway in the pursuit of vision through the negative path, or in the pursuit of self-knowledge through natural analogies. Magic, he explains to her, is a kind of domestication of science. In the act of dreaming the mind, emptying itself of fixed categories, can become a field of visitation. But Margaret is curious about whether magic, when once achieved, changes only the inner self or whether it can act also on the outer world. She wonders why a man with Faustus's power and knowledge can be so calm and sensible, but immediately makes him angry by asking him about a gold ring, with magical powers of transmutation, created by a magician who had been burned at the stake, Tremethius. Faustus had been Tremethius's disciple, but had left him when Tremethius chose the path of black magic, rather than white. Faustus, however, possesses his ring. And as soon as Faustus has gone, Margaret's aunt, the fierce Queen Katherine, bullies Margaret into stealing the ring for her. Her motive, though this is not made immediately clear, is that the ring gives power over vampires, and with it Queen Katherine will be able to raise from the grave and be eternally united with her sinister dead husband, the fierce and cruel King Eric the Red. It was for Eric that Tremethius made the ring.

The second scene is one of comedy, in which a rogue called Martin is selling, in the manner of Boccaccian or Chaucerian comedy, pardons for all sorts of sins; the more outrageously he shows himself a cheapjack and mocks his customers, the more eager they are to buy. Faustus asks Martin for news of Matthew the Hermit, a solitary wise man, whom Faustus thinks of, now that Tremethius has gone, as his teacher. In the third scene, back in his study, Faustus discovers the loss of the ring. Mephisto appears to him, for the first time materializing himself, and explains that the ring was first made by Tremethius for the vampire king, Eric, who then had Tremethius burned. Its power is so awful that Faustus has been wrong to shut it up for years. He should either have destroyed it, which is very difficult, or used its powers. But the Queen, with the aid of some stolen pages from one of Faustus's magic books, has summoned Eric from the grave and given him the ring. His bloody footprints mark the chapel and the Queen has been found there raving mad.

In the fourth scene we see Katherine in her madness, describing with awful exultation Eric's satanic power over her, her obscene love for him. She goes off to seek his grave in the forest, and the others follow her, with a stake to pierce the vampire's heart. In the fifth scene, the vampire has his heart staked, Katherine agonizingly protesting. Faustus has the ring again, but what is he to do with it? He calls up spectral figures of great magicians, of whom the last is his master, Tremethius; Tremethius tells him that the only way to destroy the ring is by the recital of a very dangerous invocation called the Great Formula. A religious friend of Faustus's, Anselm, gives Faustus a piece of the True Cross, which will resist the fires of Hell itself, and preserve Faustus from destruction. In the sixth scene, secure in his possession of this holy talisman, Faustus defies Mephisto, who wants him to use the ring, and recites the great formula, which terrifies Mephisto even more than it terrifies Faustus. They enter together a realm of flaming darkness.

In the seventh scene, it is morning, and Faustus's servant Paul and his friend Anselm, the chaplain, beat on his study door and then burst in. Faustus is lying in an exhausted sleep, his hair has turned white, his clothes have been charred to rags by the cosmic or infernal fires. But Mephisto has gone, and Faustus is himself unharmed. The ring has been destroyed, but the fragment of the True Cross has also been burnt to ashes (we later learn that it was one of Martin the Pardoner's many fakes and forgeries). Where Faustus has been has not been Hell, in Dante's sense or Milton's, but a kind of terrible cosmic foundry:

Anselm, how to tell you? Down there, in the pit
I . . . felt the very heart of process beating;
All time, the annals of our history were spread
As if in section on a huge chart before me . . .
It sounds mad no? Luxuriant panoramas of human destiny,
The contingency of human desires and wills . . .
Like all time smouldering away in the dark glare
Of furnaces such as no alchemist has ever dreamed of!
There all matter is undifferentiated, burns itself away
In an ecstasy of disappointment. I knew it all as terrible
Yet absolutely necessary—for without it we
Would have no idea of Paradise. I saw
The whole Universe, this great mine of forms
For what it is—simply a great hint . . .
Yes, I saw it all so clearly for the first time from There.
Perhaps one must go There in order to see it?
  I don't know.

In the vision of destruction, to put it crudely, Faustus has
found the vision of creation, and has been confirmed in a kind
of Blakean cosmic optimism. He feels the need to renew, refresh,
simplify his life and to go on a journey. Things are made easier
for him by Queen Katherine, now freed from her madness,
aware that she ought to be grateful to Faustus, but unable to forgive him for severing her for ever from her demon lover, Eric.
She sends him into exile. He bids farewell to her, and to his pupil
Margaret. He will not allow Margaret to follow him into exile,
but leaves her his books, which he no longer needs. He has
learned the folly of trying to control or master the plenitude of
cosmic power; one serves it best by what Wordsworth calls a
'wise passivity'.

The dark theme of the play is concluded here and the last
two scenes round off the comic theme, the acceptance of humility, the ending in simple happiness. Wandering through a
forest in exile, Faustus says good-bye to his servant Paul.
Martin, the pardoner, approaches him and talks amusingly
about his trade, telling how the more he cheats, and the more

he is known to cheat, the more he prospers, and the more people seem to benefit from contact with his forgeries. Faustus admits that Martin's forged piece of the True Cross performed a miracle for him. They go off to visit Matthew the Hermit, Faustus promising to help Martin in future with writing out indulgences. It will be quite a hard life, but, as Martin says:

> But it's not all work; in the evenings we could go down
> To the village tavern for a drink and a chat,
> Like weary Gods with bliss-bestowing hands as the poet says.
> And with your knowledge you could make the job really creative.

In the last scene, the two companions reach the log hut of Matthew the Hermit, who had been expecting Faustus for a long time. They greet each other jovially:

Matthew: So it finally happened, my poor doctor! What happened?

Faustus: Why nothing, absolutely nothing.

Matthew: Excellent; for when Nothing begins to happen at long last Everything
Begins to cohere, the dance of the pure forms begins. . . .

Matthew has known that he was not going to live till next spring, and has been waiting for Faustus, so that he can hand on to him what he calls 'the thread':

> And so nothing happened to you. How judiciously
> Nature plans; never a drop is spilled,
> Never the slender thread is allowed to break.
> But how long it takes for one to find it out.

The thread that will be handed on will be something like Taoism, both a fulness and an emptiness of being, the sense that one co-operates best with nature by striving and worrying least. The Tao works silently; Matthew says:

> . . . what I did not know
> Is just how busy all this nothingness can be.

Matthew tells Faustus also that, in succeeding to Matthew, in a sense he will have no duties:

Hm. . . . If duty is what you cannot help, then I have none;
For I am helping everything by doing nothing. I see you smile.
I help the moon rise, the sun to set. I eat and drink.
And, as a matter of fact, I play cards with the Pardoner.

Martin the Pardoner then enters, with a silent and polite
Mephisto in a mask. They all sit down to a game of cards in
which at Mephisto's suggestion they play 'the old game of
Fortune'. Hearts, standing for Love, not Spades standing for
Death, Clubs standing for Force, or Diamonds standing for
Wealth, are trumps. They may well go on playing for ever.

As with *The Black Book* earlier, I have given *An Irish Faustus*
more detailed attention than it has received before, because I
believe it is a small masterpiece, and the most coherent expression that Durrell has given of his most central beliefs. The
Faust legend exists in a mixed context of Christian dualism and
the humanistic, but in practice often anti-human, Renaissance
desire to surpass, to excel, to move over forbidden boundaries;
Marlowe's play includes both elements. Goethe's Faust, from
whom comes Spengler's 'Faustian man', is a figure of modern
Western man defeating the Devil and satisfying God by his
restlessness, his energy, his refusal to sit down and be content,
his perpetual urge for self-transcendence. Durrell's Faustus is
quite different from either of these. He has wished to pursue only
a white magic that will put him in harmony with nature, he
does not like thinking of Tremethius's black magic that produced the ring. When he is landed with the ring, he shelves it, as
one shelves a problem; in the very first scene he seems to equate
his magic with the *via negativa* of the mystics, the emptying of the
mind of images and concepts, the making it passive, that it may
be a receptacle for divine illumination. It is true that he seems
to think of the Divine as the All rather than the One, as a Cosmic
Power rather than as a Person, but a tendency of this sort is
to be found in mystics like St John of the Cross, and this natural
tendency of the mystical temperament towards a unity with
Being that gets beyond any image of God as a person is one
reason why even the greatest mystics have always been regarded,

by orthodox Muslims as well as orthodox Christians, with a certain suspicion: Taoism was similarly regarded with suspicion by Confucians in China, because it seemed to counsel a useless withdrawal from the world, and to undermine the insistence on social duty on which Confucianism was built.

Durrell's Faustus does not, however, deny or defy orthodox Christianity. He helps to stake the vampire king to death and to heal the Queen of her madness, casting out her unclean spirits, though he has not the power to replace them with any holiness or grace. But the fragment of the True Cross, even though it is burned up when he actually descends into the Cosmic Foundry, helps him to cow Mephisto. After this achievement, his course is one of renunciation, of his wordly power and position, of his mastery over Margaret's spirit, of his magical books. He allies himself with a humble but kindly-hearted rogue, the Pardoner, and seeks out with Matthew the Hermit a life in which outwardly doing nothing makes one a secret co-operator with the movement of all things. He is saved from the danger of damnation not through a terrible last-minute repentance or through asserting his humanity against both God and the Devil but by a gay and quiet submission to the cosmic order. He finds happiness or sanctification in a state in which, as in Yeats's *A Vision*, a hair separates the saint from the fool. But Durrell's Faustus talks not of the saint but of the sage: 'A hair separates the sage from the fool.' This again perhaps shows the deep influence on Durrell of Far Eastern thought, where the figure of the saint merges with that of the sage or teacher, and where the *sensei* teaches lightly, in childish jokes, in unanswerable riddles.

One should note, however, that the happy ending of *An Irish Faustus* is not quite unequivocal. The three friends at their game of cards, Matthew the Hermit, Martin the Pardoner, Dr Faustus the Magician, are joined by a fourth figure, the masked Mephisto. Mephisto is something like Jung's Shadow, the unspoken element of darkness called into consciousness, for completeness, by all bright trinities. Martin the Pardoner perhaps also is a Jungian figure. He lies, he knows he is a liar, he says he is a liar, and yet his forged relics perform miracles; for Jung

the myths and rituals of traditional religion can never be super-
seded by a purely rational view of reality since they body forth a
pattern built into the human psyche. They are a game which
homo ludens must continue to play. Mephisto, it should be noted,
has in this play not been deliberately conjured up by Faustus
but, at a moment of crisis, has emerged as the dark side of
Faustus of which he has suddenly to become palpably aware.
The use of alchemical imagery throughout the play could also
owe something to Jung's conception of alchemy (the conception,
also, of the greater alchemists themselves), of alchemical processes as a metaphor for, or analogical representation of,
spiritual processes.

What Durrell's Faustus seeks is what Jung calls integration;
and he achieves it through exposing himself to the most blasting
awareness of the shadow and through a paradoxical renunciation, the seeking of fulness in emptiness, of power in quiescence.
Durrell seems to me to have shown, in this play, profound
intuition and great artistic skill in taking ideas of the Jungian
sort, so very much of our own age, and yet weaving them into a
play, an art-transformation of folklore material, of which the
naïve medieval atmosphere is thoroughly convincing.

Faustus no doubt partly represents a spiritual path which
Durrell sees stretching ahead of him. Faustus's renunciations
would mean for Durrell renunciation of his art and his fame, a
breaking of his wand, as Shakespeare made Prospero break his
wand, a quiet turning towards cosmic mercy. But there is a
paradox. The image of Faustus or Prospero, the magician who
renounces all that is gaudier or more showy in his magic, who
submits, can only be created by the magician who has still his
wand very firmly clutched in his hand. On the other hand,
where a dark, bitter and turbulent spirit like Dostoevski creates
Alyosha as an image of a simple and relatively untormented
goodness he can never achieve, where the atheist Marlowe at
the end of *his Dr Faustus* projects his own suppressed fears of
damnation, Durrell's rational and sensible Faustus, on his small,
almost shadow-theatre scale, does present in miniature an integration which, for Durrell himself, is not an inconceivable aim.

5

An Irish Faustus is important then partly as a harmonious projection of some of Durrell's central ideas and ideals. The selection from Durrell's correspondence with Henry Miller, edited by Dr George Wickes and published in 1962, has the interest of showing us many of the ideas and ideals not yet worked up into art, coming out in a blurted, spontaneous fashion. There is also the chance, in letters, however, to work things out in a more schematic fashion. In a very important letter to Miller, written from Alexandria in the spring of 1945, Durrell works out what might be called a schema for integration, leading to revelation. It is best to quote this in his own words:

THE MINUS SIDE	THE PLUS SIDE: PURE FORMS

THE ONE

	I II III IV
All human searching for perfection as strain or disease, all concepts from Tao to Descartes, from Plato to Whitehead aim at one thing: the establishment of a non-conscious, continual STATE or stasis: a point of cooperation with time. In order to nourish conceptual apparatus, moralities, forms, you imply a deficit in the self. Alors all this WORK or STRIVING—even Yoga—aims at finding Rest or relaxation in time. It aims at the ONE.	You enter a field or laboratory of the consciousness which is not dangerous because it is based on repose. It does not strain you because having passed through the impurities of the ONENESS of EVERYTHING, you are included in Time. NOW FORMS EMERGE. Because 'contemptible' numbers are the only way to label them, you can say 1st State, 2nd State, 3rd State, like an etching. This is what I have called THE HERALDIC UNIVERSE. You cannot define these forms except by ideogram: this is 'non-assertive' form.
WHAT HAPPENS AFTER THAT IN THE FIELD OF PURE REPOSE?	THE HERALDIC UNIVERSE.

A professional philosopher, or student of philosophy, would, of course, take this passage as charlatanism and nonsense; but let us take it as a shorthand statement of a symbolist aesthetic which is also a programme for the progress of the soul (Durrell tells Miller that so far, for him, 'it is as if everything had taken place on the minus side of the equation—with the intention of producing One-ness.'). In the first column of this equation, Durrell is broadly saying that, troubled by the apparently meaningless flux of existence, many great philosophers and religious thinkers have sought, through painful striving, for some point of repose, a point at which the soul, knowing that it had perceived the true structure underlying natural change, could relax, could no longer bitterly need to assert its own separation from the whole. The self gives the whole meaning by asserting that it lacks meaning itself except in submission to the whole. Such a state of repose can be and has been attained, but it depends upon a yoking of the self. After this, there ought to come a second stage, in which, in Yeats's phrases:

> The soul recovers radical innocence
> And learns at last that it is self-delighting,
> Self-appeasing, self-affrighting.
> And that its own sweet will is Heaven's will . . .

The second column of the equation of unity, 'The Plus Side: Pure Forms', is an attempt to describe, in drastic shorthand, the progress of the soul in that recovered 'radical innocence', what happens to it in the field of 'pure repose'. There is no longer the sense of strain or striving, which is the necessary preliminary to repose; the soul no longer sets itself against the matrix, the structure of change—which Durrell on the negative side of the equation calls 'time' and on the positive, making it numinous, 'Time'—but instead feels itself 'included' in Time, enclosed, perhaps, as in a womb. It moves through a succession of states of greater clarity and beauty, like the successive states of an etching. What it becomes aware of cannot, however, be expressed in conceptual terms but only in images or emblems, like the emblems of heraldry. These emblems themselves are, even at their most abstract and mathematical, merely 'contemptible' representations of the thought-forms they stand for.

Elsewhere in this letter Durrell has spoken of the circle as the inadequate representation of the first thought-form, the square of the second. One can give these very airy notions some reference if one thinks, for instance, of the abstract paintings of Ben Nicholson or of Mondrian, which are not 'about' the possible relationships (aesthetic rather than mathematical) of squares and circles, but about a pure order or harmony which such designs can evoke for us. I think Durrell calls the emblems of his heraldic universe 'non-assertive' in the sense that they do not assert existence; they abstract our minds from what things there are, from ontology, to something even wider, the structural possibilities, the rules of the game, the germs of the crystallizing out, of any possible actual or fictive universe. Compared to this revelation the actual universe, and all the structural analogies that can be rationally deduced from it, are 'only a great hint'.

Durrell goes on to say that, if he had really passed from the minus to the plus side, he would not be able to label and conceptualize it. Of its own nature, it resists labelling and conceptualizing and yet artists can make, in a phrase Durrell borrows from Eliot, these 'sudden raids on the inarticulate'. He says:

> And so you find in the form of sculpture, or the shape of a poem, a preserving Heraldic structure sometimes which puzzles both maker and enjoyer.

Yet art is bad, in the end, because it uses the will to make these raids, and hence 'the strain and pain of the contemporary artist'. Durrell cites Rimbaud, but he could also have cited his own Lawrence Lucifer or his Campion. Throughout history, he concludes, all the artists and saints have been working at the minus side of his equation, at the subduing of the will to time, but a 'cell', a 'cabal', has been 'quietly working away for over a thousand years' at the plus side, at 'pure apprehension' (apprehension, he means, without comprehension, without labelling and conceptualizing). Who the members of this cell or cabal are one simply does not know; but one thinks of Zen Buddhism, of various kinds of neo-Platonic and Christian mystic, perhaps of Blake, perhaps of D. H. Lawrence, with his insistence on the 'pure apprehension' of otherness, his loathing of glib conceptualization. The cabal, whoever they are, should be our masters:

> These people, then, are the magicians of the new age. We are learning the inner silence. It is not, as some say, that we have potentialities which are stunted or undeveloped; there are new functions which we grow. . . . But enough of this.

Enough of this, indeed, some readers may feel inclined to say; for many admirers of Durrell such speculations may be as embarrassing as the occult and mystical speculations of Yeats are to an admirer of his like Auden. Eliot described Blake's philosophy as 'home-made' and Auden finds both Blake and Yeats slightly 'dotty'. About Yeats he once remarked, at a party where my wife and I were talking to him: 'He was underbred. And he told lies. He said he wanted to be turned into a clock-work bird.' Readers are similarly embarrassed by the more apocalyptic writings of D. H. Lawrence; I tend, though a rational sceptic by nature, to be more tolerant. We live in a period in which there is no orthodoxy, in T. S. Eliot's sense of the word; and in which, therefore, poets have to write their own sacred books, concoct their own rituals and mythologies, built schemata into which their poems may fit or seem to fit. Durrell may one day write his own equivalent of *A Vision* or *The White Goddess*, and then, like these strange but fascinating works, Durrell's sacred book will throw new light on his imagination and its creations, will show an unexpected anti-rational coherence; and yet we may find as with Yeats and Graves (or even more so with Lawrence) that much of the best of the actual writing does not really square with the canons of the sacred book.

Few passages in the letters to Miller are as difficult—or as centrally important for Durrell's development—as the Equation of the One. There is a remark on style, which is very helpful for one's approach to *The Alexandria Quartet*: Durrell, in Rhodes, is beginning to sketch out this work:

I have done a little bit of the Book of the Dead, from the beginning this time. I am using Alexandria as a locale, and it comes out bold and strong in bright colours. I'm itching to have a few months free to devote to it. It aches me. As for style, I have developed a newish kind of prose—not surrealistic but gnomic. It is lucid and yet enigmatic—I think nearer to me as a person than I have got yet. . . . But I have had such a terrible gruelling in journalism that I have developed a kind of horror of inessentials and am looking for a diamond-bright lucidity which will be QUOTABLE and MEMORABLE, not because of marvellous metaphors and bright lights, but because the thread of the EXPERIENCE shines through, as when you turn a tapestry round.

Durrell goes on to say that Miller himself tries after such a style, but is too diffuse, 'you carry about twenty tons too much supercargo.' He says that though in some parts of his work Miller has written 'the greatest prose of the century' he has never learned how to cut, and that he illustrates the fault which great American writers share with the Elizabethans of descending 'from over-exuberance to mannerism and cheapness very easily'. Durrell and Miller, though they are very fond of each other, and though they pay each other warm and extravagant compliments, come out of these letters as very critically honest. Durrell sends a cable and letters imploring Miller to withdraw or suppress *Sexus*; then apologizes, feeling that Miller is a greater man, and must know what he is doing, even if Durrell cannot admire it (he admires about twenty pages of it very much). Miller, secure in his real tradition, which is the tradition of American naturalism, is unoffended and unperturbed. The book may seem dreary and squalid to Durrell, but what Miller is recreating in it is part of his own life, and everything in his own life, including the dreary and squalid bits, exacts a certain reverence from him. Miller, similarly, to the last, thinks that Durrell's entertainments or potboilers, the Antrobus stories, for instance, are a mistake; and Durrell seems half to agree with him when he remarks that the critics do not know whether he is James Joyce or P. G. Wodehouse.

Miller, for Durrell, was primarily a father-figure. He was strong, he could be reacted against, he could be revered and made fun of, he could be relied on. Many of the great American writers of the last century, Emerson, Whitman, Mark Twain, are essentially father-figures where the typical English writer of genius is often the rebellious son, or the son, like Keats or Byron or Coleridge or the young Wordsworth, who is lucky enough to have had his father die when he was very young, and who does not have to live up to, or react against, a dominating father-image. The Father, in this sense, is the rock of ages, the repository of certainties, sometimes insane certainties. *The Black Book* suggests that Durrell in his youth was almost stifled by maternal protection, by the claustrophobia of the mother-dominated family of origin, an extension of the womb. Miller, rocky and granitic, forced the young Durrell, in their controversy about *The Black Book*, to make hard choices, to be a man. Yet Durrell, in his desire to please, to fit in, to charm, does in a sense remain a mother's boy. To put this image in another way: Durrell, in his restlessness, versatility, assertiveness, recurrent claims that he has found the key to all the mythologies, combined with fuss and worry about how the English literary Establishment will take Miller's *Sexus*, is Isaiah Berlin's fox, who knows very many little things, but longs to know the one big thing: Miller is Isaiah Berlin's hedgehog, who does know the one big thing. Durrell barks round him, cross about the little things Miller does not know, but still hankers after the solid single-minded calm of the hedgehog, after Miller's 'rock of ages' quality. It is a tribute to the genuine goodness of both men that there seems to have been no point when they were near hating each other, that Durrell never had to kill Miller in his heart.

I emphasized, in an earlier chapter, that for all Durrell's love of Greece and of the ancient Greek and Roman worlds, he is not in the ordinary sense a 'classical' writer, at least in prose. A writer in that good critical magazine, *The Review*, for April 1967, makes this point sharply. Mr Giles Sadler, reviewing Durrell's most recent volume of verse, *The Ikons*, says:

> Durrell's poems seem terrified of what, in his prose, is

usually its saving attraction: vulgarity and excess. His evident technical skills can't resuscitate such a lapidary, Landorian mode.

I do not think this at all a fair judgement on the poems, as my chapter on these will have made clear; among the great Victorian poets, Durrell more often reminds one of Browning than of Landor, and Browning is as different from Landor as could be, much as Landor admired him. The 'vulgarity and excess' of which Mr Sadler speaks are part of the richness of *The Black Book*, and could be a way of describing some of the prose of *The Alexandria Quartet*. But, more especially, 'vulgarity and excess' are part of the tradition of one kind of comic writing, the sort of writing which in its handling of language is always near parody and in its handling of character and situation always near farce. A farcical situation must always be an excessive one, one involving the physical or moral humiliation of characters who assume a factitious dignity: Robertson Hare, as a clergyman, with a bleating accent, having his trousers removed, is a paradigm case of this. The dignity of the characters of farce must be expressed in mock-heroic diction, a diction in which trivial events and feelings are given an inappropriate dignity, or even pompousness, of utterance. But the mock-heroic diction of farcical writing is not satirical.

The good farce-writer, like P. G. Wodehouse, makes us sympathize with Lord Emsworth or Bertie Wooster, since their fantasies of wisdom, of self-importance are perpetually at the mercy either of the reality-principle, as represented by the efficient Baxter, Lady Constance, Aunt Agatha, or of rival and more destructive fantasies like Bobbie Wickham's; he make us sympathize with the hero-victims of farce, because he feels that their fantasies and their trepidations are something that he and ourselves share. Good farce must always include scenes of mock-humiliation and mock-distress, but in the end the hero-victims must be given back their illusions, must recapture the dignity of the absurd. Durrell is too kind-hearted a man to be a writer, like Anthony Powell in his pre-war novels, of Jonsonian corrective or satirical comedy, the comedy of the 'dry mock', in which knaves and fools are both abhorred alike, are both equally exposed and discomfited, and in which we apply the satire, wryly, to ourselves.

In his three volumes of farcical stories about Embassy life in Slavonic countries, Serbia and Vulgaria, he is a disciple of Wodehouse, and (apart from Waugh's obvious debt to Wodehouse in, say, the character of the Colonel and the episode of the presentation of the film of the life of Wesley in *Vile Bodies*) the only really talented disciple. The stories in the three Antrobus books, *Esprit de Corps* (1957), *Stiff Upper Lip* (1958), and *Sauve Qui Peut* (1966) are, however, too short to develop the elaborate plot-mechanisms of Wodehouse's Mulliner and Jeeves short stories. They are stories of a basic simple situation, abruptly solved or reversed, and Durrell has to rely even more than Wodehouse, for laughs, on the character of his anecdotist and on a sustained parodic and inappropriately, and therefore comically, inflated use of language.

The comedy of these stories, in fact, becomes at times much more than in Wodehouse the comedy of language itself. The fun in the story 'Frying the Flag' comes neither from plot nor character but from a range of absurd misprints from a Jugoslav English-language newspaper set by Serbian compositors: MINISTER FINED FOR KISSING IN PUBIC. WEDDING BULLS RING OUT FOR PRINCESS. QUEEN OF HOLLAND GIVES PANTY FOR EX-SERVICE MEN: BRITAIN TO BUY SERBIAN TIT-PROPS. The humour of another story, 'Case History', is again verbal: the conversion of the ambassador Polk-Mowbray from old-fashioned English diplomatese, 'a sort of mental copperplate prose', 'vaguely orotund and ornamental eighteenth-century stuff which was then in vogue', spattered with Latin quotations, to Americanisms like ' "set-up", "frame-up", "come-back", and even "gimmick". I ask you—*gimmick*.' The formerly neo-Curzonian Polk-Mowbray is finally glimpsed in a *trattoria* in Italy sipping Coca Cola and he greets his former 'sidekick', Antrobus, with the expression, '*Hiya!*' To Antrobus it seems almost the end of the Empire.

More usually, however, the stories have a plot, though of

124

necessity, because of their brevity, a simple one. The diplomatic corps are invited to a *vin d'honneur*, in 'Stiff Upper Lip', to taste Vulgarian wines. The tasting takes place in a large cellar, lavishly decorated with flowers. Angela Polk-Mowbray, the Ambassador's niece, is inappropriately in love with the Russian military *attaché*, Serge, and in dudgeon her English suitor, Dovebasket, goes to sit on a corner nook which is unfortunately the ventilator of the cellar. Already rather drunk, the diplomatic corps are overpowered by the progressive rarefaction of the air. Serge drags Dovebasket off the ventilator, the oxygen pump, and some sort of order is restored. There is no detailed *dénouement*, as there would be in Wodehouse—'With your permission,' says Antrobus, 'I will draw a veil over the disgraceful scenes that ensued among the combatants'—and the fun of the story rests on Antrobus's diction as reflecting, in a Wodehousian way, his personality:

> Apparently in the middle of all this bonhomie the wretched youth [Dovebasket] crept up on Angela and breathed a winged word in her ear. It was the old fateful pattern. She turned on her heel and tossing up her little chin went over to the other corner where the crapulous Serge was swigging the least significant of wines with much smacking of the lips. It was obvious; Dovebasket was cut as if by a whiplash. A cry of fury broke from his lips to find that she preferred this revolting foreigner who had apparently been named after an inferior British export material; he banged his fist upon the nearest table and cried out, 'If I cannot have her, nobody shall!' And all of a sudden made his way to the corner of the tunnel of love and sat down. He took a copy of Palgrave's Golden Brewery from his pocket—one of those anthologies with a monotonous-looking cover— and started to read in a huffy way. Sulks, old boy, mortal sulks.

That paragraph is almost pure Wodehouse in its combination of worn poetic phrases ('breathed a *winged word* in her ear') and phrases from popular romantic novelists, the Ethel M. Dells and Ruby M. Ayreses, of the early years of this century ('Dovebasket was *cut as if by a whiplash. A cry of fury broke from his lips . . .*') with absurd allusions and metaphors (Serge, 'this revolting foreigner who had apparently been named after an inferior British export material', the nook where Dovebasket retires to sit on the oxygen pump described as 'the tunnel of love'). There is deliberate deflation by informal colloquialism— 'started to read in a *huffy* way. Sulks, *old boy*, mortal sulks.' Wodehouse, however, with a popular audience in mind would not have used the learned word 'crapulous'—he would have said 'sozzled', 'pie-eyed', 'stewed to the gills', or 'already hangoverish'—and would probably not have been quite so subtle about Palgrave's *Golden Treasury:* 'one of those anthologies with a monotonous-looking cover'.

Durrell, in fact, in the Antrobus books, models himself almost perfectly on the popular-facetious style of which Wodehouse is the great master in our century. If the literary allusions are a little above the head of many Wodehouse fans, nevertheless Wodehouse himself makes great and repeated play with a few favourite tags from Shakespeare and Tennyson, and more broadly it is a style which parodies the conventions of lending-library popular and sentimental fiction of the 1920s and 1930s. Durrell, in his youth, must have immersed himself in such fiction, as the general style and structure of *The Dark Labyrinth* shows. Wodehouse's attractiveness rests, however, not only on his style but on his gift, noted by Evelyn Waugh, John Hayward, and George Orwell, for creating an unreal but consistent pastoral world, a world deriving from musical comedy, but transforming the mechanical conventions of musical comedy into literature. The Antrobus stories do not quite create a world in this way, since Durrell does not allow himself quite enough space. But they are both a skilful tribute to a writer whom Durrell must have loved since his schooldays, and another manifestation of Durrell's extraordinary professionalism.

6

Durrell's adventure story about Yugoslavia, *White Eagles Over Serbia*, is similarly a tribute to another favourite writer of his boyhood, John Buchan. It differs completely from the spy stories of Ian Fleming or John Le Carré in the simple black and white of its political colouring, in its avoidance of sexual or sadistic elements, in its code of simple gentlemanliness, and, above all, in its leisurely amplitude. The hero is for much of the book alone in the Balkan mountains and, as in Buchan's *John MacNab*, a feeling for wild scenery, for fishing, for the delight of roughing it, for the toughness of the lone male animal lend as much charm to the story as the episodes of danger and violence. Colonel Methuen, a bachelor clubman, back from a dangerous assignment in Malay, and looking forward to a quiet life, is persuaded to go to Yugoslavia, to look into the mysterious death of a military attaché, Anson, who had been killed on what was allegedly a fishing trip in the mountains. He travels to the Belgrade Embassy disguised as a temporary clerk, meets an old war-time colleague, Vida, who is working ostensibly for the Communists but has Royalist sympathies and is working really for the Royalists, and then he is smuggled into the wild areas disguised as a Serbian peasant. He gets in touch with a Royalist organization, which is trying to smuggle a great treasure, the gold reserves held by the Yugoslav government before the war, out of the country. The gold is carried on mules by winding mountain tracks, but the Royalists are ambushed by Communists. The Royalists are destroyed, but manage to hurl gold and treasure into a great lake below, pushing the unfortunate mules over the precipice too. Methuen manages to escape, getting mildly shot up by and killing a loutish Communist soldier, but leaving behind, in the cave which has been his lair, his precious fishing-rod. The British Ambassador gives him his own even finer fishing-rod, as a tribute to his courage. Methuen comes back to England, still intent on retirement, but is met by his friends in the Secret Service with talk of an even more exciting assignment, and it is clear that, like Richard Hannay, he will not retire. Vida, for whom he felt a romantic but apparently sexless admiration, has not been killed, as he had been led to believe early in the story, and Dombey, the head of the great spider-web of Methuen's department, takes Methuen out to dinner with her on his first evening back in London. As in Buchan, there is a certain wholesomeness; Methuen, simple, decent, and brave, says his prayers before going to sleep and in moments of danger. The story, of its old-fashioned kind, is a good story. In its very simplicity, it throws light on Durrell's own political attitudes and on a wistfulness he feels for a lost hierarchical England, half imaginary, more belonging to books than reality even in his childhood; an England of them and us, of good chaps and bad hats, of plain right and wrong. It is interesting that, though Durrell's publishers immediately saw that this was an ideal story for 'teen-agers, Durrell designed it as a straight adventure story to please grown-ups, perhaps to please himself. As in the Antrobus stories, he is working within an old-fashioned popular literary convention: but out of affection, not to send the convention up. A certain persistent boyishness in Durrell's nature is one very important source of his personal and literary energies.

CHAPTER SIX

THE ALEXANDRIA QUARTET: FROM PSYCHOLOGY TO MYTH

I

A great deal has been written about *The Alexandria Quartet*, but the most perceptive piece of criticism I have seen remains unpublished. It is by one of the most powerful and original of modern poets, Christopher Middleton, and was broadcast as a talk on the Third Programme in April, 1957. I shall summarize here the main points in Middleton's talk, often in his own words. His subject was *Justine*, the only novel in the quartet to have so far appeared, but he showed remarkable insight into Durrell's intentions, and much of what he wrote remains relevant to *The Alexandria Quartet* as a whole.

Durrell's originality, Middleton thought, lay in using the conventions of the psychological novel as a framework for a vision of reality based in myth. He noted that the main characters in *Justine*, the narrator, a young Irish schoolmaster (it is later that we learn he is called Darley); Melissa, his mistress, the Greek cabaret dancer; Nessim Hosnani, the Coptish banker and merchant; and Justine Hosnani, his Jewish wife, do not have personalities that are 'discrete', in the sense of being wholly individual or separate, but act out together a patterning of various forms of love; and what the narrator is exploring is the nucleus of energies that is revealed when, under the stress of love, the façade of established identity, of accepted social personality, is shattered. Durrell, however, unlike Lawrence, does not want to shatter reflective consciousness in the name of instinctive drive, nor like Proust (or, perhaps, like Arnauti, the French-Albanian novelist whose novel about Justine Hosnani gives Darley, the narrator, some of his first clues to what she is like) does he wish to dissolve the experience of living and loving into pure reflection. 'Sex and reflection', Middleton writes, 'are simultaneous and interactive phases of a single process'.

Darley, in fact, describes purely animal sexual obsession, 'brute sex' in Middleton's phrase, as a 'terrible accident', and pure reflection as akin to the hubris and error of 'excessive desire to be united with God'. But sensuality and mysticism are, in fact, the two traditions of Alexandria, and the tension between these polarities defines the city's soul. Between these tensions, Durrell's characters, though they may not be 'discrete', are living and real. They can be related less to Freud's theory of the Id than to Groddeck's theory of the It, 'a cosmic process which transcends mind and body', a process of which 'what we call mind and body are interactive functions'. The realm between pure reflection and brute sex could be called the realm of the imagination, and it is in the erotic imagination that Durrell's characters are most alive.

For Durrell, however, as an artist and a man, mere psychological understanding is not enough. Middleton notes the importance of mirrors in *Justine*. The novelist, Pursewarden, breaks his mirror before he kills himself. He wants, Middleton suggests, 'to arrive on the other side of reflection; to know the reality behind the infinite psychological inflexions of self'— facets of self, it might be clearer to say. Justine, similarly, admiring her reflection in a triple mirror, and again in a fivefold mirror, suggests the prismatic nature of human character. Middleton might have quoted Pound:

> *She who could never live save through one person,*
> *She who could never speak save to one person,*
> *And all the rest of her a shifting change,*
> *A broken bundle of mirrors. . . !*

Justine, in fact, is desperately seeking that one person, and perhaps, even at the very end of *The Alexandria Quartet*, will not really have found him. She was raped as a child and in all her nymphomaniac activity is seeking to relive, and exorcize, that experience. Much about her, in *Justine*, Darley has still to learn, and Middleton, in 1957, could not know. But he did see that behind all her multiple facets, her Picasso-like fragmentation, Justine had one face which the psychoanalysts she consulted could not discover: what Darley calls 'the primitive face of mindless Aphrodite'.

The full complexity of Durrell's intended treatment of time, the excavation of a given area of place-time in motivational layers or strata, could not be apparent to Middleton in 1957. But he notes the complexity of Darley's narrative handling of time, the recalling of events in the order in which they first became significant to the narrator, and the mixture of tenses. Past events are presented sometimes in the historic present, sometimes in the preterite, but the actual present is used to describe the narrator's situation on a remote island and his feelings about past events as he now recreates them. In a sense, the narrator transcends time, but not in such a way as to blur the bewildering immediacy of recalled and experienced events. Middleton quotes a remark of Justine's gazing into a multiple mirror: 'I would try for a multi-dimensional effect in character, a sort of prism-sightedness. Why should not people show more than one profile at a time?'

This prism-sightedness, Middleton notes, enters into the very language of the novel. The great set pieces of elaborate and highly coloured description are not realistic: they do not evoke, so to say, one street in Alexandria as seen by Darley at one particular time. They are patterned from a multiplicity of facets, profiles, or inflexions, and thus seem, while graphic in their vividness, to carry a weight of heraldic or emblematic meaning. The city, too, speaks. It is a cosmic symbol, but it is also actual in the personal imagination, what Durrell in a poem had called 'a star entombed in the flesh'. The kind of 'right attention' which the poetic or magical meaning of the city evokes recalls to Middleton one of Durrell's remarks in *Key to Modern Poetry* about Groddeck: 'Phenomena may be individuals carrying on separate existences in space and time, but in the deeper reality beyond space and time we may all be members of one body.' And this thought is echoed, Middleton observes, in the note at the end of the book on the n-dimensional novel: 'a book which is standing above time and slowly turning on its own axis to comprehend the whole pattern'. Middleton brilliantly connects this with a sentence in *The Black Book*: 'Art must no longer exist to depict man, but to invoke God.'

Yet the invocation of God must, if the work of art is a real one, have about it the fullness of human experience. The four lovers in the book may synthesize a meeting of extremes, a fusion of brute sex and reflection in the erotic imagination, but the vividly created minor characters, in their simplicity, light up the complexity of the major characters. There may be graphic representation, of things and persons for their own sake, with no underlying symbolic purpose. There may be multiple representation, Justine in her many mirrors, her facets of self-contradiction. And the techniques of graphic representation and multiple representation may fuse in symbol or metaphor, so that we are in the realm of myth, no longer seeking for merely psychological meanings. The force that drives Justine again and again to commit 'the divine trespass of an immortal among mortals' is 'mindless Aphrodite' possessing her. At the psychological level, Justine is a sick woman, the prisoner of an imagination obsessed by a traumatic memory: at the numinous or mythical level she is Jung's 'self-sufficient psyche', 'which, in the play of its images, reflects not the world but itself, even though it may use the forms of the world of sense in which to manifest its images'.

The primacy of myth is also shown, Middleton points out, in Durrell's treatment of Alexandria. The two great hero-types of the classical Mediterranean world are Aeneas, the hero of the Foundation, and Odysseus, the hero of the Quest. Pursuing his destiny, which is to found Rome, Aeneas rejects Dido: Venus befriends him, but he rejects what Venus stands for. Odysseus founds nothing, he is on the way home to Penelope, but on the way he is beset with Princesses and Goddesses, he is in Middleton's phrase 'Goddess-haunted'. Durrell, in *The Alexandria Quartet*, sets the erotic myth of the quest within the framework of the political myth of foundation, of the establishment of the City. The idea of the Established Order was to play a greater part than Middleton guessed in the development of *The Alexandria Quartet*: the career of Mountolive; the political motives which underlie Justine's marriage to Nessim; the conflict between friendship and loyalty to his country which is one, but only one, motive for Pursewarden's suicide. Yet Middleton is right in thinking that it is the Quest rather than the Foundation, the Goddess rather than the City, which is of primary importance in the story: 'The odyssey may be made within the framework of the City; but it is undertaken in the service of the Goddess. And he who undertakes the odyssey must choose, whether this Aphrodite shall be a thorn embedded in his flesh, or a star entombed there, awaiting his call to rise from the dead.'

Much as he admired *Justine*, Middleton saw that Durrell was undertaking something not only ambitious but risky: 'Can the poet as novelist really become the visionary, the seer, the "man without qualities"? Can he master that sense of play which liberates Romantic expression from the foggy frustrations of pathos? Can he achieve that Olympian detachment which alone objectifies entirely the passion for the singular, the visionary, the irrational? Above all: can the sceptical mind focus upon this age sharply enough to discern and create a mythology for this age?' These were acute critical, and programmatic, questions. I have mentioned already my sense of Durrell as a writer 'out of phase', in Yeats's term, with his time. There is a tradition, for instance, of economy and understatement in the prose of fiction, in English, in this century running through Forster and Isherwood to, to take one of several possible examples, a young contemporary novelist like A. S. Byatt. A stylist like Durrell who, so to say, writes it up instead of writing it down, who, on the analogy of painting, is a master of colour rather than line, who likes it rich, takes some adapting to. Durrell's virtue and originality as a stylist lie in an area

THE ALEXANDRIA QUARTET: FROM PSYCHOLOGY TO MYTH

which we have all been taught to be suspicious. Almost on principle, we all distrust 'beautiful writing'.

I think Middleton ought to have seen that the 'sense of play' was already at work in *Justine*, in the depiction of Scobie, say, and even to have foreseen that the 'foggy frustrations of pathos', which seem to enwrap the presentation of the heroine herself, would be cleared away in the end. Durrell's gift as a writer is that of the lyrical comedian. I take comedy in Northrop Frye's wide sense as that area of literature that is concerned with life and fulfilment, with sympathetic not cruel laughter at failures in life and fulfilment, with unexpected happy endings following death-threatening intrigues. Durrell's gift belongs, like comedy and romance in their essence, to spring and summer, not, like tragedy and satire in their essence, to autumn and winter. He could be contrasted with Samuel Beckett, a writer as much in phase with his time, as Durrell is out of phase with it: presenting tragedy as satirical farce, presenting high art with the sap and juice squeezed out of it. Responding immediately today to the pleasures of desiccation, we are squeamish about the pleasures of over-ripeness.

Yet Durrell is aware of course, he is too intelligent a man not be, of what lies behind Beckett's world. Middleton could not have foreseen that Justine's last appearance in *Clea*, trotting along an Alexandrian street flirting with the abominable Memlek, would be one of satirical farce, and that the progression of the companion novels of *Justine* would at once ruthlessly diminish her mythical stature, expose her pretensions, and yet also bring out in her unexpected qualities or capacities of a Stendhalian type. Her story-telling gift can entrance the wretched children of the brothel district. Sex is, after all, only a secondary amusement for her. She needs the sense of danger, the whip of the fear of death, if her desire is to be aroused. She turns out to be greedy, shallow, practical in a typically Levantine way. Losing power as a myth, she gains interest as a possible actual person, a character of high comedy.

Middleton again could not foresee that it would be the blonde, benign, apparently rather tepid Clea, who spends a sexless, sisterly night with Darley at the end of *Justine*, who would prove, rather than Justine, to be Darley's real Muse. Yet he was on to most of what Durrell calls 'the workpoints': at the top of my copy of Middleton's script, Durrell has written: 'This is really *excellent*: he's twigged what I'm up to.' There is still more to twig, but I am grateful in this chapter for Christopher Middleton's pioneer insights.

2

Another generalization could be superimposed upon Christopher Middleton's view of *The Alexandria Quartet* as a cosmic myth set within the framework of the psychological novel. Both in its structure, and in the views expressed by the most important characters in it, especially by Darley and Pursewarden, the book is the expression of a fairly coherent and systematic philosophy. One might call it neo-Hegelianism. The epistemology of this system insists that there is neither absolute error or absolute truth. Our observations of life are bound to be subjective, and therefore expansible and corrigible; but the most fantastic lies and fables are not mere errors, they have some root in experience, they riddlingly reveal some truth about the world or ourselves. And, at the other end of the spectrum from subjective observation, the grandest and most general statements about what life or love or art or death means are still subject to questioning. The evidence can never be complete. For each of us, our cosmos is a construct from limited observations.

The particular relevance of such a philosophy to the novelist's task is that it leads (like the Principle of Indeterminacy in physics, with which Durrell is much impressed) to a principle, in the realm of human behaviour, of ambiguous and multiple causation. Pursewarden's suicide is a case in point. Middleton deduced from *Justine* that Pursewarden killed himself for metaphysical reasons; he wanted to break through from the mirror-world of reflexive consciousness to the real world of absolute self-identity, from Sartre's *pour-soi* to his *en-soi*. It appears later that Pursewarden killed himself on a point of honour and partly for 'official reasons'. As a friend of both Nessim, the conspirator, and Mountolive, the ambassador, who is also his chief, Purse-warden does not want to betray one or the other. He informs Mountolive that Nessim's conspiracy, whose very existence he has been pooh-poohing, is real and dangerous; with a last message scribbled on a mirror in shaving soap he warns his friend Nessim that the British Embassy now knows, in detail, of the conspiracy's most dangerous aspect, the smuggling of guns into Palestine, and knows the agents and the channels. But Mountolive feels that people do not really kill themselves for official reasons. In *Clea*, it appears that Pursewarden 'really' killed himself to leave the way clear for the marriage of his blind sister Liza (with whom he has had a long incestuous love affair) to Mountolive. Mountolive is already her lover, and has condoned the incest, but Pursewarden feels that his own continuing existence will be an embarrassment to them both. This final revelation makes Darley revalue his whole experience of Pursewarden, his interpretation of Pursewarden's character. He now feels that the mocking irony he had so disliked in Pursewarden was merely tenderness turned inside out.

But Pursewarden is not yet, so to say, fixed. We learn how beautiful his letters to his sister were; we learn also from the journalist turned soldier, Johnny Keats, who has been asked to write Pursewarden's life and decided not to, that Pursewarden's letters to his wife were mean and nasty. . . . The whole of *The Alexandria Quartet* is an archaeological excavation of motives, in which it is difficult to get down to the layer below without destroying the layer we are at, and in which the very bottom layer is perhaps never reached at all. A workpoint at the end of *Clea*, for instance, tells us that Justine's first husband, Arnauti, dies slowly from general paralysis. The supposition that he may have infected Justine and that there may be a simple medical ex-planation for much of the wildness of her behaviour, and for the slight stroke which she has suffered shortly before the beginning of *Clea*, at once springs to mind. She may be 'wounded in her sex' in a physical not a metaphysical way.

Durrell's cosmology has a mystical aspect. There is, for him, a world beyond space and time, numinous and eternal, in which we are all members one of another. In this world we are enclosed as in a womb. This sense of unity with the cosmos, for Durrell, derives from Einstein and from Groddeck, but these merely reinforce heretical Renaissance cosmologists like Giordano Bruno and Paracelsus. Since the observer creates and alters the space-time events by which he constructs his universe, he feels himself almost cosily part of the universe he constructs. The external world is no longer cold and dead. Therefore, Durrell suggests, where madness was the only way out for nineteenth-century geniuses like Nietzsche or Rimbaud, tormented by the contrast between the dead universe and the living soul, the really good twentieth-century poet does not have to go mad.

Vague and remote as such speculations, taken in the abstract, may seem, they again directly affect Durrell's art as a novelist. If there is a mystical unity of being, and if all men unconsciously work out cosmic roles, then characters in a novel cannot have discrete identities. They may seem to complement each other: Darley working up towards the state of the artist, Pursewarden moving beyond it. They may be stages on a single path: from Melissa through Justine to Clea, Durrell experiences love, in a successively greater concreteness, first as pity, then as passion, finally as ardent companionship. Characters again may be almost mirror-images of each other. Nessim and Mountolive are on opposite sides, but they belong to the same class, each has the same kind of slightly stiff public integrity. Passion irrupts into their lives, Mountolive's passion for Leila and then for Liza, Nessim's for Justine, as something out of key, something not quite belonging to their characters, something profoundly disturbing.

The non-discreteness, however, works in several other ways. Nessim is complementary to his brother Narouz, but not quite in the same way as Pursewarden is complementary to Darley. Nessim has become wholly westernized, a cool, intelligent, refined modern man; Narouz is the primitive country squire, fierce, cruel, powerful, and tender. When Nessim thinks he will have to kill Narouz his horror is partly that he will be killing the submerged part of himself. Narouz's hopeless longing for Clea is, similarly, a longing for the light, the luminous part, the Nessim part, of his own heavy dark nature: a longing for what has never been able to emerge out of his darkness. Similarly, Balthazar and Scobie, the one a sage, the other a holy fool, are both homosexuals; and the kicking to death of Scobie, disguised as a woman, could be equated with Balthazar's social disgrace (a kind of death) and attempted suicide. The dead Scobie becomes a saint; rescued from attempted suicide, Balthazar, who has been oppressed with the shamefulness and folly of his adoration of worthless objects, and with his own ugliness, discovers how his friends love him, and his wisdom deepens. Violence and pain are, in fact, seen often in this novel as a means of rebirth. The most extreme and obvious example of this is the case of Clea: she has almost to die as a woman before she can be reborn as an artist and she has to lose her painting hand before she can paint with it. And she and Darley have to renounce each other physically, to love each other at a distance, before their love runs true.

One might put all this in a slightly different way by saying that, in *The Alexandria Quartet*, as in dreams, or as in Shakespeare's *King Lear*, there are more characters than roles. Pursewarden, Darley, Arnauti are variations on the theme of the writer as Capodistria, Pursewarden and Pombal are variations on the theme of the rake. Incidents also parallel each other, in a dream-like way: obvious examples are the linkings of death with celebration; the duck-shooting and the carnival dance both ending in murder, or, the other way round, Narouz's murder and death preceding the great set piece about his funeral ceremonies at the end of *Mountolive*. In *Clea*, again, it is a minor celebration, a boating picnic, which leads to Clea's near-death but this has been preceded by the episode when Pombal, at last genuinely in love, takes his mistress out boating, and she is shot when they drift into a Vichy warship. Death needs celebration, and celebration needs death.

3

Perhaps a little too much has been written about the importance of Durrell's ideas about time in relation to *The Alexandria Quartet*. The idea that the order in which events should be presented in a narration is not the order in which they occurred but the order in which they acquire significance for the narrator is, of course, not Durrell's invention. It is, if anybody's, Conrad's and Ford Madox Ford, in *The Good Soldier*, a technical *tour de force*, worked out this method even more adroitly than Conrad had ever done, using an apparently naïve narrator who, as he tells the story, only gradually discovers both the real motives of the characters he is talking about and the real likings and dislikings, admirations, resentments and envies, that have lain behind his own actions and failures to act. The drama for Ford as for Conrad (and Ford had learned something from Henry James as well as from Conrad) is not chronicle drama but the drama of a consciousness, of the growing pains and pressures of mental re-enactment, retrospective understanding. In an interview with Kenneth Young in *Encounter* for December, 1959, Durrell, who has read *The Good Soldier* overnight on Young's advice, is recorded as writing to Young: 'I'm so glad I didn't read *The Good Soldier* before writing *Justine* or I might never have finished her! This novel is an eye-opener with its brilliant organization and gathering momentum; it's fit to put beside the best work of our time!' But he added, in conversation with Young, that whereas *The Good Soldier*, in Young's phrase, is 'all tucked in and painless . . . a Mozartian weave', 'the ragged ends' in *Justine* 'illustrate the principle of Indeterminacy. This is deliberate. I deliberately scribbled down at the end of *Clea*, for instance, five or six pieces of data which themselves could make five or six more novels, either interpolated or extrapolated—this isn't to infuriate the reader, but simply to indicate that it would be possible to expand the Quartet without it becoming *roman fleuve*.'

The pattern of the first three members of the quartet is an exploration of a given area of space-time in growing depth; in the fourth volume time, within the magnetic area of Alexandria, moves forward, but is still dominated by what has been explored before, and particularly by two characters who reach their fullness of being for the imagination only in death, Pursewarden and Scobie. But Durrell also tells us in *Key to Modern Poetry* that whereas the sense of time in a novelist of the nineteenth century is linear, beginning, middle, and end, the sense of time in modern novelists like Joyce or Lawrence is cyclical, the coming round again not only of the seasons of the year but of the seasons of the soul. Darley and Clea at the end of *Clea* are both on their own again, starting out again as artists—Darley is writing a story beginning, 'Once upon a time . . .'. Justine and Nessim, ascending the spiral stair, are engaged again on another and even grander conspiracy. (Where did it end, one wonders—Suez, 1956, or the Israeli victory of 1967?)

The sense of eternal recurrence, the turning of the great wheel, is therefore as important in *The Alexandria Quartet* as the space-time continuum idea, the revelation, as in a detective story, of 'what really happened' in successive layers. Durrell also presents the timeless, or unchanging: Muslim prayers to the one unchanging God; religious fairs and festival; the unchanging rituals of the day on the Hosnanis' country estate or in a British Embassy or on Darley's island before the Second World War breaks out, the peasant or patrician society where time is conceived of as the endless re-enactment of rituals and ceremonies not as a continuing quantitative process leading to radical qualitative change. The timelessness of life for the very sophisticated as for the very simple is very well done. It is only by a fussy and superstitious observation of the tiny rituals of protocol that a diplomatist like Mountolive acquires the moral strength, the confident distant rigidity that enables him to treat the terrifying interrelationships of sovereign states with the same detailed attention as the little problems of *placements*, of who will sit beside whom at dinner—the same detailed attention, the same indifference.

It is David Mountolive's momentary illusion, when he becomes Ambassador to Egypt, that he will be able to step outside this world of ritual, to initiate action in time. He is warned against this illusion, and soon learns that the warning was sound. Folklore and magic are also timeless: Pursewarden's anecdote about a vampire lady of Venice, Capodistria's letter about how to create homunculi, Darley's starting his real book (not the book we have been reading) with 'Once upon a time . . .'—all these devices put what is honestly tale-telling on a level with what, on Durrell's own page, we, his readers, have been pretending to take for fact. And some elements that *are* presented as fictitious 'fact', Mountolive's entrapment in the child brothel, Narouz's bullying of the soothsayer, nearly everything about Scobie, even if they are not folklore, have the feeling of Arabian Nights fantasy, of the tall story grown taller in the telling. *The Alexandria Quartet* constantly, as it were, questions its own status in time: moves from a level of jumbled chronicle, of the deceptions of perspective and memory, to the timeless level of fable. An extremely sophisticated attitude to time merges into an extremely primitive one, tentative factuality is drowned in real magic: 'Once upon a time. . . .' It is this problematicism that gives *The Alexandria Quartet* its real originality. To put it pompously, we move from a radical scepticism and relativism on the level of phenomena to a cosmic mysticism on a level of ontology. Less pompously, Durrell the joker is always there, who likes his little mystifications, who enjoys pulling our legs.

4

I want to consider briefly, in relation to the characters who embody them, the themes of love, death, art, and power in *The Alexandria Quartet*. Love and death more properly belong to the myth of the Quest, since we face death to reach love, and since fulfilled love can make death seem unreal or unimportant. Art and power belong more properly to the myth of the Foundation, since it is art and power that sustain a city. But the public man faces death, and risks love, just as the private man seeks some permanence for his memories and desires in art and needs some power in the City, just as he has some loyalty to it, or some hatred of it.

Darley's first experience of love, his first journey in the Quest, arises from his compassion for Melissa. He has rescued her from a dreadful party of Pursewarden's where she has been reduced to hysteria by an aphrodisiac. She is a dancer, an untalented one, at a low night club, and the mistress of a hideous old Jewish furrier, Cohen. She offers herself to Darley out of gratitude (suffering from a mild venereal illness, he cannot at once accept the offer). Melissa finally melts from Darley's memory, except as a linking device in a story. She compels his imagination at first by her grace, pathos, touching ineptness. She feels no lust for him. She tells Pursewarden, on the night when she reveals to Pursewarden Cohen's part in Nessim's conspiracy, that ugly old Cohen was a much more efficient sexual partner than pleasant young Darley. As gratitude rather than lust holds Melissa to Darley, pity rather than lust holds Darley to Melissa.

It is Justine who teaches Darley passion-love. Rich, bored, the Jewish wife of a Coptic banker, Nessim Hosnani, she picks Darley up in a grocer's shop after hearing him give a lecture on Cavafy. She introduces Darley to Nessim, whom he immediately likes and respects, and together they rescue her from a child brothel, where she has gone in a vain search for her lost child by her first marriage to the writer Arnauti. She is hysterical then, and she is on the verge of some sort of hysteria all through *The Alexandria Quartet*. Darley and Justine become great friends. He is obsessed with her, neglecting Melissa. She insists that sexual intimacy would add nothing to their friendship, but nevertheless comes one afternoon to the sordid little room he occupies in the flat he shares with the French diplomat Pombal. He humbly confesses that the room is dirty, the bed messy, that he has been trying to make love to himself. Nevertheless, she takes him.

Soon he discovers that she, too, is using him to make love to herself. She is trying to re-enact a childhood experience of being raped, which has acted always with her as a check against complete sexual surrender. Darley acquires a passionate desire to 'know' Justine, in the secret parts of her mind as well as her body. He seeks clues to her in the novel about her, or supposed to be about her, written by her first husband, the French-Albanian Arnauti. His passion becomes quickened by fear. After the suicide of the novelist Pursewarden, whom Darley admires but dislikes, Justine becomes convinced, or so she convinces Darley, that her husband Nessim is spying on Darley and herself, and may murder them. Invited to Nessim's great annual duck-shooting party, Darley fears that he may be assassinated, since nothing is easier to arrange in Alexandria than a disappearance or a death. Somebody is shot, but not Darley. The dead man is (or so everybody thinks at first) the comic sinister one-eyed sexual athlete, Capodistria, whom Justine has recently recognized as the man who raped her in childhood, and whom she has asked vainly (since he is a close friend and colleague of her husband) to rape her again. On hearing of his death, Justine immediately deserts Nessim, and goes to Palestine, where she becomes a worker on a kibbutz. (It is only later that we learn that none of this is true. Nessim was not sexually jealous. Justine, if she loved anybody, loved Pursewarden, not Darley, but fundamentally in all her sexual forays she is acting as Nessim's spy. Nessim and she are deep in a conspiracy against the British, which Pursewarden has discovered and revealed before his death. Nessim married Justine not out of passion but to unite the Jews with the Copts in the conspiracy. Capodistria is a key member of the conspiracy, and his pretended death, the provision of a corpse disguised to look like him, is to facilitate his escape. Justine has gone to Palestine because she is in less danger of arrest there than in Egypt. It is amazing that *Justine* should remain such a gripping novel even after one has discovered that all its central data, as Darley at first interprets them, are delusive. *Justine* remains rereadable when we know it is all hoax because Darley is a poet, his response to mood, gesture, atmosphere provides the interest, not his explanations of why things happen.)

After Justine's departure, Darley becomes emotionally blank.

He gets hospital treatment for Melissa (Pursewarden has inexplicably left him some money), teaches for a couple of years in a dull Roman Catholic missionary school in Upper Egypt, coming back to Alexandria only when he hears that Melissa is dying. She is dead before he arrives. He goes off to a Greek island, taking Melissa's daughter by Nessim with him, and there starts writing *Justine*, recreating Alexandria. (Nessim had turned to Melissa in the agony and near madness which Darley wrongly attributed to murderous jealousy.) Darley is recreating in his imagination his first great experiences of love—love as compassion, love as obsession—but his true love, Clea, is still on the margin.

In *Balthazar*, the second member of the quartet, Darley's friend, the doctor and occultist Balthazar, corrects some but not all of Darley's errors. Balthazar thinks Justine had been using Darley merely as a cover for her affair with Pursewarden, the boorishly ironical English novelist who had seduced her, like Wyndham Lewis's 'soldier of humour', by making fun of her intensities. Pursewarden mockingly describes Justine as a boring nymphomaniac, a sexual turnstile through which every distinguished visitor to Alexandria has to pass. Balthazar reveals that Justine had first come to Darley's room all on heat after Pursewarden had thrust her out of his hotel apartment. (Sex seems more brutish in *Balthazar* than in *Justine*; there is something of homosexual malice in Balthazar's denigration of heterosexual relationships, and he has also the homosexual's passion for gossip, not always accurate. As a source of information, he is no more finally reliable than Darley himself. He still believes in Nessim's jealousy.) We hear about the murder of Toto, another homosexual, who, at a ball where all guests looked identical in mask and domino, had been wearing Justine's ring. He had made advances to Narouz who, mistaking him for Justine, killed him in defence of the Hosnani family honour. Narouz confesses this to Clea, whom he has long adored from a distance, and she rings up, to discover that Justine is still alive and well; but she rejects Narouz's love with disgust, it is an intrusion.

Clea, in the end, becomes the symbol of what love should be, for Darley and the reader, and her character is therefore peculiarly interesting. She is a painter, blonde, devoted to her father and affectionate to other older men, like Scobie and Balthazar. She gives an impression of coolness and chastity, and she is certainly very fastidious. Painting a portrait of Justine, she allows Justine to make Lesbian advances to her, and discovers that this is not her direction. On a holiday in Palestine, she thinks of having an affair with a handsome young painter but, when she discovers that his paintings are vulgar, she rejects him. She does have an affair in Syria with Amaril, a doctor known for his charm and kindness. This leads to pregnancy and abortion, which she takes in her stride. She remains Amaril's friend and helps him to design a nose for the noseless beauty whom he has met, disguised by mask and domino, at the fatal ball. Yet she rejects Narouz's love disgustedly, drives only most reluctantly to see him on his death-bed, and there is a streak of squeamishness in her; Durrell does not let her discover how Scobie, whom she had adored, died. At the end of *Justine* she spends a sexless night with Darley, in *Clea* she invites him to become her lover. She achieves a calm happiness, as Darley does, but finds that this is hampering her as an artist (earlier, in the only scene in which she appears farcical, she has asked Pursewarden to take her virginity, to help her lose a painting-block). I think it is for a self-centredness, a wish to control life as if it were art, that Clea is punished, in *Clea*, by having her hand harpooned; her disgust at Narouz's love is not so much at Narouz himself, but at unasked-for intrusion, an episode in her life she had not planned and arranged for.

The cynical homosexual Balthazar, like the young romantic poet, Darley, thinks love is everything. In the third member of the quartet, *Mountolive*, we discover—a discovery that Dr Johnson praised Shakespeare for making—that sexual or romantic love is not the main driving force in human actions, but only one of many. The traditional impersonal omniscient author technique here makes this the one of the four members of the quartet that we can most nearly describe as objective, or as fact.

We discover that the main motive behind Nessim's marrying Justine is to unite Jews and Copts in an anti-British conspiracy. Justine is certainly a casually lascivious woman, but she is more interested in power and money than sex, most interested in danger, which whips up her sexual excitement. In making love to Pursewarden and Darley, both British intelligence agents, the one of major, the other of minor importance, she has been partly acting as a spy. She and Nessim are perfectly sexually well adjusted, and Nessim has never been jealous of her. And yet this is perhaps not the whole truth. Did Nessim marry Justine purely for political reasons, or use the political reasons to assuage a passion not properly part of his life-pattern? Did Justine herself care at all for the object of the conspiracy, or only for the stimulus?

The last volume, *Clea*, gets back to the pure theme of love. In *Mountolive*, David Mountolive, the Ambassador, has brutally rejected the love of his lifetime, Leila, who suddenly appears to him in a cab, an old Arab woman drenched in perfumes, begging him to protect her sons, Nessim and Narouz. Coldly and cruelly he leaves her (Aeneas leaving Dido), saying merely that he cannot discuss public affairs with private persons. Similarly, he is hesitating to marry his new love, Pursewarden's blind sister Liza, not because she has had an affair with her brother, but because it would be eccentric to have a blind Ambassadress. Darley at last rejects Justine, when Nessim leaves him alone with her at the Hosnani country house. Nessim and Justine have survived the discovery of their conspiracy, but at a price. Nessim is acting as an ambulance driver at the docks, and, like so many characters in the story, maimed, one-eyed. Justine is under house arrest. She has had a slight stroke, and nervously, before she meets Darley, spills a bottle of scent over herself. When she comes naked to Darley's bed, the smell disgusts him, as Leila's scents had disgusted Mountolive. Darley finds that all his old obsession has gone, his heart has shut on Justine like an iron gate.

The love-pattern of *Clea* is a strange one, the promising of happy endings and then the thwarting of them, in the interests of the continuing growth of all the characters, of the purposes of

146

Groddeck's transcendental It. This theme is worked out most neatly in the history of Pombal the good-hearted rake (where Capodistria was the malignant, Pursewarden—in his rake role only, of course—the humorous, heartless Restoration comedy rake). Pombal finds real love at last with a pregnant married woman, whose husband is on active service. They remain chaste, a new and delirious experience for Pombal, till she is very far gone in pregnancy, and hears that her husband is safe as a prisoner of war. They make love at last. Then she is killed when she and Pombal go boating, drift across the bows of a Vichy warship, and are fired at. But this is not finally tragic for Pombal. Our last glimpse of Pombal is when he is safely back in Normandy, after the war is over. His life-pattern has resisted deflection; glad to be rid of all this Levantine nonsense, he is smacking his lips again at French women and French cooking. Darley, similarly, seems to find happiness with Clea, but there is Clea's near death by water, her maiming, their separation; but then again the purer love of artists at a distance. Balthazar, socially disgraced, flung out of his clubs, an attempted suicide, is allowed a resurrection like Pombal's into his proper world, that of Alexandrian gossip. Justine, reduced from myth to contemptibility, from the incoherence of mystery to mere incoherence, has a proper resurrection as a lively figure of farce. Life, like water, can move around and past the most murderous rocks. Our true roles persist, in spite of ourselves.

Thus, for all its patches of the cruel, the horrible, the macabre, for all its maimings and deaths, its transformations and reductions, *The Alexandria Quartet* is not a tragic novel like *Anna Karenina*, nor an epical one, like *War and Peace*; it is lyrical romantic comedy in which the working-through of the life-force, the It, is celebrated in its very absurdity. Durrell has a gross, schoolboyish, but very hearty appetite for life. Life can be very humiliating, it tends to put one in one's place, but only the mortally sick, the broken, or incurable egoists (like Rochefoucauld, in Durrell's poem about him) reject it. Love, like art, like death, like power-games, is a means by which the It or the Life-Force (Shaw's phrase) works itself out; nothing is a final consummation, nothing is an end-stop. But the working out leaves in our mouths not only the taste of grapes or of wine but the taste of iron, a tingling and dangerous sadness. And the wild laughter that echoes through *The Alexandria Quartet*, Pursewarden's laughter, *is*, as Darley says, a reversed glove: tenderness turned inside out.

5

One reason why *The Alexandria Quartet* is not tragic or epical is that true tragedy implies the finality of death. For a Jacobean audience, King Lear and Cordelia, after all their sufferings, will be happy in heaven; which makes Christian Renaissance tragedy something more than, but also other than, true classical tragedy. Epic allows a meagre and shadowy after-existence but depends on heroic death and survival in fame, in the poetry of the people. The only heroic death among many deaths in *The Alexandria Quartet* is Narouz's, and Narouz with his primitive simplicities of violence and tenderness is the only epic hero. Yet, with his unbasted hare-lip, he is a maimed and abashed epic hero; his abasement before Leila and before Clea is not, even if one thinks of Samson and Delilah, properly epical. The extraordinary number of physical injuries, statistically improbable, suffered by the characters in *The Alexandria Quartet*, untreated hare-lip, one-eyedness (Capodistria—and others), loss of an eye and a finger (Nessim), loss of a nose through lupus (Amaril's Arabian Nights loved one), loss and replacement of the painter's hand (Clea), a drooping and inauspicious eye after a stroke (Justine), suggests perhaps corrosive Time slashing and chipping at archetypal images, old statues: Balthazar also loses his teeth, symbolically standing for virility, the possibility of fierce physical love. Balthazar also slashes his wrists (he has learned from Darley's first narrative that his hands are ugly). The archetypal, the heroic cannot survive. Physical injury induces the humility before time which makes survival possible.

Pursewarden's death might appear tragic: at least, a heroic

148

choice. Scobie's death deems tragical farce, but proves sacrificial; he become a saint. Pursewarden also becomes heroically transformed in the imagination of his survivors, the artist as hero, after he has killed himself. Wittgenstein said death is not an experience we live through. Durrell thinks rather of a proper dying as the full flowering of life; this is clear both from a speech of Petronius's in *Acte*, quoted in my chapter on the verse plays, and from Durrell's approval of Rilke's attitude to death in *Key to Modern Poetry*. Durrell thinks of death not as limit, the edge over which everthing falls into nothingness, but as the rounding off of being. Thus, in Shakespeare's *Antony and Cleopatra* the deaths of the protagonists are not tragic, since they have worked out their full trajectory, they are the ripe fruit falling from the tree; the death of Enobarbus, the good and loyal servant seduced into deserting his master by the treacheries of common sense, is properly tragic because he has broken his trajectory. A tug between competing loyalties is one of the multiple motivations of Pursewarden's suicide, but this is not tragic like Enobarbus's. Pursewarden has had everything, achieved everything, that lay within his life-pattern. And the death of Melissa is not tragic, but belongs to the *Vie de Bohême* tradition of pathos and sentiment. Durrell sings a hymn to growth, to completion. His dead characters are more alive than his living characters in the imagination, the place where the artist lives.

6

Let us turn from the theme of love in *The Alexandria Quartet* to the theme of art. There are four writers in the story, Arnauti, Darley, Pursewarden, and the journalist Johnny Keats; one painter, Clea. (There are no musicians.) Arnauti appears only in extracts from his novel about Justine. This has all the qualities that irritate English readers in French fiction: it deforms, or reduces, raw experience into aphorism and reflection. The 'slow death' with which Arnauti is threatened in the final work-note about him, at the end of *Clea*, is the proper punishment of the

artist who lives in order to reflect about life, who has wholly
'expurgated'—a pet word of Durrell's, as we have seen in my
chapter on his poems—the roughage of life out of art. Arnauti
does not in the end remember whether his novel was about
Justine or not; the raw material, whatever it was, has been so
completely absorbed and digested.

The young Darley, a lyrical consciousness, is at the opposite
pole from Arnauti. Passively though eagerly receptive, he is the
vulnerable young man for whom all experience is so exciting
that he has not yet learned to distance himself from it, to shape,
discriminate, reject. Life, all life, is so wonderful! Pursewarden is
the artist who, without having any illusions about life, knows
art, the rage for order, at least to be holy, and respects the rough
energies of life. He is an admirer of D. H. Lawrence; the act he
puts on, of the boorish *farceur*, reminds one of Lawrence's
antithesis, Percy Wyndham Lewis; his fondness for paradoxical
aphorisms reminds one of Auden, except that Auden's aphorisms
are so much better. He is, at any rate, presented as a healthy
shocker of the prim *bourgeoisie*. His politics are of the romantic
Right (like Wyndham Lewis's or Roy Campbell's) rather than
of the Left. He is a loyal if cynical British public servant. But
from what we learn (and we learn comparatively little, we have to
guess a great deal, Durrell arranges for the key documents to
be destroyed) about his incestuous love for his blind sister Liza,
the girl he brought up to think of herself as a princess in a tower,
we realize that he started off with romantic emotions far deeper
than Darley's; he links with the Brontës and with Byron. (Inci-
dentally there is a puzzle, which Durrell uses sleight of hand to
avoid our noticing, about his letters to Liza. Blind, she could
not read them herself; if they were, in an open sense, love letters,
whom could she get to read them to her . . . and if they were not
in an open sense love letters, why need she, or Darley for her,
decide to destroy them?) Pursewarden, anyway, is intended to be
deeper than Darley. Darley is saved from the disasters he courts
throughout *The Alexandria Quartet* by what might be called a
widespread sensitive shallowness. He is quickly and accurately
sensitive, but his wounds heal quickly: Melissa vanishes for him

except as a novelist's connective device. Liza, Nessim, Mount-olive, Darley himself do not vanish for Pursewarden.

Arnauti, Darley, Pursewarden thus represent three aspects of creative activity: withdrawal from the rawness of experience, fluid involvement in that, masterly command over it: retreat, engagement, victory. Clea is much more of a puzzle. She is from the beginning at what might be called a sympathetic distance from life. Horrified by unexpected, unwanted adoration, like Narouz's, she can nevertheless calmly make pictures of the injured parts of venereal patients for Balthazar, without being overcome by pity or horror. Her attitude to sex is an experimental one; she does not repulse Justine's Lesbian advances but is grateful to learn from them that her own sexuality is normal. Her virginity, at one stage, she thinks of as an impediment to her progress as an artist, and it is in a self-improving and self-educating spirit that she asks Pursewarden to deprive her of it. She realizes that she has been waiting for Darley but realizes, more clearly than he does, that their calm togetherness is stifling them both as artists. Yet, cool and rational as she seems, she tells fortunes and has obscure and frightening pre-monitions; her calm gift has to be outraged by pain, terror, near-death, mutilation, in the harpoon incident, before it can break through into proper art. But one notices that even after this very bad shock her *persona* seems to reassemble very rapidly; so also does Darley's. Both, at the end, are at last discovering themselves as artists, without seeming to have changed very radically as people.

One should add to this list a semi-artist, the journalist Johnny Keats, the restless, inquisitive pryer (too much interested, in Durrell's own phrase about me in Cairo, in 'whether the poet picks his nose') who is shaken into proper creativity by his experience as a tank-captain in the Western Desert. (In this later development, in his picture of Johnny Keats as transformed by active service, Durrell has told me he drew a little on his memories of somebody who was never vulgar and never a journalist, the poet Keith Douglas.) For Johnny Keats, in *Clea*, anyway, active service in war is a kind of very rough shock-therapy which can shake non-artists into the kind of awareness that born artists acquire more slowly, naturally, and peacefully. Art, like love, like death, like power, is not for Durrell something to be pursued for its own sake, to be pursued as a 'final solution'. Art is one of the many roads to Rome, one of the many bifurcating paths on the way to full consciousness, to 'right attention'.

It is tricky for an artist to present an artist in a work of art: 'Mirror on mirror on mirror all the show!' Durrell solves the problem easily with Darley: Darley's narrative talent, and his poetic imagination, these are Durrell's own, more or less. But in Pursewarden, Durrell has attempted to create an artist who is, in Yeats's phrase in *A Vision*, more or less exactly Durrell's own 'antithetical mask': an amalgam of Wyndham Lewis and D. H. Lawrence, both artists who were preachers or prophets as well as pure artists, with a touch of Henry Miller added, and touches also (it has been suggested to me) of Dylan Thomas, Roy Campbell, and Lord Byron—though these are not all quite such clear examples of 'the artist who is a preacher or prophet as well as pure artist.' (Campbell and Byron were, in fact, dogmatic satirists. Pursewarden seems to me utterly unlike Dylan Thomas, they were both socially outrageous, but in different ways; and yet I could find a preacher and prophet in Dylan Thomas, too, a coherent doctrine that life is terrible and yet must be celebrated, that death and oblivion are welcome yet must be defied.)

Pursewarden does not seem to me a wholly successful creation (I know that friends of Durrell's whom I respect disagree with me about this).[1] It is partly that *The Alexandria Quartet* itself validates Darley's (or Durrell's) claim to be an artist. We are not given any fragments of Pursewarden's novels, we get only examples of his aphoristic brilliance, as in 'My Conversations with Brother Ass', and these seem to me to smack of mock-heroic hearty polemical journalism. If Pursewarden really *was* a great novelist, why did he forever have to be putting on such a

---

[1] Durrell also tells me in a letter that *he* disagrees, he thinks Pursewarden his most successful character creation in the Quartet; he may be right; re-reading my proofs, I notice that I display towards Pursewarden the irritation which one feels, not with a fictional character, but with an actual living person. My annoyance may be Durrell's triumph!

heavy comedian's act? Pursewarden's social manners and behaviour also make me profoundly uncomfortable. Darley, in *Clea*, repents of having felt socially superior to Pursewarden, feels that Pursewarden was socially superior to him.

There are the upper classes (often unmannerly and arrogant) and there are the gentry, often poor and struggling, to whom the essence of good manners is consideration for others. Pursewarden is a member of the upper classes—art-proud rather than purse-proud. Darley is, in his odd, untidy way, a gentleman. Even when he rejects Justine, even when he neglects Melissa, Darley is never without compunction; that he can tell the story at all proves that he is a gentleman, for, even if he is exploited and deceived by Justine and Nessim, they also turn to him as an unfailing source of help and sympathy. Only an unaffected generosity of heart, for instance, could make him undertake the upbringing of Melissa's baby by Nessim. Darley never boasts about his own gifts or greatness and Pursewarden's aphorisms, as recorded by Johnny Keats and in 'My Conversations with Brother Ass', are nothing if not boastful. Pursewarden has something, in fact, of the paranoia and megalomania of Wyndham Lewis, without Lewis's excuse of having been socially snubbed and critically neglected.

The real evidences of Pursewarden's greatness as a writer—Darley, praising these, nevertheless slips in the damning word 'prolix'—namely, his letters to his sister, we never see. Pursewarden wanted them burned and Darley, having read them, sadly helps the half-unwilling Liza to burn them. Henry Miller, Durrell's best friend and critic, should have the last word about Pursewarden. In a letter to Durrell about *Clea*, written on the 7th September, 1959, Miller writes:

> To be frank, of all the characters in the quartet Pursewarden is the least interesting to me. Darley and he seem to be the two halves of a coin—like Lawrence in *Aaron's Rod*. I never get the conviction that he was the great writer you wish him to seem. I think he'd come off better—forgive me! —if you sliced down his remarks or observations. They get sententious and feeble sometimes. Too much persiflage. . . .

What I mean, more precisely, is that one is not sure at times whether the author is taking his double-faced protagonist seriously or ironically.

And how good, or how great, were the other artists? Clea, for instance? Was she potentially as good as Prunella Clough? She is obviously taking a long time to learn, and Mountolive does not think her portrait of him, which he might send back in the Embassy bag to his mother, can be properly classified as a 'work of art.' But she is such an enchanting personage that we take, I think, her potential painterly gifts on trust. The gifts of Johnny Keats, brought to birth by the shock of war, are utterly believable: he is right in supposing that he rather than Darley, if he is not killed in the war, is the proper bridegroom of Clea, the Muse. I am glad to see that Henry Miller has again anticipated me:

> Keats you handled wonderfully, I thought, and in the few pages devoted to him, in *Clea*, you gave a picture of war with its multiple aspects that was tonic. Keats we feel will become a writer. As for Darley, one feels sometimes that the self-deprecation he employs is unwarranted, exaggerated— false modesty. The man who recounts and observes, whether the author in disguise or not, can not be this crippled writer!

'Recounts and observes': it will be noticed how Henry Miller, essentially himself a naturalist, a realist, a kind of moralist, praises Durrell as a traditional novelist (what Durrell presents rings true to experience), not, like Christopher Middleton, as a mythographer. Wallace Stevens thought that though reality is meaningless and alien to us until the imagination gets to work on it, nevertheless imagination incestuously exhausts itself when it is feeding only on imagination. Only by pecking, among the dunghills, farmyard crumbs of fact, can Durrell's heraldic cock crow.

7

The farmyard, the dunghills, the pecking order, the scattered grain! The foxes and the hens! It is only in *Mountolive*, the traditionally constructed, omniscient-author novel, the anchored book which ties to itself the three other light bobbing crafts, that Durrell's naturalistic and realistic gifts, or 'observing and recounting', are at their height. After considering the themes of Love and Art as woven into this great elaborate fiction, we are now considering the third theme, more frightening than either of the last two, of Power. Power! It is a terrifying word and in a passage of *Mountolive* Nessim keeps repeating to himself, in parentheses, as in agony one might say in illogical hysterical recurrence *God* or *death* or *syphilis* or *treachery* or *torture* or *cancer* or *Hell* or *murder*, the name of the most terrible holder of power in Egypt: *Memlek:* Memlek, murderous, bribable, corruptible, a prey to Turkish sloth which can be volatilized only by sadistic lust or gluttony for money, represents in *The Alexandria Quartet* the nadir of power. The moral zeniths of power, the possibilities of the transformation of power into just or justifiable authority, are represented by Mountolive and Nessim. Both have been trained to use power, not for their own sakes, but within the contexts of public service and family tradition.

The family tradition can be rigid. Nessim's brother Narouz has a hare-lip. So Nessim has to take up all the business and social and political interests of his very rich Coptic family, leaving Narouz to live in the country and look after the estates. Nessim likes every Englishman he meets, but feels that the English have deprived the Copts (the remnant of Christian Egyptians, who resisted conversion to Islam after the Arab conquest of the eighth century) of the traditional role as key administrators that they held under Turkish rule. Lord Cromer's great book *Modern Egypt* bears this out. Cromer felt that he could deal with Moslems, who might be slothful and corrupt but were simple and direct, whereas the Copts were subtle and unpredictable. In a sense, Cromer was like an English administrator in India, preferring the Sikhs, farmers and soldiers, or the Muslims, to subtle Bengali Brahmins. Nessim seeks alliance with another minority group in Egypt, the Jews, who want to get the English out of Palestine and make Israel an independent state. Though Nessim's conspiracy is a fiction of Durrell's, it makes perfectly good sense in the context of the actual recent history of the Near East. What is perhaps implausible is that a Coptish-Jewish conspiracy would seek material support, would seek arms, from anti-Christian and anti-Semitic Hitlerian Germany.

Nessim marries Justine partly out of passion-love but partly because the marriage of a Coptic patrician with a lower-class Jewess, who was more or less edged her way into good society, will be a token for the Egyptian Jews of Coptic goodwill. And it is the excitement of power and danger, the prospect of wealth and status, rather than any positive emotional attraction that induces Justine to marry him. Once she has married him, shared danger and power can breed in her an impersonal sexual passion. Very much of the sex in *The Alexandria Quartet* is, in a psychical rather than a physical sense, mutual masturbation. A key incident, of this sort, is Narouz's making love to an elderly prostitute whose low, rich voice reminds him both of Clea's voice and of the voice of his mother, Leila, who has never loved him as much as she loves Nessim. And it is very important that when Justine first gives herself to Darley, he has been attempting to masturbate, and that she is using him to live out fantasies either about her rejection by Pursewarden or her rape by Capodistria.

Power is a sort of passion for Justine, partly because it is one of the fantasies by which she excites her own sexuality. Power is only a duty for Nessim. He sets Justine to spy on Pursewarden and Darley, knowing that she will sleep with them both, for dutiful reasons. Neither he nor Justine realize that the insignificant little cabaret dancer, Melissa, is in the end a far more dangerous person than either Pursewarden or Darley (both inept intelligence agents) because her keeper, hideous old Cohen, is a key figure in their conspiracy. Though Cohen, unlike Darley, is a master of 'brute sex', Melissa finds him merely disgusting (her disgust is one of the many doublings in the book, a doubling of Clea's disgust with the unwanted adoration of Narouz). Cohen pathetically adores Melissa. To impress her, to make himself seem important to her, he lets her know that he is the key agent for smuggling German arms to the Jews in Palestine. And if Nessim and Justine had decided, as they almost decide, to have Melissa disposed of, the discovery by the British Embassy of the whole range of their conspiracy might have been indefinitely postponed.

The conspiracy is discovered, and Mountolive, who has the greatest personal respect and liking for Nessim, has to report it to the Egyptian authorities. Power, for him as for Nessim, is a burden and a responsibility one has inherited; certainly not something to be relished, as Justine relishes it, or sought out for its own sake. Nessim buys life, from week to week, by bribing the atrocious Memlek with beautiful manuscripts of the Koran stuffed with banknotes. But Memlek himself is being pushed, both by the British Embassy, and by a jealous colleague. In the end he decides that Nessim has money, which Memlek can use, and Narouz has only land, which is useless to Memlek. (Memlek wants to invest lots of money abroad, to have a bolt-hole in, say, Switzerland.) Narouz plays into Memlek's hands because he has become a fanatic, a rabble-rouser, a kind of miniature Mahdi; he has come to despise Nessim, to whom he has always deferred, while being in his deep heart profoundly jealous of him, as a mere intellectual. Nessim's distress in *Justine*, which Darley attributes to an Othello-like jealousy of Justine, is distress at the possibility that he may have to commit fratricide as a duty. But Memlek gets in first, his agents kill Narouz, Nessim is not forced to saddle himself with the primal guilt, a brother's murder. . . . And Nessim and Justine do survive, poorer, less important, Justine under house-arrest, Nessim doing war-work as an ambulance driver, both now profoundly bored with each other. Darley, as has been said already, meeting Justine again finds all her glamour gone; there is nothing left but a meaningless talkativeness, a sullen humility. Only a bigger and better conspiracy resurrects Justine, at the end of *Clea*, to farcical life.

8

Power! Mountolive is all his life near the centres of power, yet he will never be able to initiate anything, only to check or delay. Perhaps in the 1910s, perhaps in the early 1920s, the young David Mountolive had been sent to Egypt by the Foreign Office to improve his spoken Arabic. As a guest at the Hosnanis' country estate, he becomes the lover of Leila, the mother of Nessim and Narouz, who is in her later thirties or early forties, and married to a crippled husband much older than herself. Young, beautifully well-bred, but well-bred at the expense of a rawness of inner sensibility, a lack of emotional self-knowledge, Mountolive finds that Leila's love opens springs of feeling and interest in him that he had never guessed at. Leila is the new Egyptian woman, interested in books, in art, in poetry, in the theatre, but forced by circumstances to live the life of the wife of a country squire. When Mountolive has to leave Egypt, he keeps in touch with her by letters, and, to keep her interested, educates himself in the arts. Leila's husband dies only a few years after Mountolive has left her, but at the same time she is stricken with confluent smallpox, which spares only her beautiful eyes. She becomes mildly eccentric, always wearing a veil, spending much of her time in a summer-house with a pet snake, but she keeps up her correspondence with Mountolive. When at last he comes to Egypt as Ambassador, she is at first afraid to meet him, and dodges an assignation at the terrible masked ball at which Narouz kills Toto, who makes advances to Narouz, disguised in a mask and domino, and wearing Justine's ring.

Before he goes to Egypt, Mountolive is told by the very nasty personnel head at the Foreign Office, the plumply reptilian Kenilworth, with his crepitating flesh, that he ought to dismiss Pursewarden. As first political officer (or Embassy Intelligence agent) Pursewarden is unreliable. He drinks, he writes novels which shock the Establishment, his sexual life is a wild one. He is what would be called today a security risk. Already a friend of Pursewarden's, already in love with Pursewarden's sister Liza, Mountolive snubs Kenilworth. He is wrong. It is always a mistake, in the world of the Foundation as distinct from the world of the Quest, to ignore expert official advice, even from the most repulsive adviser. Pursewarden, a man of genius, has in fact been totally wrong in belittling the rumours about the Hosnanis' conspiracy; Maskelyne, the stiff, dull, limited and snobbish head of military (as distinct from Embassy) intelligence in Alexandria has been right in taking these rumours exceedingly seriously. Mountolive has already been warned by his old chief in Moscow that he will blunder badly if he thinks that, once an Ambassador, he can become a source rather than a channel. And his first independent decision, to keep Pursewarden on, proves a very bad blunder both from a public and personal point of view.

As has been said, Pursewarden's discovery through Melissa, to whom he casually makes love, that her former keeper, Cohen, was Nessim's chief agent for smuggling arms into Palestine leads to his suicide. Yet Mountolive is right in thinking that men do not kill themselves for official reasons. Perhaps Pursewarden's deepest reason for killing himself is to leave the way clear for his sister to marry Mountolive (once Mountolive has got over the streak of meanness and conventionality that makes him feel that a blind Ambassadress would be an odd thing). Durrell, in fact, does a very skilful thing in creating Mountolive; we accept Mountolive as a perfect specimen of a very specialized type, the dedicated professional member of the English ruling classes, and yet the more we admire his rectitude, the more we wonder about the immature heart. Have all these letters from Leila over the years really taught him maturity of feeling? Does he deserve Pursewarden's last gesture of generosity to him, Pursewarden's insistence that Liza should destroy those brilliant letters of his to her, which are the final proof of Pursewarden's greatness as a writer? He has his moment, anyway, of terrible shock and punishment, when, after rejecting Leila, he disguises himself as a Syrian merchant and is lured into a child brothel, where the children rend his clothes. This is a revelation to him of the power and horror of the world of the Quest, as against the ritual impotence of his role in the world of the Foundation. Nessim, Mountolive's double in the world of the Foundation, is also punished: he loses an eye, a finger, a brother, much of his wealth, his love for his wife. Narouz is a figure of more primitive power, with his great whip, his charismatic eloquence, his fanaticism. But his very peasant simplicity make him an obvious target for Memlek, and it cannot give him his loved one, Clea. One might say that if Durrell's visions of love, of art, and of death are in the end lyrical and comedic visions, the vision of the nature of politics is a very bleak one indeed.

9

There is one more vision, the vision of holiness. Scobie, for Durrell, is the holy fool who knows nothing and everything. If Pursewarden is, as Henry Miller thinks, the great failure in the Quartet, Scobie (though Miller rather misses the point of him) is the obvious grand success. All the other characters are within a convention. We have met people like Nessim, Darley, Justine, Clea, Mountolive, Balthazar, Leila, even Narouz, in life or in other novels. And if Pursewarden is an attempt at something stranger and more original, still we can see out of what ingredients in literature and literary history he has been concocted. I have been told that Scobie draws a little on an elderly eccentric whom Durrell knew in Cairo, and one has met funny old things who were like him in this or that respect. Yet he remains an original. Like other great comic originals of literature, Falstaff, My Uncle Toby, Sir George Sitwell, he is incredible yet we believe in him, he is larger than life yet real. His is a more real immortality, in terms of the fable, than Pursewarden's; long after his death those who loved him can recreate him in pages of inspired mimicry.

Scobie is not merely a great comic character, but a symbol. He fuses the two extremes of sexual kinkiness, of the most absurd kind, and childlike innocence. Though he has annoyed his Moslem neighbours, especially his *protégé*, Abdul, the barber-surgeon, by his very proper horror of female circumcision, he becomes after his death a Moslem saint, El Scob, confused with another saint, El Yacoub, whose neglected shrine had been bricked up at the bottom of his garden. The bathtub in which he brewed hooch which, after his death, poisoned half of his immediate neighbours and killed some of them, becomes a sacred object. In the mimicry of his friends he is, as I have said, more alive and funnier than he was in life.

It is Durrell's triumph, in the character of Scobie, to link images of ineptness and degradation, rough old music-hall jokes, with an idea of the holy. Scobie is an aged queer and, when what he calls his Tendencies get the better of him at the full of the moon, transvestist. It is dressed up as an old woman that he is kicked to death by sailors. Yet he lives, in his conversations with Darley, through two friends, purely loved. One is Toby Mannering, who converted him to Roman Catholicism, teaching him the function of the Virgin Mary. (This function Durrell does not define, expecting us to know it: it is to intercede with her Son, Christ the Pantocrator, for those who sin mortally, knowing the nature of their sin.) Scobie's other great friend has an earthy rather than a spiritual significance; he is the inventor of a patent earth-closet, whose lid, when it has been used, automatically snaps down releasing a mechanism that trip-kicks earth over human excrement. Thus the wicked, for Scobie, can be saved; and human nastiness can be wholesomely buried, becoming part of living soil. His very ineptness has a kind of holiness about it; instructed to offer a woman suspect on the train to Cairo a drugged chocolate, so that he can inspect her handbag, it is typical of him that he eats the chocolate himself and arrives at Cairo in a coma. He is a silly old rip, yet represents holiness and innocence just as Clea, in spite of the experiments of her sexual life, in spite of her harshness to Narouz, represents purity and benignity. The choice friendship between the two characters who most definitely, in *The Alexandria Quartet*, stand for spontaneous goodness is important; I have noted already that Durrell never lets Clea, who seems to know everything, know how Scobie died.

10

I have said enough about *The Alexandria Quartet*, Durrell's most impressive single achievement so far. I have found myself tied pretty closely to its structures, its main characters and the way in which they echo and complete each other, and its themes. Readers who would like now to think of the novel in a larger literary context are referred back to my first chapter and to what I have to say there about Durrell's affinities with modern writers like Lawrence and Joyce and writers of the last century like Dickens and Poe. Meanwhile let me summarize briefly what I consider Durrell's main gifts to be, bearing in mind his versatility and his unpredictability.

Durrell's gifts as a writer are those of a lyrical and sympathetic comedian, with an occasional taste, but not a dominating one, for the frightening and the grotesque. His gifts as a master of language are for bravura, for rich excess, though he can write when he wants to with a plain elegance, as in many pages of *Mountolive*. In his deep self, he is a quietist and almost a mystic. Bubbling over though he is with ideas, one does not have to accept the ideas behind *The Alexandria Quartet* to enjoy the book—to accept them, that is, other than as elements in a composition. His personality is in a sense everything in his books and yet it is a remarkably elusive one, what he himself calls an 'ingenuous mask'. He is a great conjurer. '*Étonne-moi, Jean:*' Diaghilev once said to Cocteau, and one might well say something similar to Durrell; the power to astonish is all the more impressive if it arises out of a new kind of manipulation of scenes, characters, and situations that might at first seem to be out of stock. In this as in many ways, Durrell is at the opposite pole from his friend Henry Miller, whose gift as a commentator is for naïve, direct, piercing reflection, in the tradition, say, of Thoreau, Emerson, Whitman, and whose gift as a story-teller lies in an unbowdlerized version of the rugged comic naturalism of Mark Twain. Durrell is always on the verge of the precious, sometimes on the verge of the perverse, he plays with the sinister fancies that fascinated the English 1890s, but only plays. Even Capodistria, the one-eyed libertine, the black magician, in a roundabout way is seeking the light. When I think of an image for what is central in Durrell's art I do not think of Beardsley but of slim, almost sexless Cycladic goddesses, of the frescoes of Knossos, of the absurd saintliness of Scobie, of the benignity of Clea, of the serene and taut melodic line of some of Durrell's short poems, of his strange but moving vision of a converted Faust; when I think of the man I have known so intermittently, but so vividly, I think of Durrell's own phrase: 'we must break the ring', and I think of Pursewarden's insistence that the truest love is 'loving-kindness'. Durrell is a near-mystic, or a near-mage, who has to 'rejoice that all things are'. He has to see evil as a dark and puzzling aspect of a cosmic unity which ultimately has to be accepted as good, or as beyond good and evil. Nevertheless, in the realm of charity, of the spirit, for all his dallyings with darkness, he strikes me as a more compassionate man than some of the critics who dismiss him as immoral, amoral, a mere belated aesthetic fantasist. Alas, the terror of life, which he sometimes represents so frighteningly, is no more a fantasy than life's promise, its delight, its painful power of growth and of rebirth. He is a serious, though never a solemn writer.

CHAPTER SEVEN

NOW OR NEVER

The title of Lawrence Durrell's new novel, which I have been reading in typescript and in rough proof, the title *Tunc*, would have utterly puzzled me, if he had not in a letter kindly given me a clue. I must keep the clue secret from my friends, he wrote, but I might confide it to my typescript. *Tunc* is the first of two novels, the first instalment of what Durrell calls a 'double-decker'. He told me to look up a passage on pages 74 and 75 of the Loeb Petronius (the Latin on one side, the English version opposite it) where I would find the phrase *aut tunc aut nunquam*, in English 'then or never'. The scene is Trimalchio's banquet and a freedman named Ganymedes is having a long grumble about the decay both of honesty among municipal officials and of piety towards the gods. Everybody, nowadays, lacks any sort of reverence and is merely on the make. The whole passage, in John Sullivan's lively and colloquial Penguin Classics version, reads thus:

'Take me, I've already sold the rags off my back for food, and if this shortage continues, I'll be selling my bit of a house. What's going to happen to this place if neither god nor man will help us? As I hope to go home tonight, I'm sure all this is heaven's doing.

'Nobody believes in heaven, see, nobody fasts, nobody gives a damn for the Almighty. No, people only bow their heads low to count their money. In the old days high-class ladies used to climb up the hill barefoot, their hair loose and their hearts pure, and ask God for rain. And he'd send it down in bucketsful right away—it was then or never—and everyone went home like drowned rats. Since we've given up religion the gods nowadays keep their feet well wrapped up. The fields just lie. . . .'

Durrell's clue about this passage comes in a letter to me, of which I think he would allow me to quote the following sentences:

You may note a resemblance to some characters in Q. This is intentional. It is the same sort of puppetry, but with another accent, another angle of view—really, I suppose, another subject, i.e. culture. The full title by the way (but this is a dead secret, so confide it only to your manuscript) is *aut tunc aut nunquam*—you will find the relevant para on page 75 of the Loeb Petronius; I am sure the University has that . . . it begins *Quid enim futurum est . . . si nec dii nec homines. . .* ? ('What's going to happen to this place if neither god nor man will help us?') What indeed? In the culture sense it's always now or never.

Petronius's speech is given to a low character, who speaks vulgar Latin, and has a jocular air; the high-born ladies who have been imploring Jove for rain come home like drowned rats. Still, excessive or ill-judged help from the gods or men is better than no help at all. *Tunc*, which is more fantastic, and less romantic, than any of Durrell's previous novels, has also a more exact and disturbing social relevance. It is about an age which, at the springs of power, is perhaps both anti-religious and anti-humanist, perhaps satanic. Full of grim and gamy humour and of fantastic invention as *Tunc* is (the brothel scenes in Athens in fact very much recall Petronius), it is a frightening book, though Durrell himself is not frightened, and though his high spirits and delight in his own artistry infect the reader.

I think Durrell would permit me to quote a very useful passage from an earlier letter about his thematic and structural intentions in *Tunc*:

. . . I know that a work stands or falls by itself—it carries instant conviction or not as the case may be: and that all 'explanations' are futile, if it don't. But in case you are interested in the latter. . . . In the Quartet I tried to see people as a function of place which has also a source-place for our western culture. . . . Ahem, the Septuagint and all that. 1066 to 1984, so to speak. Now in this 'ere spunky little work I am attempting to set my people against a backcloth of an idea of culture as something generic. . . . They will lose a little as individuals and gain as puppets; will be swallowed by the Firm, which I am using as my top symbol of culture. BUT please DO NOT regard this as a critique of any special culture, much less of our own technocratic etc etc I spit me of all that ploy. Culture starts with an association, a kiss, an invention like fire, an alphabet; this is a study in associations so to speak. Of course it will have much to say about our contemporary preoccupations because alas I am writing it from the standpoint of my own life in the here and now, I can't escape that. . . . But the beam is really on the back-cloth idea of what makes a culture gell, be, exist? Monuments? Big pricks? Small kisses? House Tombs wombs bombs? Well, this is roughly the stance; apart from that I have tried to use all the time-honoured pantomime effects and hope you get a laugh here and there. . . .

I am very grateful to Lawrence Durrell for all this help about his intentions; though, in fact, before I had studied these letters carefully, *Tunc* had carried what he calls 'instant conviction' to me.

Tunc is only, of course, the first instalment of a 'double-decker' that may quite possibly expand itself into more than two volumes; and, unlike *Justine*, it is not constructed so as to seem deceptively complete in itself but rather so as to leave the reader in a state of acute suspense. But already one can say that it is the best written of all Durrell's fictions, combining the poetic density (but not the clottedness) of *The Black Book* with the flow (but not the occasional improvisatory straggliness or prolixity) of *The Alexandria Quartet*. Here is a passage about making love in Athens whose cadences would reward the close examination I gave to the cadences of some passages in *The Black Book*. But the mature Durrell has acquired ease. We no longer feel that he is trying a little too hard, there is no sense of *pastiche*, parody, or uneasy self-mockery:

> ... The quiet wind blew dustily uphill among the moon-keepers. To make love in this warm curdled air seemed an act of unpremeditated simplicity that placed them back once more in the picture-book world sacred to the animal kingdom where the biological curve of the affect is free from the buggerish itch of mentation. Warm torpid mouth, strong arms, keen body—this seems all the spiritual instruction the human creature needs. It is only afterwards that one will be thrown back sprawling among the introspections and doubts. How many people before Iolanthe? Throats parched in the dry air we drink thirstily from the sacred spring. She washes the sugar from her lips, washes her privates in the icy water, drying them on my old silk scarf. No, Athens was not like other places; and the complicated language, with its archaic thought-forms, shielded its strangeness from foreign eyes. Afterwards to sit at a tin table in a tavern, utterly replete and silent, staring at each other, fingers touching, before two glasses of colourless raki and a plate of olives. Everything should have ended there, among the tombs, by the light of a paraffin lamp. Perhaps it did?

That is the prose of elegy, dense with all the richness and sadness of the retrospective sense of a fulfilment that, when it happened, was not sufficiently valued. But the prose can have other cadences, hard and clangorous as iron. As in this passage, again with its Athenian setting:

> ... She came from no island but from the mulberry-starred plateaus where the Vardar flows, and where the women have voices of steel wire. The fish-markets of Salonika had been her only school. Pitiful black eyes of a mooncalf adorned this kindly personage. Her freshly washed hair, though coarse, was delicious as mint. But then ideas turn sideways in their sleep, seduced by the lush combing of waves upon sand, and one turns with them, sliding towards the self possession of sleep and dreaming. Once more I

saw Harpalus among the tombs. 'Harpalus the Macedonian, who plundered large sums from Alexander's funds, fled to Athens; there he fell madly in love with Pythonice the courtesan and squandered everything on her. Nothing like her funeral had ever been seen, choirs, artists, displays, massed instruments. And her tomb! As you approach Athens along the Sacred Way from Eleusis, at the point where the citadel is first seen, on the right you will see a monument which outdoes in size every other. You halt and ask yourself whose it is—Miltiades, Cimon, Pericles? No. It is Pythonice's, triple slave and triple harlot.'[1]

Pater, who seems to haunt *The Black Book*, with his yielding and feminine temperament, is all too easily imitable; Landor's prose of steel and marble, his unyielding masculinity, has not, it seems to me, been properly resurrected by any English writer, except Durrell in *Tunc*. But what is important, also, is that these two passages I have quoted are not inorganic 'purple panels' but have their exact place in the thematic development of *Tunc*. Iolanthe, the little Athenian prostitute, with her coarse hair as delicious as mint, her pitiful black eyes of a mooncalf, becomes a great film star, will have a memorable tomb, without ceasing to be a harlot or a slave. Julian, who vainly dotes on her, has plundered richer treasures than those of Alexander and is ready, vainly, to squander them on her. Charlock, the hero and narrator of *Tunc*, will realize in retrospect that, for all his later worldly success and fame, for all the tortured and pitying love which he is to feel for another woman, his wife Benedicta, perhaps his real life ended when he was an obscure and struggling inventor, making love to Iolanthe, eating sugared apples with her, drinking raki and nibbling olives 'among the tombs'. The note of the treatment of love in *Tunc* is what Matthew Arnold calls 'the eternal note of sadness'.

It is the style, then, of *Tunc* that will to any reader of proper sensibility first carry instant conviction. But the reader who has followed Durrell's development all through will be growingly

[1] The passage in quotation marks about Harpalus and Pythonice is (Durrell tells me) from the English translation in the Loeb edition of Athenaeus.

impressed also by the fusion, or the weaving together, in *Tunc* of various strands of interest that had previously been laid out in separate books. Durrell himself mentions in a note deliberate echoes from *The Alexandria Quartet* and *The Black Book*. But the element of submerged allegory (hinted at to the reader by the flavour of proper names), the use of characters as what Lionel Trilling, in reference to Scott Fitzgerald's *The Great Gatsby*, calls 'ideographs', carries on also from what is positive and promising in that generally unsatisfactory fiction, *The Dark Labyrinth*. What Durrell himself calls the pantomimic humour, black farce rather than comedy, of such a character as the clown Sipple, owes something to Durrell's practice with farce in the Antrobus stories, even more perhaps to his translation of the Rabelaisian Greek novel, *Pope Joan*. Even the more or less pot-boiling task of writing a thriller like *White Eagles Over Serbia* may have contributed something to the remarkable pace of the narrative. The great descriptive and atmospheric set pieces—in *Tunc* about Athens, Constantinople, London, and Paris—do not here seem to clog the flow, to make the mere story lag a little, as they sometimes do in *The Alexandria Quartet*. Finally, the interest in folklore, black and white magic, diabolism, that comes in the inset vampire and homunculus tales in *The Aelxandria Quartet*, and that makes *An Irish Faustus* the most successful of Durrell's plays, is now incorporated into the main substance of a serious fiction. *Tunc* has a dream-like quality, the passage of time is not quite real in it, things seem to happen magically by fearing or wishing or breaking a taboo or *not* breaking a spell, but the dream is, in a Freudian sense, doing dream-work. In dreams we try to escape from reality but are brought back to it. Durrell's draws the reader's attention to the magical, wish-fulfilling and fear-fulfilling, element in the story by his epigraph from a famous story of Dostoevsky's, translated into French as *Voix Souterraine*: '*Deux fois quatre, c'est un mur*.' But, as in a disturbing dream which draws attention to memories or hopes and fears one thought one had buried (Eliot's 'That corpse you planted last year in your garden'), two and two do make four—very frighteningly!—at the end of this story. 'In dreams begin responsibilities.'

2

Let me first summarize (and it is quite difficult to do) what happens in the story. We meet the hero, Felix Charlock, the 'happy weed', first at an expensive but unsatisfactory London restaurant where he is having a heavy lunch with his wife Benedicta's psychiatrist, Nash, and a friend whom he first met in Constantinople, the publisher Vibart. These two names have their own reverberations. Nash, whom Charlock rightly dislikes, has a name that suggests the gnashing of teeth; Vibart, a would-be writer who has become a publisher on realizing that he has no real creative gift, vibrates excitedly to the rhythms of life, but in an ultimately sterile way. Charlock and Nash are both employed under strict contract by a world-wide firm of investors, merchants, and merchant-bankers, Merlin's, which started off modestly as an *entrepôt* firm in Turkey under Abdul Hamid II. Nobody quite knows what happened to the founder, Merlin, but Charlock is married, very unhappily, to Merlin's neurotic daughter, Benedicta, who was brought up among the women and eunuchs of her father's harem in Istanbul. Charlock has been parted for some time from Benedicta. After the birth of their son Mark she wished to have nothing more to do with Charlock, sexually. Charlock thinks the senior London partner of the Firm is both Benedicta's lover and responsible for keeping her mad by keeping her drugged. Julian has also been in love with Charlock's early mistress, the little Athenian prostitute, Iolanthe, who, after a meteoric rise to fame as a film star, is to die dreadfully of cancer, brought about by an injection of paraffin wax in a cosmetic operation on her breast. Julian likes to control everything, and has resented Iolanthe's wish to make herself independent of him by setting up her own film company. He controls Vibart, whose publishing firm is a subsidiary of Merlin's; and Vibart will help him to control an unworldly mystic, Koepgen, who is one of the sources of wisdom in the story, by offering to publish Koepgen's poems. The Firm's net-

work is so wide and sensitive that practically all the main characters are caught up in it in the end. At the centre of the network,
Julian sits like a spider.

Though he has been under contract to the Firm for a number
of years, and has often conversed with him on the telephone,
Charlock has never met Julian face to face. Only once, through
the window of a railway carriage, has he glimpsed Julian's small,
Napoleonic hands. He has not been able to discover even an
authentic photograph of Julian. Revenge on Julian has become,
at the beginning of *Tunc*, the main motive of his life and for over
three years he has been living in eccentric retirement in the
country, working on a strange machine called Abel which enables him to spy not only on the voices but the thoughts of other
people, with relative accuracy. Charlock, a briliant inventor in
many fields, but particularly in the field of sound-engineering
and communication theory, has tried to break free from Merlin's,
but is bound by an unbreakable contract. The sanctity of contracts, as Julian explains to him over the telephone, is the one
matter about which the Firm, very flexible and often very con-
siderate to its employees over other matters, has to be rigid. It
buys brains, and it uses them for its own ends. Attempts to break
free are dangerous. One may be brainwashed at a private mental
hospital, the Paulhaus, in Switzerland. One may die suddenly
and unexpectedly, not even having attempted to break away,
when one's usefulness to the Firm is apparently exhausted. One
important character, the architect Caradoc, has apparently died
in an accident, but there are clues that suggest he is still alive,
and he is glimpsed in fact, sitting outside a wooden house he has
built for himself, on a South Sea island.

The Firm has, at the beginning of the story, generously
approved of Charlock's taking a long holiday, also in the South
Seas. In fact, he intends to go back to Athens, where the firm first
became aware of his potentialities as an inventor, and where he
had his first really serious and, as it turns out, only really happy
love affair with the prostitute Iolanthe. In Athens, he intends to
record his memories on a small recording machine he has invented, the dactyl (*dactyl* of course is the Greek word for *finger* and

by metaphor for a metrical foot of one long and two short syllables, like the one long and two shorter bones of the finger; poetically, Charlock is refingering past time). The dactyl records human whispers and turns them out as perfectly typed pages of foolscap (it is these pages that we are reading, and the tone of *Tunc*, even in such elaborate passages as I have quoted earlier, is always that of a possible speaking voice: it is one difference between *Tunc* and the exceedingly graphic *Alexandria Quartet* that in *Tunc* we are being rather more invited to listen than to look). Charlock's dactyls are keyed to his personal register, his individual tone of voice. He turns them on by saying *Konx*, and off by saying *Om*. His object, in Athens, is not merely to leave a record of his memories before the Firm tracks him down. He wants to pull his whole story together for himself, to make sense of it. This narrative device permits the combination of an exciting forward thrust of narrative with an intensity and depth of retrospective reflection, and a note of elegy.

In a broader sense, Charlock himself is of course a narrative device, like Lawrence Lucifer in *The Black Book* or L. G. Darley in *The Alexandria Quartet*: he is a stand-in for Durrell, a focus for Durrell's authorial authority. But in a sense he is more distanced from his creator than these other two; not merely in that he is a scientist rather than an artist, rational rather than mystical, middle-aged rather than young, but in that there is a certain dryness and detachment in his character, an ironic and sad submissiveness to circumstances, a certain grey justice, and also, at moments, a very strong, determined, and obstinate will. Stendhal, who so much detested romantic prose, *la cime indéterminée des forêts*, would have detested the prose of *Tunc* also, yet would have felt an affinity with Felix Charlock: Durrell's admiration for Stendhal here, for the first time, works itself fruitfully into his art. He had not before achieved this effect of witty desolation, polite surprise, mocking and dry and intense sadness. Charlock is, in a sense, much more of a *man* than Lawrence Lucifer or L. G. Darley.

Through the dactyls, Charlock gives us an account of his background. He hardly remembers his parents, who were mostly stationed overseas, and he was brought up by aunts (one remembers Auden's 'the long aunts'). Charlock's interest in mechanical inventions, particularly those concerned with the recording of sound—the first toy that interested him as a child was a stretched-string nursery telephone—springs from the ingenuity and loneliness of a small boy with no parents handy and no brothers and sisters, plagued, perhaps, by a wish to spy aurally, to overhear. (Julian, one of the most powerful ideographs in *Tunc*, makes his sinister effect by being never properly *seen* but by being very articulately, in his whole register and idiolect, *heard*.) As a scientist, Charlock is more or less self-taught (as Durrell himself is an autodidact in literature). In Athens, Charlock's early and primitive recording machines attracted, when he was young (at the temporal not the narrational beginning of the story) the attention of an important great lady, Hippolyta, who wished to record a speech to be made in the Parthenon by a distinguished visiting architect, Caradoc.

Charlock meets Caradoc and some other members of Hippolyta's entourage at her castle in Attica. Caradoc, Welsh as his name suggests, though his important early commissions were in Australia, is a strange bardic figure, fond of inventing improper rhymes and making punning bawdy jokes, slightly overpowering but life-giving, perhaps fonder of talking about sex than enacting it. He is also a heavy drinker. In a broad sense, he corresponds to Pursewarden in *The Alexandria Quartet*, but he is also a Tiresias-figure like Scobie and Balthazar. He is not homosexual, but he is becoming fat and feminine, a baggy breasted figure, as self-indulgent middle-aged men do, and our last glimpse of him is on a South Sea island, where, with a native wife, he lives in a wooden house he has constructed according to his biological principles of architecture, suckling two 'kids'. (His assistant Pulley speaks demotic English, and one does not know whether Caradoc, who now calls himself Robinson, is suckling two small children by his native wife, or two baby goats.)

After dinner with Hippolyta, Caradoc takes the male members of the party to a brothel in Athens, a friendly establishment kept by a lady called Mrs Henniker, who has some characteristics in common with Hilda of *The Black Book*, though a much more practical and successful person. Caradoc's favourite whore there is a fat Turk, who revolts Charlock's aesthetic feelings. There is a funny but scabrous account of the antics in the brothel of a famous performing clown, called Sipple, who needs to be beaten with broomsticks before he can have an erection and an emission. On his dactyl, in between the Rabelaisian accounts of conversations and doings at Mrs Henniker's establishment, Charlock intersperses his own more intense and, in a sense, purer memories. His mistress, Iolanthe, has just signed on at Mrs Henniker's, and a doctor is looking over her to see whether she has some venereal disease. (Mrs Henniker is a very conscientious Madam, with a great regard for the health of her customers.) Charlock recalls his visit with Iolanthe, on a Sunday, a non-working day for prostitutes, to the much humbler seamen's brothel in the Piraeus, the port of Athens, where she at first worked: the image of the Piraeus brothel is strangely one of chastity of the spirit, of sparseness, of humility, of qualities that are basically Greek.

Caradoc, in the brothel scene at Mrs Henniker's, is in a wildly exuberant state, but though, later, he turns up at the Parthenon drunk, agonizing Hippolyta with worry and expectation, he in fact makes a wonderful speech, about the biological roots of architecture, the relation of all architecture to infantile needs and resentments (in an Anna Freud sense, good and bad breasts) and to the shape of the human body. Our physical exits and entrances, our cooking machines and thinking machines, the belly and the brain, our windows out to the world, like the eyes and the ears, our legs that support us, our arms and hands that we reach out with, our receptive vaginas and our aspiring towering phalluses, these are the basic shapes of all architecture: the study, the drawing-room, the bedroom, the kitchen, the ways in and the ways out, the need both for protection and openness, the need for an ear and an eye, the need to prop the whole thing up, the need to make it a riddling human image.

Just as Caradoc is beginning to lose coherence, he is interrupted by the clown Sipple, who seizes the bottle with which

Caradoc has been refreshing himself, pushes through the audience (who, mostly Greeks with an imperfect command of English, have admired Caradoc's eloquence but not followed what he was saying), and jumps madly off an outer wall of the Acropolis: apparently to his death in the street below, but in fact to a safe ledge.

Hippolyta, whose motives are obscurely connected with her love for a sick but noble Greek politician called Graphos, is for reasons she promises to explain but never does, anxious to get both Sipple and her peculiar friend, the eccentric Count Banubula, out of Greece to Turkey. In a nightmarish sequence, Charlock tracks Sipple to his house, finds him locked in the lavatory, but finds also, in Sipple's bed, a beautiful dead youth with a cut throat who is the double of Charlock's mistress, Iolanthe. Charlock, after Sipple has assured him that he has not murdered the boy, and has left, goes back to his own cheap hotel. There, opening Iolanthe's door, he sees her dabbling herself ritually with menstrual blood. It is she who has killed her brother (though he does not learn this till much later, when he meets Iolanthe, now a famous film star, in Paris). The brother is a male prostitute, has 'gone to the bad'. (When first hearing this, Charlock sardonically wonders whether Iolanthe, a female prostitute, can be said to have 'gone to the good'.) Iolanthe has killed her brother to save her old impoverished peasant father, who had made an oath to kill his son to save the family honour, from doing so. The strange —and when it first irrupts into the story, totally inexplicable— incident of Iolanthe's dabbling herself with menstrual blood links thematically with the fact that Benedicta, the blessed or cursed witch whom Charlock is to marry, has never had a period, or been capable of bearing a child, till she marries him.

Sipple and the peculiar Banubula are got out of the country. Partly in gratitude for Charlock's services, Hippolyta and Graphos send Charlock to Constantinople, to meet Jocas Pehlevi, the Turkish representative of the great firm of Merlin's, who may be able to help him to patent and develop his inventions. Charlock is met by a charming, timid, and uxorious clerk, Mr Sacrapant (to Mr Sacrapant, as his name implies, *everything* is

holy or *sacred*, but especially his own job with Merlin's) who gives
him some more information about Merlin's. It is a very exclusive
firm, and Count Banubula has been trying vainly for years to
worm himself in. Very respectable and scholarly in Attica,
Banubula comes to Stamboul, to indulge in orgies which—he
describes one, that he has never tried, as *en brochette*—sound more
like cooking recipes. He confides his peculiar tastes to Charlock,
at the same time asking him to guard his confidences as if they
were state secrets. He and Charlock peer in at Sipple giving an
obscenely comical performance at a Seamen's Club, to the sound
of barbarous and inane laughter.

Merlin, the founder of the Firm, was a cabin boy who deserted
from a privately owned British yacht (though, in *The Times*
obituary, Vibart thinks it more proper to describe him as a
'naval cadet') and started modestly in Stamboul with a wine-
shop for sailors. He lived slyly and secretly in a converted seraglio, where his daughter—if she was his daughter—Benedicta
was brought up. Brought up though she was in Istanbul, Benedicta's total atmosphere is North European, Gothick. Merlin,
when he died, if he died, left the whole business to two brothers
(but in fact they are not brothers, merely orphans brought up in
the same monastic orphanage), Jocas and Julian. Julian, an
Oxford man, manages the London end, the general administration, the paper work, telephone calls, constant flights to attend
international business conferences. Jocas, who reads and writes
with difficulty, and speaks rather imperfect English, has never
been farther away from home than Smyrna. He looks after the
great Istanbul warehouses, packed with spices, carpets, furs.
Shy and awkward though he is, Jocas is almost magically in-
tuitive; he can read Charlock's thoughts.

Charlock stays the night at Jocas's, and likes him, but dislikes
Benedicta. He has glimpsed her before he meets her, a slim girl
with dark hair, though we learn later that this dark hair is a wig.
She does not join Jocas and Charlock in their evening meal but,
while they are eating, feeds one of her hawks with little birds,
which she crushes with her bare hands, and Charlock is disgusted
both with this performance, and with a pervading smell of

decaying meat which the hawk has rejected. Yet, though he finds Benedicta repellent, he also finds himself possessed by an absorbing pity for her. He gathers from Jocas that her health is uncertain, and that she goes from time to time to a nursing home in Zürich, but he does not yet know that her illness is a mental one.

One fine morning, Jocas and Charlock go hawking with Benedicta. Benedicta has taken off her black wig and her real fair hair is streaming in the breeze; she has an aquiline nose and it is difficult not to think of her as a hawk and poor Charlock as a snipe or woodcock. Jocas is called home on business and, having dismissed their attendants, Charlock and Benedicta spend the night together outside a hunter's lodge, near a fountain. Benedicta excites Charlock but at the same time herself seems to find love-making a kind of agony. After they have made love, Benedicta in the morning, after bathing herself in the fountain, strips a plaster from her right foot, and reveals that on that foot she has twin small toes, a deformity which in the Middle Ages was called 'the devil's teat' and was regarded as one of the marks of a witch. Benedicta wants to marry Charlock, and this no doubt influences him in finally signing a contract with the Firm, though he does not do so without a great deal of doubt and inner questioning. Benedicta has to go to Switzerland for some time, before she and Charlock can meet in London and arrangements for the marriage can be made. Charlock is meanwhile briefly to return to Athens. It is disconcerting to him that before he goes, Sacrapant, the little clerk whose gratitude to the Firm seemed almost effusive, commits suicide by jumping from a tower. It is disconcerting also that his announcement in Athens, to Hippolyta and her friends, that he is going to marry Benedicta Merlin is met, before the formal congratulations come, with a moment of awkward silence. (Much later, in London, Hippolyta is to tell him that all other women instinctively detest Benedicta.)

Benedicta, indeed, does not seem to bring good luck. Her first husband, who like Charlock was an inventor, though of a minor kind—he had devised a machine for copying music scores—died in the Far East of a fever on their honeymoon. The sense of

Benedicta as a 'possessed' person is important throughout the novel. Often unbalanced, at the climax of the story she attempts to hack off her double toe, her witch-mark. Her name, of course, means *blessed*, and her fair hair and blue eyes (like those of Clea in *The Alexandria Quartet*) should be the colours of virtue. But she is in a black wig when we first see her. And we remember that in French, say, *sacré* means both 'sacred' and accursed, or, more obviously, in Greek, the Eumenides are the Furies. Julian, also, who has complete power over her, more and more seems to resemble, as the novel progresses, in his mysteriousness and elusiveness, in his icy suavity, traditional representations of the Devil.

Yet perhaps Benedicta *is* blessed, and *will* escape from the Devil in the end: we see her at one point trying to say the Lord's Prayer (though punctuating her phrases with rifle shots at her reflections in a row of mirrors). She does tell Charlock at one time: 'I only really loved you when I thought you were determined to be free from the firm.' She certainly makes an odd disquieting effect. I have mentioned Hippolyta's horror of her. Yet Charlock (though there comes a time when he almost hates her) feels: 'Her case is so hopeless that one must, absolutely must, love her,' and also that she is 'born to be loved, yet doomed to die, in solitude like a masterless animal'. One cannot help comparing her a little with Justine, a Justine more thoroughly a victim; perhaps the final impression is that of the Princess under a dark spell. At one point on their honeymoon Benedicta tells Charlock that he may ask her any question he pleases, and he lets the chance go by; in a fairy tale, of course, the right question at the right time breaks spells, and to pass over the chance to ask it is very dangerous.

Charlock comes to London, but his new wealth has an oddly unreal taste. The furniture in his Mayfair house is 'sumptuous' and 'impersonal'. Savouring wealth, he orders a bowl of strawberries and a glass of the finest sherry at eleven o'clock in the morning, while he is busy with his papers; still busy, he only half notices that the strawberries are watery, the sherry very ordinary. Though Benedicta is sharing his bed, time has to go past till their marriage contract, which is financially very gener-

ous to him, can be drawn up. Julian speaks to him on the telephone but never meets him in person. (Very few people have
actually seen Julian, as very few people have actually seen Benedicta's father, Merlin.) The atmosphere of Charlock's actual
wedding is strange and macabre. With Benedicta, he drives out
to a great house in the country, where preparations have been
made as for a great ball, but there are only sheafs of congratu-
latory telegrams, and the firm's solicitor, Shadbolt, to drink the
couple's health. The ceremony is a civil one (that is, not sacra-
mentally binding). Charlock only discovers much later that the
great library in which the ceremony takes place is full of beautifully bound books which are, in fact, 'empty dummies':

> Yet to browse among the titles one would have imagined
> the room to contain virtually the sum total of European
> culture. But the books were all playful make-believe, empty
> buckram and gilt. Descartes, Nietzsche, Leibniz. . . .

The little detail is important, suggesting something sham and
hollow about anything the Firm can offer Charlock. But the
ceremony does not take long. Within an hour, Benedicta and
Charlock are whirling off to Southampton for the long sea voyage
which is to be their honeymoon. This is like a royal tour. Everywhere they go, they meet the Firm's representatives. Benedicta
becomes jealous when Charlock sees a film in which little
Iolanthe has a part. They make love passionately, she has begun
at last to menstruate, she becomes pregnant.

The pregnancy unsettles her; for the time being, at least, after
she comes home, she wants nothing more to do with Charlock
sexually. And in his absence other disturbing things have been
happening. A small invention which he had intended for peaceful purposes is to be turned into a new gunsight, by one of the
Firm's more professional scientists, Marchant. Julian is suavely
apologetic over the telephone. Marchant tells Charlock that he
himself hates the human race, and is glad to work on armaments,
but that the gunsight is comparatively harmless compared to
some of the other things the Firm is working on.

Charlock's life is now a lonely one. He rarely sees Benedicta,
he fails ever to see Julian. Hippolyta cheers him up a little by a

visit to London, during which they several times see films of
Iolanthe's, who in the two years or so since Charlock last saw her,
and after her marriage to the greatest box-office draw in Holly-
wood ('triple slave and triple harlot'), has become a world-
famous film star. Charlock is obsessed by her great images on
posters and the screen, by his inability to connect the honest
little whore whom he loved, without quite knowing that he loved
her, with Iolanthe's new unreal glamour. Hippolyta hates
Iolanthe because she was the mistress of Graphos, whom Hippolyta loved. She feels that a touch of Graphos's genius has rubbed
off on Iolanthe, who has, in Benedicta's phrase, such 'a common
little face' on the screen. Agreeing that the film cannot possibly
be a true art-form, Hippolyta and Charlock nevertheless become
unwilling fans of Iolanthe's.

Charlock does, in fact, quite soon meet Iolanthe, the star
visitor at a great exhibition of Impressionist paintings which
Merlin's has arranged as an advertising stunt. At the opening
reception, everybody has eyes for Iolanthe, nobody eyes for the
paintings. He finds that she has taken on the genial Mrs Henniker, who was as kind as a mother to her in the Athens brothel, as
her personal companion. He learns also that she is being harried
by the elusive Julian. Julian has seen her once and fallen in love
with her. He is using all the Firm's resources to drive an independent film company which she has started, into bankruptcy.
If Julian cannot possess her, he wants at least to possess shares in
her. Furtively, because of their nervousness both about Julian
and her husband, Charlock and Iolanthe meet in Paris. She
disguises herself as a girl he knew in Paris, before he met her,
Solange; they meet in the café where Charlock and Solange
used to meet. They discuss the past wistfully, they are on easy
and comradely terms with each other. He learns that Iolanthe
could have been permanently his if he had chosen only to
dominate her, to claim her as his slave. What touched her
about him in Athens was the courtesy he always showed her:
women, she says, ask for very little, only 'the iron ration, consideration'. The meeting is not amorous. Iolanthe shows Charlock her bandaged breasts, the scars of an operation to make

them tauter and more youthful still unhealed. The operation, involving the injection of paraffin wax, has not been successful. Quite soon, Iolanthe, though Charlock does not at the time foresee this, will have to face a lingering and painful death.

Charlock's exasperation with Julian is growing more intense. All his attempts to confront Julian in person, even to find an authentic photograph of him, have been thwarted. Julian has stepped between himself and Benedicta, seems to wish to step between himself and Iolanthe. He asks Julian, over the telephone, to let him give one of his inventions away free to the public. The conditions of his contract will not permit this. All his inventions belong to the Firm. Julian suggests that he should give some of his money to charity but, if he does so, income tax rebates and his marriage contract with Benedicta will leave him as rich as before. Julian has in the past expressed gratitude for the consideration Charlock has shown to Benedicta, in not forcing himself on her or their young son Mark, in not asking for a divorce. His suspicions of Julian now come to a head. He accuses Julian fiercely: 'Julian, for how long has Benedicta been your mistress, and what is the name of the drug?' Earlier in the conversation, Julian, as if talking to himself, has said: 'Who can gauge the feeling of a man in love who is forced to sit and look on at the steady deterioration of a fine mind and lovely body?' Julian might be referring to his own feelings for Benedicta, or his own feelings for Iolanthe, by this time mortally ill. He might be referring to Charlock's feelings also. Though they never in *Tunc* meet face to face there is between Julian and Charlock a sinister mind-reading intimacy. Later, after Iolanthe's death, Julian is to say to Charlock (over the telephone it must have been, since in this first deck of the double-decker they never meet face to face): 'The unlucky thing was her loving you; it was completely unsuitable, and anyway you did not care.' Julian has also said earlier: 'We must celebrate the people who set us on fire.' Shadowy and sinister as Julian's image is, cold and almost diabolical as he seems in his manipulations of others, he is not presented as someone wholly devoid of human passion.... The option, anyway, which Julian leaves Charlock with is that if he likes he can retire from active participation in the Firm, and live on his winnings (winnings which he would never have had if he had not signed his contract in the first place). But Charlock cannot consider any invention of his his own property; the best he can do, if he is sulky is to stop inventing.

Charlock, who lives in London, and rarely sees Benedicta these days, feels that he owes it to her to consult her about his decision. He goes out to the strange country house where they were married and where she lives with a staff of servants and nursemaids and their small son Mark and finds her, in the most dramatic episode in the novel, in a state of raging insanity. The dummy books from the library, their shamness now revealed, are scattered all down the staircase. There is a trail of blood leading up to the bedroom—Charlock does not guess that Benedicta has been hacking at her double toe with a kitchen knife!—and Benedicta is standing naked on the bed, surrounded by torn papers (some of them the papers that Charlock uses in his dactyls), and staring up through the ceiling at an imaginary heaven opening above her. She gets into the gunroom, loads a rifle with cartridges, and in the ballroom—Charlock has seized a stick to defend himself with, fearing that she means to shoot *him*—starts shooting at her reflection in a long row of mirrors. Charlock brings her down with a rugby tackle and, in a panic, starts beating her with his stick. She has been reciting the Lord's Prayer while destroying mirrors and now she moves her lips in silent prayer. Attendants come, and she is taken away to the Firm's asylum in Switzerland, leaving Charlock alone in the great house with servants and governesses—'the harpies'—and his strange, shy little son Mark. (Let me notice in passing how many names in this story come out of the *Matter of Britain*: Merlin, Avalon— the name of Merlin's seraglio in Constantinople—Mark; and Charlock somewhere describes himself as behaving like a Galahad. Durrell, by choosing such names, is calling attention to the element in his story of traditional romance and magic, with ancient roots.)

Now is the turn in the story of what one might describe as white magic. It is now or never—*aut tunc aut nunquam*—that

Charlock must exert his own powers against what he thinks of as the black magic of Julian. He experiments with the extraordinary recording machine called Abel (and Julian is Cain, I suppose) which can be orientated on any person about whom Charlock has certain primary data. It can predict fragments of the future, bits of the four-dimensional continuum that are not yet here, as well as sorting data of the past. Charlock uses Abel to probe Julian's secret thoughts, his fears, to make a voice just like Julian's ring Julian up. He worries Julian, tortures him, by predicting the deaths both of Iolanthe and Graphos. He writes to Iolanthe, offering to 'exorcise her house' provided she comes away with him. But it is too late, Iolanthe is already mortally ill. Charlock is to meet the dead Iolanthe's companion, Mrs Henniker. Julian, of course, had been there, but had managed to slip in and out while Mrs Henniker was sleeping, had somehow managed to avoid the press photographers who came crowding round like vultures towards a carrion at the end. Julian is to remain invisible or opaque to Charlock's imagination. We know merely that he is stricken with terrible grief. Mrs Henniker gives Charlock a lock of Iolanthe's hair and a little green book that has fallen from her bed. Nothing is marked in it, so it gives no clue to Iolanthe's last thoughts. It is a volume of Flaubert's letters, and Charlock lights on one very moving passage. Can Iolanthe have been reading it, or perhaps Julian, as he watched her dying? I translate, of course inadequately:

'You are fatefully linked to my best youthful memories. Do you know, we have known each other for more than twenty years? It all plunges me into gulfs of daydreaming that have the smell of the old man I am. People say the present hurries away too fast. For my part, I find it's the past that eats us up.'

How far are we to take Abel seriously? (Charlock's colleagues, like Marchant, think he has, because of Benedicta's breakdown and his estrangement from Julian, become slightly unbalanced.) We are not given any scientifically very plausible description of the machine. But Charlock, we have learned much earlier, has a foredivining gift: he can concentrate on his image of a person, and foresee or forehear moments of their fate. Through Abel, or through his own mediumistic gift, or more probably through the working of the two together, he has at any rate learned enough to worry Julian. He works at Abel like a hermit but, after a time, allows his son Mark to watch him, and Mark sees him fix up a booby-trap (a loaded twelve-bore, that will be triggered off by pressing 'an inviting red button') that may kill Julian. Finally, Charlock goes off to Athens, where he records his memories and reflections on his dactyls: memories that are picked up by the Firm when, leaving his clothes and the dactyls behind, Charlock has staged a mock suicide, an apparent death by drowning. There is a tiny noise on the last dactyl which Benedicta, now re-covered, reports Marchant as saying 'one *could* take for the sound of oars, a squeaky rowlock'.

The last section is in third-person omniscient-author style: it is no longer Charlock recording. Benedicta is back at the great house, and Nash, her psychiatrist, and Julian drive down to see her. This is the first appearance of Julian in the story, beyond a glimpse of his hands in a train, a knowledge that he is in a car shrouded by fog, as a person rather than a disembodied voice; but Durrell carefully refrains from giving any description of what he looks like. Poor little Mark is bullied into going upstairs to dismantle the lethal booby-trap. Julian first appeals to Mark's conscience—somebody might get killed accidentally—and then says horribly: 'Mark, you know the story of the Princes in the Tower?' Mark agrees to do the dismantling. Nash and Julian visit the convalescent Benedicta. Propped up by pillows, she looks like 'a Victorian poetess', perhaps Elizabeth Barrett Browning (is this a touch of satirical comedy, like the deflation of Justine at the end of *Clea*?). Julian suggests a scheme for Benedicta's seduction of a young German baron, another scientist, 'a botanist travelling about in Turkey with his yacht. He has found a flower which he says could give us something like perfect insect control in a natural way . . . I won't bore you with the details.'

Benedicta—has she suffered some fundamental transformation?—agrees with a 'curious, furtive wolfish look, beginning to

184

bite her nails as she listened'. Has she become a werewolf or a vampire—was she only half human, a devil's daughter, to start with? Who was Merlin? We are told he died of general paralysis softly caressing his Rolls Royce. But Koepgen, Durrell's wisdom figure in this novel (not one of the novel's great successes, I think) claims to have met an aged leper in a leper colony who said he was Merlin and also said that the only point of joining the Firm was to try to get out of it. We certainly do have an odd superstitious feeling at moments that the Firm may have existed, for ever, and that Merlin may be King Arthur's Merlin. But while we are brooding, and they are brooding, a shot rings out. Has Mark deliberately killed himself? Probably not, for Abel gave Charlock an audition of Mark, in the future, as a young man working in one of the Firm's offices. But Durrell has certainly left us with a splendid cliff-hanger situation.

Durrell has also left us with a deep emotional problem about the relationship between Benedicta and Julian. They have heard the muffled report of a shot through the thick walls of the building:

> She still stared at him with admiration and pity, and he gazed down at her as he had always done—his eyes full of an impenetrable sadness.

The loves of devil and devil? The loves of tormentor and victim (but which is which?)? The loves of the damned or of the nearly lost still struggling against damnation? The ambiguity is like that of 'perfect insect control': what would be the purpose, an enormous improvement in yield, in non-wastage, of world agriculture—or, on the other hand, biological warfare of an unspeakably awful and devastating sort? How far, in fact, is the Firm—which corners talents and products, to exploit and sell them—on the side of good, on the side of evil, or perhaps quite indifferent to such problems, like Shaw's Andrew Undershaft? The image of the Firm both shrinks and expands according to the way one thinks about it. But Durrell has said, in the letter I quoted earlier, that the Firm is the top image in *Tunc* of human culture, of the interests that force combination and co-operation on men of similar appetites and talents; there are hints that the

Firm has always existed, in one form or another; and that it has such a large, ancient, various, and permanent momentum that its general pattern of progress is well out of even Julian's control. If Julian is the Devil, the Devil, in his modern guise, is perhaps merely a top organization man in a Hell that more or less runs itself.

3

In a note at the end of *Tunc*, Durrell calls attention to echoes, intended not inadvertent, of both *The Alexandria Quartet* and *The Black Book*. Let us look at a number of these echoes, first of all at echoes of certain basic philosophical ideas. In the last chapter, I drew attention to the fact that there are so many reasons why Pursewarden might have killed himself that any attempt to explain his act for *one* main reason becomes ridiculous; there are also quite a number of reasons why he might wish to go on living, and in a sense his suicide becomes for the reader a free or inexplicable or spontaneous act. Yet philosophers might also describe it as an 'over-determined' act, an act for which there are more explanations than, in one context of thought, one can use. In *Tunc*, Jocas Pehlevi, the Hierophant, says this more neatly about Sacrapant's suicide: 'We look at things from the wrong point of view. I mean, how many reasons could you give for wanting to go on living? The list would be endless. So there is never one reason, but scores. . . .'

I have spoken already of some similarities and differences between Lawrence Lucifer and L. G. Darley as hero-narrators and Felix Charlock. These could be summed up thus. Charlock is at once a more active and decisive hero than the first two, more aware of the importance of choice and the force of hostile circumstances, and yet at the same time more mature, more emotionally detached. He is never wholly 'by love possessed', except, perhaps, when he thinks back to his relationship with Iolanthe, retrospectively; he hesitates and weighs issues before making decisions; he is a character of will and reflection, aware of his own weaknesses and inadequacies in an often sharply critical way; often revising his opinion of other characters, like Pulley and Marchant whom he at first dislikes but comes to think of as friends, in the light of more mature experience. He is very much contained within himself. He is in a sense an objectively created character, not mainly, though he remains in part, a mouthpiece for Lawrence Durrell.

Of the three heroines, Iolanthe in her beginnings and her death recalls Melissa; Hippolyta in her coolness and calm sense, Clea; and Benedicta recalls Justine, both as the possessed and tormented person and as the *femme fatale*. And yet one has an odd feeling that the cards have been somehow shuffled. Dealing with Durrell's use of the Tarot pack in *The Alexandria Quartet*, Carl Bode associated Clea with the Key card called the Star. 'Water is one of the card's prime qualities; with it go associations of fish-hooks and fishing.' Durrell's character-squeeze of Clea, at the end of *Justine*, Bode reminds us, is 'still waters of pain'. But water also stands for meditation, for depth. There is another Tarot card, the Priestess, associated with 'obedience, the quality of being "below" ' which Bode associates a little less confidently with Melissa. A third card, the Empress, regal, highly sexed, wise and foolish by turns, Bode associates with Justine. In *Tunc*, the cards fall differently. Though Hippolyta resembles Clea in the clarity and charity of her mind, she has a touch of silliness, and she is a princely woman, so perhaps she is the Empress rather than the Star. Though Iolanthe starts as if she were going to be Melissa, she is not naturally obedient, she is ambitious, she does literally become a Star, a film star: and in the end suffers terribly. Therefore in some sense Hippolyta equals Justine, Iolanthe equals Clea (in Athens, and later in Paris, she offers Charlock a kind of cool comradeship). Benedicta, strangely, is thus left with Melissa's archetypal role. The Priestess, in the lore of the Tarot pack, 'bows meekly to necessity' and is 'celibate'. Benedicta, like Melissa, seems to suffer sex as something inflicted on her; like Melissa, she 'bows meekly to necessity', is utterly submissive to Julian. I said that there are more characters than roles in *The Alexandria Quartet*, as in dreams, or as in *King Lear*. Durrell is teasing us in *Tunc* by presenting character-masks that he has made familiar, but by redistributing underneath them the archetypal roles.

Something similar happens to the character-masks and roles of the men. The lively, ebullient, sometimes scabrous Caradoc seems more or less the equivalent of Pursewarden, whom Bode identifies with 'the Tarot Fool, by no means a figure of fun but a person of airy, cosmic energy'. His brilliant drunken lecture on the biological roots of architecture seems to me much more profound than Pursewarden's dicta on the novel. Yet he has a benevolence, and a touch of amiable silliness, which Pursewarden lacks, and in the end we see him as a Tiresias-figure, on a Robinson Crusoe island, starting off architecture from its beginnings, and suckling two children from his ancient breasts, his old man's dugs. So he is to be equated perhaps more with the saint or sage figures in *The Alexandria Quartet*, Scobie and Balthazar. The Card of the Devil Bode associates in *The Alexandria Quartet* with Capodistria, who has 'the lust of a goat and the look of a serpent'. The character who is most worryingly near to our traditional notions of the Enemy of Mankind is, as I have suggested, Julian; yet Julian in his poise and polish, in the genuine and conscientious distress and sorrow which he seems to feel at times, recalls Nessim. Perhaps, like Nessim, he has accepted the role assigned to him out of duty rather than ambition. He has, at least, a dignity and a self-awareness that suggests Milton's Satan rather than a sexy, half-animal medieval Fiend. Jocas seems to me (but we must wait for the second deck) an instance where the cards have not been radically reshuffled. He corresponds to Narouz, to Bode's description of Narouz as 'suggested at least in part by the Key Card of the Hierophant. The Hierophant has the gift of Revelation. . . . Psychologically, the Hierophant represents intuition.' On the other hand, a kind of basic moral impulse in Jocas seems to be a helpless and slightly bewildered kindliness, where Narouz grows more and more fierce and fanatical.

A symbolically important character, not very fully presented, is Koepgen. His name to anybody who was in the Middle East during the war suggests somebody who *keeps the gen*, who is the custodian of the relevant secret information. He is a wisdom character, like Balthazar, but unlike Balthazar is sexless. He is snared by the Firm partly through his wish to recover an ikon, which his teacher in obedience has asked him to recover, and partly through the undue personal ambition which is mixed up with his genuine mystical bent, through the wish to have his poems published. The Firm is expert in all men's weaknesses.

4

This novel covers a considerable number of years (how many exactly depends on how old the boy Mark is in the last chapter) and yet because of a continuous flow from elaborately described background to vividly presented scene, because of the lack of blank or explicitly omitted areas ('Several years now elapsed, in which things went on much as usual. It was not till May 1966 that my relations with Benedicta and Julian again came to a crisis') we feel more as if we were reading the chronicle of several crowded months. Only the sense of continual, ungapped visual flow, the cinematic feeling—odd that both Charlock and Hippolyta insist so strongly that the film is not an art-form!—stop us asking questions about Charlock's independent social, and perhaps sexual, life in the years in which he was separated from Benedicta. That he would *never* have met Julian face to face would, in a naturalistic novel, be plainly impossible. Durrell cashes in on the impossibility with a number of cinematic devices (the car in the fog, the abortive visit to the flat, the hands through the railway carriage window, the photograph which is really a photograph of Jocas) that might remind one of Antonioni's *Blow-Up*.

One might define the cinematic technique in the novel as one by means of which that which is not presented, especially the lapses of time, does not exist; and by means of which contiguous blocks of presentation (whatever their order in simple chronicle-sequence, whether, for instance, they go back or forward in time) are felt as continuous, in the narrational flow. As in the cinema, also, we do not really feel that the characters in *Tunc* grow older, change, or develop in any significant way with the passing of time. The director fixes time upon them, for a particular shot, as the make-up men might put on a grey wig or a false beard.

5

Yet, yet. . . . In another sense, the effects of time are very much what this novel is about. It is the first fiction of Durrell's in which I sense the peculiar agony of middle age, other than comically presented. Marchant, Charlock's scientific colleague, who, like another character, Caradoc's assistant, Pulley, starts off as boorish and awkward but becomes sympathetic, says to Charlock:

> '. . . Do you care for this age particularly? I mean, once our hero was a St George doing in a dragon to free a damsel; but now our hero seems to be a spy doing in a damsel in order to escape the dragon. The genius of suspicion has entered the world, my boy. And then, what do you make of the faces of the young? As if they had smashed the lock on the great tuck-box of sex only to find the contents had gone mouldy. Sex should be like King's drinking, not piglets at teat.'

Charlock delightedly hails Marchant as a true romantic, of an old-fashioned kind, and himself elsewhere recoils in disgust from the hairy faces of the London young. An old-fashioned romantic Durrell, too, very much is: and there is a bitter appropriateness, perhaps for Durrell as well as Charlock, in that sentence of Flaubert's: '*On dit que le présent est trop rapide. Je trouve, moi, que c'est le passé que nous dévore.*'

There *is* this devouring sadness in *Tunc*, something not felt in *The Alexandria Quartet*. At the very beginning of the novel, a scene of drinking, the wine comes from greasy barrels, the chestnut stuffing is dubious, the drunken humour (Nash accused by Charlock of raping a woman patient whose confidences on the psycho-analyst's couch excited him too much) has the personal malice and the heavy scabrousness of middle age. The panto-

190

mimic humour of Sipple the clown is similarly broad and funny, but rank: a ribald performance for a piss-up in a war-time Sergeants' Mess. Even the name of the restaurant, Poggio's, in which the novel starts, is suggestive: Poggio was a late medieval humanist who wrote short stories much more lubricious than Boccaccio's. The appetite of middle age is queasy, but it is not going to give up; it forces itself to force things down. Yet, if Durrell's attitude to life is faltering in *Tunc*, his appetite for language, as I have suggested by my quotations, is at its most discriminating and mature. And the sadness of middle age comes partly from our realization of how beautiful youth was, how much more beautiful it could have been, if we had only realized how beautiful. Because partly of this new sense of the poignancy of memory, *Tunc*, just as a piece of writing, an exercise by a various master in the possibilities of English prose, seems to me Durrell's finest achievement so far. I have given what Durrell himself would call a 'character-squeeze' of the novel rather than a properly objective critical analysis of it. But I hope I have at least conveyed the *feel* of the book; and have managed to suggest how Durrell, taking more risks—carefully calculated risks—about our general educated expectations of what a novel should be than ever before, simplifying psychology, condensing presentation, stripping many of his main characters to their archetypal bones, has nevertheless produced a fiction which, macabre, bawdy, fantastic, sounds a new note in his writing: the note of regret.

RECOLLECTIONS OF A DURRELL
COLLECTOR

by Alan G. Thomas

The credit of publishing Lawrence Durrell's first book, *Ten Poems*, goes to J. A. Allen, who was not then primarily a publisher, but a bookseller in the heart of Bloomsbury. He issued small editions of books by his somewhat bohemian customers, including one other author who has since achieved a considerable reputation, Mulk Raj Anand. As with most pioneers the way was hard, and these small editions had by no means sold out when his premises, his remaining stock, and his records were all destroyed in the Blitz.

Pied Piper of Lovers, Durrell's first novel, was entered for a fiction competiton organized by Cassell's. Although it was not the prize-winner, Cassell's decided to publish it—to their financial loss. Once again the publisher's records were destroyed by the Luftwaffe and the number of copies sold cannot be ascertained, but *Pied Piper* has become a rarity. It achieved only a few reviews, one rather bitchy one in a 'little magazine', *Janus*. Durrell replied on a post card:

> *'We've just read a review in your* JANUS
> *Which it seems was intended to pain us,*
> *But the joke's on your title,*
> *What an endless recital.*
> *Not of head, my dear——, but* ANUS.'[1]

[1] *In justice add that I wrote the following epigraph in many copies:*
'There was a young fellow called Lawrence
From whose pen the tripe trickled in torrents;

Cassell's did not exercise their option on Durrell's next book, *Panic Spring*, and with it began the connection with Faber and Faber which has lasted to this day. The faith and enthusiasm of T. S. Eliot and Alan Pringle remained unwavering through the lean years, and they must have been gratified indeed by the growth of Durrell's international reputation.

I first met 'Larry' Durrell in 1934 when he and Nancy, soon to become his first wife, used to haunt the bookshop in Bournemouth where I was working as an assistant. I realized immediately that he was one of the most remarkable men I had ever known, a judgment I hold with the same conviction more than thirty years later. Life in his company took on a new dimension. I was swept off my feet by his wonderful gusto, his power over words, his perception, his all-embracing Rabelaisian sense of humour, the warmth and kindness of his friendship, and his intoxicating joy of life. I remember one February night when we were walking along the sea front; Durrell was so full of high spirits that he kept running into the sea, filling his hat with water and showering it over us. If only I had been an S. C. Cockerell I would have preserved that hat and put it into Sotheby's.

In those days we were half-hoping to make our fortune by writing jazz songs. (Durrell had played the piano in the Blue Peter night club for a short time.) *Love's Just a Noose Round Your Neck, First Love Must Die, When You Go I Know that it's Paradise Lost, Dear*, were among our *chefs d'oeuvre*; another fragment which sticks in my memory ran: 'I don't like your face —it's a disgrace, but your hips, oh your hips, are a poem.' Durrell went to London and played them over to some Tin Pan Alley king, who commented: 'I've enjoyed your songs, but I'm not going to publish them, they're too highbrow, they ought to go into a show.' Durrell retorted that he had no intention of sleeping with—, came home, wrote a waltz entitled *Three*

> *Though this carries a greeting*
> *He can't help repeating*
> *He regards the whole thing with abhorrence.'*
> L.G.D.

Pawnbroker's Balls, and sent it off inscribed, 'Dear Sir, you say my songs are too highbrow, this isn't a song, it's a disease'.

In 1935 the whole Durrell family were planning their move to Corfu. Durrell, knowing my bibliophily, announced that one should travel light through life, and that he proposed to tear the favourite pages out of his books and bind them up in two volumes, one verse, one prose. Watching my horror with a gleam of friendly malice, he went on to suggest that I should buy the residue of his library; after all, most volumes would still contain ninety per cent of their pages, and I should surely be able to offer ninety per cent of their value.

I happened to be staying with the Durrells in Corfu when news came through that an American publisher had taken *Panic Spring*. There was a typically Ionian touch about this message; it had come halfway across the world by telegraph, and the last few miles were accomplished by a lunatic, peddling furiously on his bicycle. Greeks believe it lucky to employ the insane, as they are held to have been touched by God. Elated by this first success outside England, we went into town to celebrate; it happened to be Ascension Day, a general holiday, and we ate an immense lobster while a radiogram of ear-splitting power played Greek tangos. Peasants in national costume poured into the town for the traditional dancing.

Jack Kahane, founder of the Obelisk Press, and publisher of *The Black Book*, was a native of Manchester who lived in Paris. He specialized in books which had been banned in England or America, and did a great trade with tourists. The repressive activities of Sir William Joynson-Hicks, Home Secretary, James Douglas, Editor of the *Sunday Express*, and Sir Archibald Bodkin, Director of Public Prosecutions, brought plenty of grist to Kahane's mill, and when that ran short he wrote suitable works himself. English and American authors, suppressed by the puritan tradition at home, had reason to be grateful for the spiritual freedom to be found in Paris between the wars. Among them was an American writer of remarkable talent and character, Henry Miller, whom Kahane published, doing 'the right thing for the wrong reason'. In his autobiography, Kahane

recalls with pride that he published Durrell, but in truth, Nancy
Durrell put up the money, while Miller not only persuaded him
to accept *The Black Book,* but took immense pains seeing it
through the press.

Greatly as they differ in most respects, Durrell and Kipling
have three things in common: they were born in India, they
exercise superb mastery over words, and they have produced,
to the joy and chagrin of book-collectors, scarce and fragile
items printed in far-flung and out of the way places.

The first serious Durrell collector was John Gawsworth, the
poet and critic who succeeded M. P. Shiel on the throne of
Redonda, in which regal capacity he created dukedoms for
both Lawrence and Gerald Durrell. Some years ago his collection was purchased by Messrs. Hollings and sold to America,
where, I understand, it remains intact. My own collection,
begun in 1934, has benefited from Durrell's generous friendship.
Lawrence Clark Powell was the first, and has remained the
most enthusiastic and loyal, of Lawrence Durrell's American
admirers. He used his influential position as Librarian of the
University of California to promote interest in Durrell's books
when they were hardly known in the States. To his private, as
to his professional, collecting he brought a flair for locating the
all but impossible. From a distance of six thousand miles he
purchased for 7s. 6d., out of the catalogue of an English specia-
list in modern first editions, a copy of *Quaint Fragment,* then
unrecorded, and for long the only copy known to exist. Powell
and I joined forces to compile the first bibliography of Durrell;
we each listed our own collections and collated the results. At
that time most of Durrell's own books and papers were stored in
the loft of my house and this enabled me to catch such rare pieces
as *Premature Epitaphs and All,* of which only six copies were
produced in Alexandria. Durrell himself bombarded me with
postcards whenever some point occurred to him, and he inter-
spersed the final typescript with pungent comments. This
bibliography appeared in *The Book Collector,* Spring 1960.

John Hayward rejected our sections 'Contributions to
Periodicals' and 'Ana' as not being 'strictly Book Collector

material' and they were later handed to Anthony Knerr, who wove them into his own much-expanded study entitled 'Regarding a Checklist of Lawrence Durrell' in *The Papers of the Bibliographical Society of America*, LV, 1961.

On retiring from his position as head of the Library, Powell presented his Durrell collection to the University of California and this was the occasion of an exhibition for which Robert A. Potter and Brooke Whiting compiled an illustrated catalogue. All of these scholars added to the corpus of knowledge about the works of Lawrence Durrell and I have drawn on their researches. And to these acknowledgements I must add the name of Bernard Stone, the Kensington bookseller specializing in Durrell, who lent me numerous items from his files and stock.

In this bibliography I trust that the sections devoted to Books, Prefaces and Translations are both complete and accurate. I cannot hope to achieve these standards for Contribution to Periodicals and Ana. No library, not even the British Museum or that of the University of California, contains all the items listed here, and no one person has actually *seen* them all. Perhaps I ought to have modelled myself on Hain, the bibliographer of incunabula, who placed a star against all books he had examined himself. Once one relies on even the best hearsay, inaccuracy creeps in. Thus, Curtis Brown informed me of a contract with an American magazine for publication in December of a story which actually appeared, under a completely different title, in the following February. Even the great copyright libraries fail to secure complete runs of all 'little magazines' whose editors are seldom organization men and whose standards of production do not always ensure preservation. My friend Walter Goldwater, when working on his bibliography of American Left-Wing Journals, sometimes opened the cloth boxes in which national libraries preserved fragile rarities only to find that the poor quality paper had disintegrated into powder.

As for interviews, comments by journalists and critical articles by scholars, etc., since the publication of *Justine*, these have gone beyond control. I used to subscribe to a press cuttings agency, but what began as a modest stream developed into a torrent.

Almost any review of a novel set in modern Egypt contains some phrase like 'the author fails to bend the bow of Durrellian prose', while passages in travel books are frequently compared with *The Alexandria Quartet*. The climax was reached when Durrell, as was inevitable, became involved in the film world. The Argus eyes of Durrant's (the press cuttings agency) picked out even such fringe items as the divorce proceedings of film stars currently engaged on a Durrell story. By this time the bills, four guineas per hundred cuttings, were in danger of exceeding my annual income and I had to stop them. But I still miss those little green bundles coming through the post, for in addition to information about Durrell they provided such a curious slant on the phantasy world in which journalists live. 'Do intellectuals get the best girls? . . . Who would wonder that . . . small but dynamic Durrell should have more than a share of female admiration', pondered *The Queen*, 18th August 1960; while the London *Evening Standard*, the *Nottingham Evening Post* and the *Middlesbrough Evening Gazette* syndicated a piece: 'What can an author say to women who hound him?'. A correspondence in *The Times Literary Supplement* on 'Literature and Alcoholism' inevitably dragged in Durrell. Devotees include Robert Allerton, author of *The Courage of His Convictions*, a professional criminal convicted of armed robbery, safe-blowing, smash-and-grab, and grievous bodily harm, who has served twelve and a half years in prison. He admires Danilo Dolci and Albert Schweitzer . . . he reads Claud Cockburn, Hugh Klare, Simone de Beauvoir and Lawrence Durrell.

Predictably, the obvious psychological parallels between *The Alexandria Quartet* and the Resnais film 'L'Année Dernière à Marienbad' brought a further crop of critical cuttings. But it was the entry of Sophia Loren which finally almost bankrupted me and gave an insight into the mad world in which we live: 'The countries of the Arab League will ban all films starring Sophia Loren unless she withdraws from a picture being made in Israel about a Jewish refugee, it was announced in Rome yesterday', *Aberdeen Press and Journal*, 20th August 1964.

Finally, I should like to add a few words regarding Lawrence

Durrell's unpublished works, some of which are unfortunately no longer extant.

On moving to Corfu, Durrell left a package of stories and poems in my care. Some months later he asked me to post these out to him. Feeling that my temperament as a hoarder, and my training as an antiquarian bookseller, were more likely than the carefree nature of the Durrells to ensure the preservation of these early works, I dragged my feet. At last, exasperated by the long delay, Durrell quite naturally exploded. And so the typescripts were despatched to Corfu. Here, left in store on the outbreak of war, they were used by the occupying German soldiers for lighting fires. Among them I remember two stories, *The Prurient Duck* and *The Large Field*. The latter described a band of brothers, all writers and each the leading authority on his subject. Reviewers of their vast publications invariably used the phrase '. . . he covers a large field'. United by an intense mutual attachment, so often found in Jewish families, the brothers travelled around the countryside in a private char-à-banc until they perished together in a terrible motor accident. As the story closes, a critic is visiting the country churchyard which has been enlarged to contain their many new graves. 'Aye, Sir', says the old sexton, 'they cover a large field'.

Of all these lost works I especially regret a pyrotechnic attack on Bournemouth, that innocent seaside resort to which Mrs. Durrell had moved her home, believing that the sun shone there while it was raining in London. In those inter-war days there was probably no town which preserved so entirely the smug and stuffy puritanism of Victorian England. No subject was better calculated to provoke Durrell into a coruscating flow of invective and I have never ceased to reproach myself for failing to make a copy of this jeu d'esprit. There was also a play about the Elizabethan statesman Walsingham but a carbon copy of this is said to be in existence.

Black Honey, a farce in three acts, dealing with imaginary incidents in the lives of Baudelaire and Meryon, was written for a group of amateur players in Alexandria at the end of 1942 or the beginning of 1943. It has never been printed or produced, but there is a typescript in the library of Iowa State University.

The recent emancipation of Anglo-Saxon publishing has resulted in numerous reprints of erotic classics. One American asked Durrell ('as the greatest living authority on love') to write a preface to the *Kama Sutra*. In refusing, Durrell replied: '. . . the Kama Sutra is primarily a religious book, and I cannot help suspecting that you are reprinting it for pornographic reasons. And, anyway, of the hundred-and-eighty positions I've only tried about twelve—and some of those didn't work.'

BIBLIOGRAPHY

A. BOOKS BY LAWRENCE DURRELL

All 8vo. and publisher's cloth, unless otherwise stated. Lawrence Durrell's comments printed in italic.

1. QUAINT FRAGMENT. Poems Written Between the Ages of Sixteen and Nineteen. London, The Cecil Press. 1931. Portrait.

'Never published. Cecil Jeffries bought a hand press and asked me to give him something to practise with; poems were easier than prose so I gave him an old notebook with roughs. Title was his. We took two pulls I think before the type was dispersed. One copy bound.' This book *is* extremely rare, but Durrell's statement that only one copy was bound is an exaggeration. Three or four have passed through the antiquarian book market in the last ten years, and one copy, left behind in Corfu, was destroyed.

2. TEN POEMS. Wrappers. London, The Caduceus Press. 1932.

— Edn. de Luxe. Limited to twelve copies, signed by the author. Buckram. London, The Caduceus Press. 1932.

The author's and the publisher's recollections of the number printed differ so widely that it seems wiser not to quote them. The number was quite small, the book did not sell out and the residue stock was destroyed in the London blitz. The same applies to No. 4. The device on this book was designed by Nancy Myers, Durrell's first wife.

2A. BALLADE OF SLOW DECAY. [Bournemouth]

Christmas 1932. Two leaves. A Christmas card. A device by
Nancy Myers on p.i.

3. BROMO BOMBASTES. A Fragment from a Laconic
Drama by Gaffer Peeslake, which same being a brief extract
from his Compendium of Lisson Devices. London, The Caduceus Press. 1933. Boards. Limited to 100 copies.

A squib, satirizing Shaw's *Black Girl*.

4. TRANSITION: Poems. London, The Caduceus Press.
1934. Boards. See note to No. 2.

5. MASS FOR THE OLD YEAR. [Bournemouth] New
Year 1935. Two leaves on Jap. vellum, 9 × 6 ins.

A New Year card, with poem on p. iii. A device by Nancy
Myers on p. iv; she drew caricatures on p. i of some copies.
Only two copies are known to have survived; one bears a pen-
and-ink caricature of A.G.T. suffering from post-Christmas
dyspepsia, the other, sent to George Wilkinson, is now in the
British Museum.

6. PIED PIPER OF LOVERS. London, Cassell. 1935.
Dust jacket designed by Nancy Myers.

Spine incorrectly lettered: Pied Pipers of Lovers.

7. PANIC SPRING. A Romance by Charles Norden.
London, Faber & Faber. 1937.
— New York, Covici-Friede. 1937.

The first of Durrell's books to be published by Faber who
suggested a pseudonym because *Pied Piper of Lovers* had been a
failure.

8. THE BLACK BOOK, An Agon. Paris, The Obelisk
Press. 1938. Wrappers. Villa Seurat Series, edited by Henry
Miller, No. 1.
— Second edition, with a new preface. Paris, The Olympia
Press. 1959. Wrappers.

Promptly banned in Eire.
— U. S. edition advertised by Circle Editions, Berkeley,
California on the back-flap of jacket of *Zero*, 1947, but was never
issued.
— New York, E. P. Dutton. 1960. Introduction by Gerald Sykes.

Contains the preface of the Olympia Press edition, 1959.

9. A PRIVATE COUNTRY. [Poems.] London, Faber & Faber. 1943.

10. 'PREMATURE EPITAPHS AND ALL'. Alexandria. 1944. Sm. 8vo. Six copies only produced for friends, typescript, handbound in wrappers.

11. PROSPERO'S CELL. A Guide to the Landscape and Manners of the Island of Corcyra. London, Faber & Faber. 1945. Illus.

— U. S. edition advertised in *Chimera* V (2), Winter 1947, p. 61: 'Two works of his [Durrell's], *The Dark Labyrinth* and *Prospero's Cell*, have been published recently by Reynal & Hitchcock.' Both books are listed in *The Publishers Trade List Annual* 1946 under Reynal & Hitchcock. The firm went bankrupt before the author's contracts were signed, however, and neither book was published.

— New York, E. P. Dutton. 1960.

Issued together with *Reflections on a Marine Venus*. See: A21.

— London, Faber & Faber. 1962. Paperback.

12. CITIES, PLAINS AND PEOPLE. [Poems.] London, Faber & Faber. 1946.

13. ZERO AND ASYLUM IN THE SNOW. Two Excursions into Reality. Rhodes. 1946. Privately printed. Wrappers. Block depicting ship and fish on cover and title.

— TWO EXCURSIONS INTO REALITY. Berkeley, California, Circle Edition. 1947.

14. THE PARTHENON. For T. S. Eliot. [Rhodes. 1945 or 1946.] 4 pp. and decorated card cover. $7\frac{7}{8} \times 6\frac{1}{4}$ ins.

Durrell's own copy bears the following note in his hand: '*Lawrence Durrell, his copy. This was set and printed in 25 copies at the Govt. Press in Rhodes, Dodecanese Islands, and issued as a Christmas Card to friends. The cover had been especially cut by an artist for the Governor of Rhodes (Italian).*'

15. CEFALÛ, A Novel. London, Editions Poetry London. 1947. Two bindings, green and light brown cloth. Author's and British Museum copies both green cloth.

THE DARK LABYRINTH. London, Ace Books, The Harborough Publishing Company. 1958. Paperback.

A reprint of *Cefalû* with alterations limited to a few sentences.
— On U. S. edition, 1946, see 11. New York, E. P. Dutton. 1962.
— London, Faber & Faber, 1961.
— London, Faber & Faber. 1964. Paperback.

16. ON SEEMING TO PRESUME. [Poems.] London, Faber & Faber. 1948. First binding brick red cloth, second binding light red cloth.

17. A LANDMARK GONE. Los Angeles, Reuben Pearson. 1949. $8\frac{1}{2}$ × $5\frac{3}{8}$ ins., wrappers, 125 copies privately printed for Lawrence Clark Powell.

Contains 'A Note on Lawrence Durrell' by Lawrence Clark Powell. *A Landmark Gone* was first published in *Middle East Anthology*. London, 1946.

18. DEUS LOCI, A Poem. Ischia, Di Mato Vito. 1950. $6\frac{1}{4}$ × $4\frac{1}{4}$ ins., wrappers, 200 copies privately printed, signed by the author. Variant colours of covers, red, buff, green, and grey, with no precedence of issue.

19. SAPPHO, A Play in Verse. London, Faber & Faber. 1950.
— New York, E. P. Dutton. [1958].
Sheets of English edition with undated cancel title.
— London, Faber & Faber. 1967. Paperback.
— Acting edition in German. Hamburg, Rowohlt Verlag. [1959?]

Margaret Rawlings took the title role in a rehearsed reading of this play at the French Institute, London, 1952.

Jill Balcon took the title role in Terence Tiller's production broadcast in the BBC Third Programme on 25 March 1957.

Margaret Rawlings took the title role in the first stage production in English at the Edinburgh Festival, Royal Lyceum Theatre, 28 August 1961.

Elizabeth Flickenschildt took the title role in the first German stage production, Deutsches Schauspielhaus, Hamburg, 21 November 1959. The programme contains an article on Durrell by Henry Miller. See Section D. No. 27 for photographs of this production.

ALTERATION OF THE TEXT FOR GERMAN PRODUCTIONS OF VERSE PLAYS

'Sappho was cut and mounted under the advice of Gustav Gründgens; Acte went through about four drafts, and some parts were written in as afterthoughts while the play was in rehearsal. An exchange of letters between myself and Gründgens was published by Rowohlt Verlag as a booklet for the opening night. This was the most successful of the plays in terms of number of performances. Remember it played in a repertory cycle with two other plays—Shaw's Caesar and Schiller's Mary Stewart, and the advance bookings determined whether people wanted it again or not. It lasted the season out. Faustus was mounted by Oscar Schu in the same theatre in its printed version quite entire. It is well constructed whatever other demerits it has as a piece. I was unhappy about the hasty writing in Acte and revised it completely for English publication.

'Maria Caesares holds a Paris option on Sappho, but so far no production has come out.'

20. KEY TO MODERN POETRY. London, Peter Nevill. 1952. Lectures given in Argentina for the British Council.

— A KEY TO MODERN BRITISH POETRY. Norman, University of Oklahoma Press. 1952.

Sheets of the English edition.

— An edition (in English) has been published in India.

21. REFLECTIONS ON A MARINE VENUS, A Companion to the landscape of Rhodes. London, Faber & Faber. 1953. Illus.

— New York, E. P. Dutton, 1960.

Issued together with *Prospero's Cell*. See: A11.

— London, Faber & Faber. 1960. Paperback.

The Dorset County Library once advertised for 'The Submarine Venus'.

22. PRIVATE DRAFTS. Nicosia, The Proodos Press. 1955. $3\frac{1}{2} \times 2\frac{5}{8}$ ins., pictorial wrappers, 100 copies privately printed, signed by the author.

23. THE TREE OF IDLENESS and Other Poems. London, Faber & Faber. 1955.

24. SELECTED POEMS. London, Faber & Faber. 1956.
— New York, Grove Press. 1956.

Published in wrappers, also in blue-black cloth with dust-jacket, as Evergreen Books of Poetry (E-57). Also an edition limited to 100 copies in brown half-cloth and grey boards, with a *justification de tirage* tipped in before p. 7. *'Which the author has never seen! What a publisher!'*

— SELECTED POEMS, 1935–1963. London, Faber & Faber. 1964. Paperback.

'This new paperback selection of Lawrence Durrell's poetry contains the whole of *Selected Poems*, which was published in 1956 and is now out of print, together with a number of additional poems, of which some are of more recent date and a few have not previously been published in book form.'

25. BITTER LEMONS. London, Faber & Faber. 1957. Illus. The advance proof is entitled 'Bitter Lemons of Cyprus'. *'Yes, title changed on advice of V. S. Pritchett for Book Society Choice.'*

The plates were used to publish an edition for The Book Society. This imprint follows that of Faber & Faber on the title-page; the inside front flap of the jacket states: 'The Book Society Choice for July', and the price is 16/–. The top edges of this printing are stained lemon yellow; on the verso of the t.p. appears (top) in italics: 'This edition issued on first publication by/The Book Society Ltd in association with/Faber and Faber Ltd/July 1957.'

No plate changes are recorded.

Another printing was made for the Readers Union.

— New York, E. P. Dutton. 1958.

— London, Faber & Faber. 1959. Paperback.

26. ESPRIT DE CORPS, Sketches from Diplomatic Life. Illustrated by V. H. Drummond. London, Faber & Faber. 1957.

'Written in the hope of making a little money from Punch (*I was "in extremis"*). *Submitted as a book and rejected "in toto"! The dear old British sense of Humour at work again! On publication had numerous fan-letters from prolapsed ancients who (subscribers to* Punch) *thought it was in the tradition.'*

— New York, E. P. Dutton. 1958. Illustrated by Vasiliu.

The Dutton edition has two sketches not in the English edition: 'La Valise' and 'Cry Wolf'.

— London, Faber & Faber. 1961. Paperback.

27. JUSTINE, A Novel. London, Faber & Faber. 1957.
'*1st edition had about 250 errors which were put right in the 2nd, though some caused some beautiful muck-ups in the French translation, notably 'her tree' for 'her knee'. . . .*'
— New York, E. P. Dutton. 1957.
— London, Faber & Faber. 1961. Paperback.

28. WHITE EAGLES OVER SERBIA. London, Faber & Faber. 1957.
— New York, Criterion Books. 1957.
— London, Faber & Faber. 1962. Paperback.
— Edited and Abridged by G. A. Verdin. London, Chatto & Windus. 1961.

A note in a presentation copy: '*Purely as a curiosity. I decided in Yugoslavia to resign and make some dough out of 12 detective stories which I had planned—but I was puzzled I couldn't sell it. Much later I showed it to Faber. "A juvenile" they shouted in a high pitched tone. The trouble was it was mental age 12: I thought detective stories were about that—but no: they are nearer age 15 apparently. Anyway!*
'*Some snatches of landscape not too bad—all accurate—and the story founded on a true recital I'll tell you about one day*'

29. BALTHAZAR, A Novel. London, Faber & Faber. 1958.
— New York, E. P. Dutton. 1958.
— London, Faber & Faber. 1961. Paperback.

30. MOUNTOLIVE, A Novel. London, Faber & Faber. 1958.
— New York, E. P. Dutton. 1959.
— London, Faber & Faber. 1961. Paperback.

31. STIFF UPPER LIP, Life among the Diplomats. London, Faber & Faber. 1958. 'Nicolas Bentley drew the pictures'.
— New York, E. P. Dutton. 1959.
— London, Faber & Faber. 1966. Paperback.

The Faber edition contains 'La Valise' and 'Cry Wolf' which are not in the Dutton edition, while the Dutton contains 'A Smircher Smirched' which is not in the Faber edition.

32. ART AND OUTRAGE. A Correspondence about

Henry Miller between Alfred Perlès and Lawrence Durrell. (With an intermission by Henry Miller.) London, Putnam. 1959. Portrait.
— New York, E. P. Dutton. 1960.
33. CLEA, A Novel. London, Faber & Faber. 1960.
— New York, E. P. Dutton. 1960.
— London, Faber & Faber. 1961. Paperback.
33A. THE ALEXANDRIA QUARTET. Justine, Balthazar, Mountolive, Clea. With numerous revisions in the text and a new Preface. Limited to 500 copies signed by the author. London, Faber & Faber. 9th November 1962.
Also ordinary trade edition.
— New York, E. P. Dutton. 4th December 1962.
Dutton's signed limited edition consisted of 199 copies for distribution in the United States in addition to the 500 copies distributed by Faber. Faber printed both editions but giving Dutton their own imprint and other necessary alterations in the prelims. Dutton produced their own binding, their own box, and their own endpapers.
Also ordinary trade edition.
An order for *The Alexandria Quartet*, sent to one of England's leading bookshops, was passed to the music department.
34. COLLECTED POEMS. London, Faber & Faber. 1960.
— New York, E. P. Dutton. 1960.
35. BRIEFWECHSEL ÜBER ACTIS. With Gustaf Gründgens. Hamburg, Rowohlt. 1961. Wrappers. Frontispiece.
See: Theater Heute. Hannover. 1962. Section E.
36. THE FIFTH ANTIQUARIAN BOOK FAIR. Handlist of Exhibitors. London, National Book League and Antiquarian Booksellers' Association. June 1962. $3\frac{1}{2} \times 8\frac{1}{8}$ ins. Wrappers.
In addition to the ordinary edition which was distributed gratis, one copy was printed on pink hand-made paper for Lawrence Durrell and ten copies on Barcham Green hand-made paper, signed by Durrell; the latter were auctioned in aid of the Antiquarian Booksellers' Benevolent Fund.
Contains Introductory Essay on Book-collecting.

— Reprinted in The Antiquarian Bookman. New York. May–June 1962.

37. LAWRENCE DURRELL AND HENRY MILLER. A Private Correspondence. Edited by George Wickes. New York, E. P. Dutton. 1963.

— London, Faber & Faber. 1963.

Publication of the American edition preceded that of the English edition by a few weeks.

Two pages of text were omitted from the subsequent American paperback edition.

38. BECCAFICO *LE BECFIGUE*. English text together with a translation into French by F.–J. Temple. 150 copies privately printed on pink paper, signed by the author. Montpellier, La Licorne. 1963. $6\frac{1}{4} \times 4\frac{3}{4}$ ins. Wrappers.

39. A PERSIAN LADY. [Edinburgh.] The Tragara Press. August 1963. Folio broadsheet; limited to 6 copies.

40. AN IRISH FAUSTUS. A Morality in Nine Scenes. London, Faber & Faber. 1963.

— New York, E. P. Dutton. 1964.

41. LA DESCENTE DU STYX. Traduit de l'Anglais par F.–J. Temple et suivi du Texte Original [in English]. 250 copies privately printed and signed by the author. Montpellier, La Murène. 1964. 4to. Wrappers.

EXHIBITION OF PAINTINGS BY OSCAR EPFS [Lawrence Durrell]. Paris. 1964.

Was there a catalogue or poster?

'*Not really. A few typed sheets with titles. 200 copies of a hand-painted poster, half by me and half by Nadia Blokh were carried round and placed in the indulgent bars and bistros of the Latin Quarter by Epfs and his wife and two artloving girl friends.*'

42. ACTE, a play. London, Faber & Faber. 1965. With 4 photographs of the production of the play in German by Gustav Gründgens at the Deutsches Schauspielhaus, Hamburg, November 1961.

— New York, E. P. Dutton. 1965.

— For German acting text see: Theatre Heute, Hannover, 1962. Section E.

43. SAUVE QUI PEUT. London, Faber & Faber. 1966. 'Nicolas Bentley drew the pictures.'
— New York, E. P. Dutton. 1967.
Nine Antrobus stories.

44. THE IKONS. New Poems. London, Faber & Faber. 1966.
— New York, E. P. Dutton. 1967.

45. TUNC, A Novel. London, Faber & Faber. 1968.
— New York, E. P. Dutton. 1968.

B. TRANSLATIONS

1. SIX POEMS from the Greek of Sekilianos and Seferis. Lawrence Durrell. Rhodes. 1946. Wrappers.
   Contains note signed L.D. '*Fifty copies I think.*'

2. THE KING OF ASINE and other Poems, by George Seferis. Translated from the Greek by Bernard Spencer, Nanos Valaoritis, Lawrence Durrell. With an Introduction by Rex Warner. London, John Lehmann. 1948.

3. THE CURIOUS HISTORY OF POPE JOAN. Translated out of the modern Greek of Emmanuel Royidis by Lawrence Durrell, and illustrated by John Buckland-Wright. 13 illustrations. Demy 8vo, $9\frac{3}{4} \times 6\frac{1}{8}$ ins., pp. i–xxiv; 1–134. London, Rodney Phillips & Green. 1948.

Never issued. The firm of publishers who planned it went out of business before the book could be produced. Three sets of proofs have survived. There was also to have been an edition limited to 150 on mould-made paper. Copies survive of a Prospectus bearing one of the illustrations.
— Frontispiece only. London, Derek Verschoyle. 1954.
— Revised edition with new preface but no frontispiece. London, André Deutsch. 1960.
— New York, E. P. Dutton. 1961.

C. PREFACES

1. Stephanides, Theodore. CLIMAX IN CRETE. London, Faber & Faber. 1946. Maps.

BIBLIOGRAPHY

1A. GEORGHIOU, GEORGIOS POL, Cypriot painter. Catalogue of Exhibition of paintings in Athens. ?

'*I did a general article on him in the Cyprus Review* [April 1955] *with pics. and he used it afterwards as a catalogue blurb* [in Greek].'

2. Nin, Anais. CHILDREN OF THE ALBATROSS. London, Peter Owen, 1959.

The New York edition, E. P. Dutton, 1947, does not contain the preface.

3. Venezis, Ilias. AEOLIA. Translated from the Greek by E. D. Scott-Kilvert. London, William Campion. 1949.

4. Tremayne, Penelope. BELOW THE TIDE. London, Hutchinson. 1958.

— Boston, Houghton Mifflin. 1959.

5. Guirdham, Arthur. CHRIST AND FREUD. A Study of Religious Experience and Observance. London, George Allen & Unwin, Ltd. 1959.

In a review entitled 'Couch-Bound Christians', the *Irish Times* printed the title as 'Christ and Friend'. '*Too good to change*! ! !'

6. A HENRY MILLER READER. Edited with Introduction by Lawrence Durrell. New York, New Directions. 1959.

— THE BEST OF HENRY MILLER. London, Heinemann. 1960.

7. Wideson, Reno. PORTRAIT OF CYPRUS. Privately Printed. The Hague, Deppo Holland. n.d. [1961.] Illus.

8. Groddeck Georg, DAS BUCH VOM ES. Verwort von Lawrence Durrell. Wiesbaden. 1961.

9. Brandt, Bill. PERSPECTIVE OF NUDES. 4to. London, The Bodley Head. 1961. 90 photographs.

— English edition distributed in America by Amphoto Ltd.

10. Nimr (Smart), Amy. Preface (in French) to an exhibition of paintings. Paris, Galerie de Marignan, 5–27 May 1961.

11. Rouff, Marcel. THE PASSIONATE EPICURE, translated by Claude (Mrs. Lawrence Durrell). Illus. by Charles Mozley. London, Faber & Faber. 1961.

12. Stark, Freya. THE JOURNEY'S ECHO, A Selection. London, John Murray. 1963. Illustrations.

13. Blokh, Nadia. Preface (in French) to an exhibition of paintings, Paris. 1963.

14. Lear's CORFU, An Anthology Drawn from the Painter's Letters by Maria Aspioti. Corfu Travel. 1965. 4to, wrappers. 8 views of Corfu reproduced from Lear's lithographs.

15. Peyre, Marc. CAPTIVE OF ZOUR. Trans. Claude. London, Alan Ross. 1966.

16. Douglas, Keith. ALAMEIN TO ZEM ZEM. London, Faber & Faber. 1966.

17. Seignolle, Claude. THE ACCURSED (Les Malédictions). London, George Allen & Unwin. 1966.
(French edition published by G. P. Maisonneuve et Larose, Paris.)

18. Miller, Henry. ORDER AND CHAOS CHEZ HANS REICHEL. Illus. Tucson, Arizona. Loujon Press. 1966.

Cork Edition of 1399 copies. Leather Edition of 99 copies, signed and dated. Leather Edition of 26 copies, signed, dated and lettered by the author from 'A' to 'Z', the autograph page inscribed to the collector, etc.

19. 100 GREAT BOOKS. MASTERPIECES OF ALL TIME. Edited by John Canning. Odhams Books Limited. 1966.

D. SOME CONTRIBUTIONS TO BOOKS

1. MASTERPIECE OF THRILLS. [Edited by John Gawsworth.] n.d. [1936.] London, Daily Express.
Contains 'The Cherries'.

2. PROEMS. London, The Fortune Press. 1938. Edited by Oswell Blakeston.
Contains 'Unckebuncke/A Biography in Little'; 'Five Soliloquies Upon the Tomb'; selections from 'Themes Heraldic'. This is not the first appearance of Durrell's poems in book form, as the prefatory note erroneously claims.

3. NEW DIRECTIONS IN PROSE & POETRY 1939. Norfolk, Connecticut. Edited by James Laughlin IV.
Contains 'Gracie', a selection from THE BLACK BOOK, with an introduction by Laughlin. This is the first publication

of any part of The Black Book in America. Prefaced by a lengthy editor's note praising Durrell and recommending purchase of the book 'through your Paris bookseller'.

4. NEW DIRECTIONS IN PROSE & POETRY 1940. Norfolk, Connecticut. Edited by James Laughlin IV.

Contains 'Poem in Space and Time'; 'A Noctuary'; 'Self'; and 'At Corinth'.

5. DAYLIGHT/EUROPEAN ARTS & LETTERS/ Yesterday Today Tomorrow. London, The Hogarth Press. 1941.

Contains translation of George Seferis, 'Myth of Our History' [with G. Katsimbalis].

6. Miller, Henry. THE COLOSSUS OF MAROUSSI. San Francisco, The Colt Press. 1941.
— London, Secker & Warburg. 1942.

Appendix contains a letter from Durrell, dated 10th August 1940, concerning George Katsimbalis.

7. THE FORTUNE ANTHOLOGY. London. n.d. [1942.] Contains 'At Epidaurus'.

8. POETRY IN WARTIME. Edited by Tambimuttu. London, Faber & Faber. 1942.

Contains 'Epitaph', 'Island Fugue', 'The Green Man', 'In Time of Crisis', 'Letter to Seferis the Greek', (the latter since suppressed from Collected Edition).

9. NEW ROAD 1944/New Directions in European Art and Letters. London, The Grey Walls Press. 1944. Edited by Alex Comfort and John Bayliss.

Contains 'For a Nursery Mirror'.

10. SELECTED WRITING. London, Nicholson & Watson. 1944. Edited by R. Moore, poetry selected by Tambimuttu.

Contains 'On Looking into the Loeb Horace'.

Two variant bindings.

11. PERSONAL LANDSCAPE, An Anthology of Exile. Compiled by Robin Fedden, Terence Tiller, Bernard Spencer, Lawrence Durrell. London, Editions Poetry London. 1945.

12. THE HAPPY ROCK, a Book about Henry Miller [by numerous writers]. Berkeley, California, Bern Porter. 1945.

'The Happy Rock', the book's opening essay.

13. ATLANTIC ANTHOLOGY. London, The Fortune Press. 1945. Edited by Nicholas Moore and Douglas Newton.

Contains 'Tribes'; 'Sea Music'; 'Pearls'; 'Air to Syria'; 'Heloise and Abelard'; 'The Pilot'; and 'La Rochefoucauld'.

14. NEW WRITING AND DAYLIGHT 1946. London, John Lehmann. 1946.

Contains 'Blind Homer' and 'Rodini', also 'The Death Feast of the Greeks' by Angelos Sikelianos, trans. by Durrell.

— New York, New Directions. 1946.

Sheets of the English edition.

15. MIDDLE EAST ANTHOLOGY. London, Lindsay Drummond. 1946. Edited by John Waller and Erik de Mauny.

Contains 'A Landmark Gone'; 'Alexandria'; and 'Conon in Alexandria'.

16. TRAVELLERS' VERSES. London, Frederick Muller. 1946. Edited by M. G. Lloyd Thomas, lithos by E. Bawden.

Contains 'Nemea'.

17. AND SO TO BED. An Album compiled by Edward Sackville-West, from the B.B.C. Feature. London, Phoenix House. 1947.

Contains 'Corinth'; 'On Ithaca'; 'Standing'.

18. T. S. ELIOT. A Symposium compiled by Richard March and Tambimuttu. London, Editions Poetry London. 1948.

Contains a poem, 'Anniversary'.

— Chicago, Henry Regnery Company. 1949.

19. PLEASURES OF NEW WRITING. London, John Lehmann. 1952. Edited John Lehmann.

Contains 'From a Winter Journal'.

20. NEW POEMS 1952. London, Michael Joseph. 1952. A P.E.N. Anthology edited by Clifford Dyment, Roy Fuller and Montagu Slater.

Contains 'Sarajevo'.

21. NEW POEMS 1953. London, Michael Joseph. 1953. A P.E.N. Anthology edited by Robert Conquest, Michael Hamburger and Howard Sergeant.

Contains 'Clouds of Glory' and 'Chanel'.

22. NEW POEMS 1956. London, Michael Joseph. 1956. A P.E.N. Anthology edited by Stephen Spender, Elizabeth Jennings and Dannie Abse.

Contains 'The Octagon Room, National Gallery, '55'.

23. POETIC HERITAGE, A Sunday Times Anthology, edited by John Press. London, André Deutsch. 1957.

Contains 'Lesbos'.

24. HOMMAGE À ROY CAMPBELL. [In French.] Edited by F.-J. Temple. Montpellier. 1958. (Actually issued 1959.) Wrappers. Illus.

Two contributions by Durrell. Other contributors include: F.-J. Temple, Richard Aldington, Edith Sitwell, Wyndham Lewis, etc.

25. THE GUINNESS BOOK OF POETRY: 1956–7. London, Putnam. 1958.

Contains 'The Meeting'.

26. DYLAN THOMAS: THE LEGEND AND THE POET. A Collection of Biographical and Critical Essays. London, Heinemann. 1960. Edited by E. W. Tedlock.

Contains a personal tribute to Thomas.

27. Clausen, Rosemarie. THEATER, Gustaf Gründgens Inszeniert. Hamburg, Christian Wegner. 1960. Oblong 4to.

Contains numerous photographs taken during the production of Sappho at Hamburg, with a brief note (in German) by Durrell.

28. THE GUINNESS BOOK OF POETRY: 1959–60. London, Putnam. 1961.

Contains 'Cavafy'.

29. THE WRITER'S DILEMMA. Essays first published in The Times Literary Supplement. Introduced by Stephen Spender. Oxford University Press. 1961.

Contribution by Durrell, 'No Clue to Living'.

30. PENGUIN MODERN POETS. No. 1. Lawrence Durrell. Elizabeth Jennings. R. S. Thomas. Harmondsworth, Penguin Books. 1962. Wrappers.

31. INTERNATIONAL WRITERS CONFERENCE. Edinburgh, August 1962. Transcript, roneoed on foolscap

sheets, unbound and held in place by office paper-holder threaded through punched hole in left-hand top corner. Each day's proceedings numbered separately:

20 Aug. (1)—23; 21 Aug. (1)—28; 22 Aug. (1)—25; 23 Aug. (1)—27; 24 Aug. (1)—35.

100–110 copies said to have been made.

(The 'Programme & Notes' of the Conference; contains brief note on and portrait of Durrell.)

32. KAREN BARONESS BLIXEN. Redigeret af Clara Svendsen og Ole Wivel. Copenhagen, Gyldendal. 1962. Portrait.

Contains tribute by Durrell (in Danish), reprinted from Nordisk Verlag.

— BARONESS BLIXEN, Isak Dinesen, A Memorial, edited by Clara Svensen. Random House, New York. 1965.

33. WALTER SMART BY SOME OF HIS FRIENDS. [Edited by Robin Fedden.] Limited to 500 copies. Wrappers. Chichester. Privately Printed by Lady Smart. n.d. [1963].

Contains 'Thinking About "Smartie" '.

34. HENRY MILLER AND THE CRITICS. Edited by George Wickes. Carbondale, Southern Illinois University Press. 1963.

Contains 'Studies in Genius: Henry Miller' reprinted from Horizon.

35. NEW POEMS 1963. A P.E.N. Anthology of Contemporary Poetry. London, Hutchinson. 1963. Edited by Lawrence Durrell.

A somewhat uncomplimentary review in The Times Literary Supplement brought forth a blistering letter from Edith Sitwell (T.L.S. 5 Dec. 1963.) 'Sir,—Mr. Lawrence Durrell, who is the editor of the new P.E.N. Anthology, is in trouble with the reviewer of that book because he is a fine writer, and therefore famous. I do not know from under what dull, meaningless stone the writer of that review crawled! But I understand that persons of that kind think I am laughing at them. (They are all exactly alike.) There is nothing to be said against them as writers (apart from the fact that a pathological hatred and malice are unattractive) excepting for three things: *A* that they have nothing whatsoever in their heads. *B* that they do not know one word from another. *C* that they can't write. Etc., etc.'

36. THE VAMPIRE. All the Best Vampire Stories in the World. Presented by Roger Vandin. London, Pan Books. 1963. Paperback.
Contains 'Carnival' from Balthazar.

37. PERMANENCES MEDITERRANÉENNES DE L'HUMANISME. Paris. Société d'Editions Les Belles Lettres. 1963.
Contains 'Langue d'Oc'. Translated by F.-J. Temple. First published in the revue ATLANTIQUE, daily newspaper of the liner 'France', English text and translation. February 3 1962.

38. RICHARD ALDINGTON, An Intimate Portrait. Edited by Alister Kershaw and F.-J. Temple. Carbondale and Edwardsville, Southern Illinois University Press. 1965.
Contains a short memoir by Durrell.

39. THE POETRY OF RAILWAYS. An Anthology by Kenneth Hopkins. London, Leslie Frewin. 1966.
Contains 'Night Express'.

40. I BURN FOR ENGLAND. An Anthology of Poetry of World War II. Selected and Introduced by Charles Hamblett. London, Leslie Frewin. 1966.
Contains 'Epitaph'. 'In a Time of Crisis'.

41. LONDON MAGAZINE POEMS. 1961–66. Selected by Hugo Williams. Introduction by Alan Ross. London, Alan Ross. 1966.
Contains 'Leeches'. 'Geishas'. 'Io'. 'Troy'.

JOHN GAWSWORTH, a short essay for a volume celebrating his fiftieth birthday: (as yet unpublished).

E. ANA
In Chronological Order

Kahane, Jack. MEMOIRS OF A BOOKLEGGER. London, Michael Joseph. 1939.

Memoirs of the founder of the Obelisk Press, Paris, publisher of Henry Miller and The Black Book.
Coward, Noel. MIDDLE EAST DIARY. London, Heinemann. 1944. 'August 22nd:
'The day broke fair and excessively warm but I didn't notice it as I slept until twelve o'clock when, with my breakfast tray on my knees, I gave an interview to Larry Darrell (sic) who lived in Corfu and writes poems.'
Stanford, Derek. THE FREEDOM OF POETRY, Studies in Contemporary Verse. London, The Falcon Press. 1947.
Contains critical essay on Durrell, with plate and select bibliography.
LEAVES IN THE STORM, A Book of Diaries, edited with a running commentary by Stefan Schimanski and Henry Treece. London, Lindsay Drummond. 1947.
Contains John Waller, Athens in Spring (Katsimbalis and Durrell).
POETRY REVIEW. May–June 1947.
Contains John Waller, Lawrence Durrell: A Clever Magician.
Waller, John Stanier. THE KISS OF STARS. London, Heinemann. 1948.
Contains poem 'Didcot'. A note by the author: 'This parody of Durrell's *Nemea* was to have appeared in a parody number of *Personal Landscape* but the issue never materialized.'
ΕΦΗΜΕΡΙΣ ΤΩΝ ΕΙΔΗΣΕΩΝ (Daily Newspaper) Athens. 10th March, 1950.
Contains "Ένας ποιητής μιλεῖ γιὰ τὴν Κέρκυρα. (A poet speaks about Corfu.) Signed: M.I.Δ
THE PENGUIN BOOK OF CONTEMPORARY VERSE. London, Penguin Books. 1950. Edited by Kenneth Allott.
Contains a biocritical sketch of Durrell along with three poems: 'Carols'; Sections I, III, and V from 'The Death of General Uncebuncke'; and 'A Ballad of the Good Lord Nelson'.
WORLD REVIEW: January 1952.
Contains D. J. Enright, The Cultural War: A Note on the Intelligentsia of Alexandria.

Durrell, Gerald. MY FAMILY AND OTHER ANIMALS.
London, Rupert Hart-Davis. 1956.
— New York, Viking. 1957.
A charming account of the idyllic life led by the Durrell
family in Corfu between the wars. With an affectionate, if
somewhat caricatured, portrait of Lawrence Durrell as seen
through the eyes of a younger brother.
Now available as a talking book for the blind.

COMMENTARY, XXVII: 4 April, 1959.
Contains R. W. Flint, A Major Novelist.

TWO CITIES. Paris 1 (1). 15 Avril, 1959.
Contains *Hommage à Durrell*, which includes: Henry Miller,
The Durrell of the Black Book Days; Alfred Perlès, Enter
Jupiter Jr.; F.-J. Temple, Construire un mur de pierre sedre;
Richard Aldington, A Note on Lawrence Durrell; Edwin Mul-
lins, On Mountolive; Durrell answers a few questions.

L'ARC, cahiers méditerranéens. Aix-en-Provence. No. 7.
Juillet, 1959.
Contains François Erval, Lawrence Durrell. Portrait.

SOUTHWEST REVIEW, XLIV. Summer 1959.
Contains Mary G. Lund, 'Submerge for Reality: The New
Novel Form of Lawrence Durrell'.

NEWS CHRONICLE. London. 9th September 1959.
Contains David Holloway, Why Mr. Durrell Can't Afford to
Write Poetry. (Interview.)

DIE ZEIT. Hamburg. 27th November 1959.
Contains Ein Abend mit Lawrence Durrell.

LES LETTRES FRANÇAIS. Paris. 17th December
1959.
Contains Hubert Juin, Paroles avec Lawrence Durrell.

ENCOUNTER, XIII: 6. London. December 1959.
Contains Kenneth Young, A Dialogue with Durrell.

PARIS REVIEW. No. 22. Autumn-Winter 1959–60.
Contains Julian Mitchell and Gene Andrewski, The Art of
Fiction XXXIII, Lawrence Durrell. An interview with Durrell
in Provence.
See Writers At Work, 1963, below.

Rodis, Roufos. THE AGE OF BRONZE. London, Heinemann. 1960.
A novel about the Cyprus troubles by a Greek diplomat. In
an earlier version, which I read in typescript, there is a recogniz-
able portrait of Durrell as Maurice Ferrell, a poet (author of
Sour Grapes and The Bench of Idleness), who is working as
Information Officer. In the published version this character
appears as Harry Montague and much of the resemblance to
Durrell has been discarded.

THE OBSERVER. London. 28th February 1960.
Contains Profile, Lawrence Durrell. Portrait.
BOOKS AND BOOKMEN. London. February 1960.
Contains Lawrence Durrell, Is he the only great novelist of
the Fifties? Durrell Interviewed. Two portraits.
20th CENTURY. 167 (997). London. March 1960.
Contains C. Mackworth, Lawrence Durrell and the New
Romanticism.
HORIZON, II: 4. London, March 1960.
Contains Gilbert Highet, The Alexandrians of Lawrence
Durrell.
THE BOOK COLLECTOR, IX. London. Spring 1960.
Contains Some Uncollected Authors XXIII: Lawrence
Durrell by Alan G. Thomas and Lawrence Clark Powell.
CRITIQUE. Paris. May 1960.
Contains J. P. Hamard, L'Espace et le Temps chez Lawrence
Durrell.
ENCOUNTER, XIV. London. May 1960.
Contains Hilary Corke, Mr Durrell and Brother Criticus.
YALE REVIEW, XLIX: 4. New Haven, Connecticut. June
1960.
Contains Lawrence Durrell: Two Views, The Baroque Novel
by George Steiner; A Minority Report by Martin Green.
ESQUIRE. New York. September 1960.
Contains Thomas B. Morgan, The Autumnal Arrival of
Lawrence Durrell.
PREUVES, 109. 1960.

Contains Dominique Arban, Lawrence Durrell.
HUDSON REVIEW, XIII: 3. Autumn 1960.
Contains Benjamin DeMott, Grading the Emanglons.
LIFE, 49: 21. New York. 21st November 1960.
Contains Nigel Dennis, New Four-Star King of Novelists. Illustrated.
RÉALITÉS. No. 178. Paris. November 1960.
Contains, Lawrence Durrell Vous Parle.
PARIS MATCH. No. 608. 3rd December 1960.

Contains Guillaume Hanoteau, Lawrence Durrell, riche et glorieux grâce à quatre femmes, ce carré de dames apporte la gloire et la fortune à ce poète inconnu. Illustrated.

Perlès, Alfred. MY FRIEND LAWRENCE DURRELL. With a Bibliography by Bernard Stone. Northwood, Middlesex, The Scorpion Press. 1961.

Also an edition specially bound, limited to 50 copies signed by the author.

BIBLIOGRAPHICAL SOCIETY OF AMERICA, 57: Second Quarter. 1961.
Contains Anthony Knerr, Regarding a Checklist of Lawrence Durrell.

LAWRENCE DURRELL: A CHECKLIST. Compiled by Robert A. Potter and Brooke Whiting. Issued on the occasion of the presentation of Lawrence Clark Powell's Durrell Collection to the UCLA Library. Preface by Powell. Los Angeles. 1961. Illustrated.

Jennings, Elizabeth. POETRY TO-DAY. London, Longmans, Green for The British Council and The National Book League. 1961. Portrait.

LIFE. New York. 27th January 1961.
Contains Durrell Reunion at the Family Zoo. Excellent photographs.

SEWANEE REVIEW, LXIX: 1. Sewanee, Tennessee. Jan.–March 1961.
Contains Bonamy Dobrée, Durrell's Alexandrian Series.

ΕΙΚΟΝΕΣ, 282. 17th March 1961. Athens.
Also published in English as PICTURES FROM GREECE.

Contains "Ἕνας μεγάλος μυθιστοριογράφος ἀνατέλλει.
(A great novelist rises.) Illustrated.
RÉALITÉS. No. 125. Paris and New York. April 1961.
Contains Lawrence Durrell An Exclusive Interview. Illustrated.
THE GUARDIAN. Manchester. 6th May 1961.
Contains W. J. Weatherby, The Durrell Brothers. Illustrated.
CRITIQUE, IV: 2. Spring-Summer 1961.
Contains Matthew N. Proser, Darley's Dilemma: The Problem of Structure in Durrell's Alexandria Quartet. Frank Baldanza, Lawrence Durrell's Word Continuum.
ANTIOCH REVIEW, XXX: 1. Summer 1961.
Contains Mary G. Lund, The Alexandrian Projection.
THE OBSERVER. London. 27th August 1961.
Contains Kenneth Tynan, Durrell in Three Dimensions. (Review of Sappho.)
THE SUNDAY TIMES. London. 27th August 1961.
Contains Harold Hobson, The Quick and the Dead. (Review of Sappho.)
EVENING STANDARD. London. 5th October 1961. & (same night) MANCHESTER EVENING CHRONICLE.
Contains Lawrence Durrell by his brother Gerald; No. 4 in a series of brotherly articles (Tomorrow: Robert Graves—by his brother Charles.) Portraits. Probably appeared in other papers.
THE ATLANTIC. Boston, December 1961.
Contains Curtis Cate, Lawrence Durrell.
WATERLOO REVIEW, 6. Winter 1961.
Contains R. A. O'Brien, Time, Space and Language in Lawrence Durrell.
PRAIRIE SCHOONER, XXXV. 1961.
Contains Mary G. Lund, Durrell, Soft Focus on Crime.
THE PERSONALIST, XLIII. 1961.
Contains John Arthos, Lawrence Durrell's Gnosticism.
Rexroth, Kenneth. ASSAYS. Norfolk, Connecticut, New Directions, 1961.
Contains Lawrence Durrell.
Moore, Harry T., edited by, THE WORLD OF LAW-

RENCE DURRELL. Carbondale, Southern Illinois University Press. 1962.

Contains essays by seventeen authors; Durrell Answers a few Questions; The Kneller Tape (Hamburg); Durrell, Letters to Jean Fanchette.

MONITOR, Anthology, edited by Huw Wheldon, a selection of talks from the television programme. London, MacDonald. 1962. Illustrated.

Contains interview with Lawrence Durrell.

Gordon, Ambrose. SIX CONTEMPORARY NOVELS. Austin, Texas. 1962.

Contains Time, Space, and Eros: The Alexandria Quartet Rehearsed. (The others are Pasternak, C. P. Snow, Hemingway, Faulkner and Beckett.)

Foley, Charles. ISLAND IN REVOLT. London, Longmans. 1962. Illustrated.

— Revised edition, Harmondsworth, Penguin Books. 1964.

An account of the Cyprus troubles, contains several references to Durrell.

THEATER HEUTE. Hannover. January 1962.

Contains Gründgens last Durrell hinter sich. Illustrated. Briefwechsel über Actis (with Gustaf Gründgens.) Actis, Drama in drei Akten von Lawrence Durrell. (German text of the play.) See A35 a finely printed edition of one item in this book.

GRANTA, LXV; 1215. Cambridge. February 1962.

Contains Tony Tanner, Lawrence Durrell.

THE SUNDAY TIMES. Colour Section. 18th March 1962.

Contains Joyce Emerson, A New 'Faust' from Durrell. Illustrated.

LE MIDI LIBRE. 3rd May 1962.

Contains F.-J. Temple. Lawrence Durrell Parmi Nous.

ANGLO-SOVIET JOURNAL. Summer 1962.

Contains I. Levidova, A Four-Decker in Stagnant Waters. Levidova, irritated by the acclaim which the Quartet has received from the 'bourgeois press', described it as a 'vividly painted' ship unable to set sail.

ETUDES ANGLAISES. Paris. Juillet-Sept. 1962.

Contains Curate's Egg. An Alexandrian Opinion of Durrell's Quartet. By Mahmoud Manzalaoui.

THE SCOTSMAN. Edinburgh. 21st August 1962.

Contains photograph of Lawrence Durrell conversing with Henry Miller at the Writers' Conference, Edinburgh Festival. The conference was widely reported in British newspapers and magazines during this week.

REVUE GÉNÉRALE BELGE. October 1962.

Contains Albert Gérard, Lawrence Durrell, Un Grand Talent de Basse Époque.

COLLEGE ENGLISH, 24:1. October 1962.

Contains Eleanor N. Hutchens, The Heraldic Universe in The Alexandria Quartet.

ΕΙΚΟΝΕΣ, 368. 9th November 1962.

Contains Λώρενς Ντάρρελ: "Μαγεία ἡ 'Ελλάδα!' Illustrated.

PICTURES FROM GREECE. No. 84. January 1963.

English version of the foregoing—Lawrence Durrell, Enchanted to be back in Greece! Illustrated.

MOTIVE. No. 23. November 1962.

Contains David Littlejohn, Lawrence Durrell, The Novelist as Entertainer.

TEXAS QUARTERLY, V: 4. Austin. Winter 1962.

Contains Stanley G. Eskin, Durrell's Themes in the Alexandria Quartet.

ACTUELLES. No. 1. Janvier 1963.

Contains F.-J. Temple, Avec Lawrence Durrell. Photograph.

WRITERS AT WORK, The Paris Review Interviews, Introduced by Van Wyck Brooks. London, Secker and Warburg. 1963.

Contains Lawrence Durrell.

— New York, Viking. 1963.

Unterecker, John. LAWRENCE DURRELL, Columbia Essays on Modern Writers, No. 6. New York, Columbia University Press. 1964.

ΕΙΚΟΝΕΣ, 404. 19th July 1963.

Contains Λώρενς Ντάρρελ, Φίλιππος Σερράρντ.

Illustrated. Philip Sherrard, Lawrence Durrell.

CRITIQUE, Studies in Modern Fiction, VII: 1. Spring 1964.
Contains John V. Hagopian, The Resolution of The Alexandria Quartet.

EDGE. No. 2. Canada. Spring. 1964.
Contains W. F. Smyth. Lawrence Durrell. Modern Love in Chamber Pots and Space Time.

MODERN FICTION STUDIES, 10: 2. Summer 1964.
Contains Romantic Anachronism in The Alexandria Quartet.

ΕΙΚΟΝΕΣ, 457. 24th July 1964.
Contains 'Ανάμνηση καί στόχος. Memories and plans. Illustrated.

Weigel, John A. LAWRENCE DURRELL. New York, Twayne's English Authors Series. 1965.
Contains useful summaries of many of the items recorded in this section.

— New York, E. P. Dutton. 1966. Paperback.

ΤΗΛΕΓΡΑΦΟΣ, (TELEGRAPH) Corfu. 25th May 1965.
Contains Πηγή έμπνεύσεως ή Κέρκυρα γιά τόν Ντάρρελ.
(Corfu is a well of inspiration for Durrell.) Portrait.

ECRIVAINS CONTEMPORAINS. Paris. Editions D'Art Lucien Mazenod. 1965.
Contains page about Durrell by F.-J. Temple. Coloured photograph.

REFLETS MEDITERRANÉENS. Avignon. June–July. 1965.
Contains R. Allan. Entretien avec Lawrence Durrell and F.-J. Temple. Lawrence Durrell, L'Homme et L'Oeuvre.

Jennings, Paul. OODLES OF ODDLIES. London, Max Reinhardt. 1963.
Contains East Bergholt Quartet. '(I read Mr. Lawrence Durrell's 'Alexandria Quartet', rather belatedly, at a time when we were looking after Twemlow, an Abyssinian guinea-pig belonging to neighbours on holiday. We have a female cat (Elliot), a neuter (William Byrd) and a spaniel (Barker).)

ΚΕΡΚΥΡΑΙΚΑ ΝΕΑ, (CORFU NEWS) 17th January 1966. Corfu.
Contains 'Η Κέρκυρα όπως τήν είδε ό Χένρυ Μίλλερ.

'Ο' Ἀμερικανός ποῦ τή γνώρισε μαζύ μέ τόν Ντάρρελ. (Corfu as seen by Henry Miller: the American who knew the Island as the guest of Durrell.)

Stephanides, Theodore. THE GOLDEN FACE. Poems. London, The Fortune Press. 1965. [1966.]

Contains The Submerged Garden (Kassopi, Corfu, 1939), with reference in the notes to Lawrence Durrell. Dr Stephanides is one of the leading figures in Prospero's Cell.

Fedden, Robin. PERSONAL LANDSCAPE. London, Turret Books. 1966.

An account of the Genesis of the magazine Personal Landscape. (See section F.) A portion of this book appeared in The London Magazine, Vol. 5. No. 12, March 1966. Limited to 1,000 copies, the first 50 numbered and signed by the author. Two illustrations. Limited edition bound in cloth, ordinary edition in paper wrappers.

THE HENRY MILLER LITERARY SOCIETY, 121 North 7th Street, Minneapolis 3, Minn. issues a Newsletter and broadsheets which sometimes contain references to Durrell.

F. CONTRIBUTIONS TO PERIODICALS

L'ARC. No. 15. Aix-en-Provence. Summer 1961.

Contains 'Le Becfique' translated by F.–J. Temple.

ARGOSY. London. August 1966.

Contains 'Aunt Norah'. Antrobus story.

THE ATLANTIC. Boston, September 1957.

Contains 'Liberation Celebration Machine'.

— May 1965.

Contains 'The Other T. S. Eliot', portrait.

This tribute had previously appeared in French: PREUVES, Paris. April 1965.

THE BOOSTER. Paris. A monthly in French and English, edited by Alfred Perlès, Lawrence Durrell, Henry Miller, and William Saroyan. It was the magazine of The American Country Club who handed its direction to Alfred Perlès in the mistaken belief that his brilliant friends would turn it into a sort of New Yorker. As far as I know their opinion of the result has not been recorded. For the history of THE BOOSTER and its successor, DELTA, see Perlès: MY FRIEND HENRY MILLER. London, Neville Spearman. 1955; New York, John Day. 1956.

Contains numerous contributions by Durrell and Charles Norden. Also the first appearance in print of Gerald Durrell, then aged eleven. Durrell thought that Gerald's tutor, Patrick Evans, had written the piece. 'Do you suppose', said Pat, 'that if I could write as well as that I would waste my time on being a tutor?' The back page usually carried a poem in some exotic script, Persian, Japanese, etc., produced by means of a line block. Meanwhile the stolid bourgeois advertisements continued to appear, flanked by 'The House of Incest' and 'Nightmare'.

II: 7. September 1937.

II: 8. October 1937.

3ᵉ Année, No. 9. November 1937.

4ᵉ Année, Nos. 10–11.

CHIMERA, III: 3. New York. Spring 1945.

Contains 'Byron'.

— V: 2. Winter 1947.

Contains 'Eternal Contemporaries'.

CIRCLE NINE. Berkeley, California. 1946.

Contains 'Eight Aspects of Melissa'.

The magazine appeared in four different covers, all executed by Bezadel Schatz.

COUNTERPOINT, I: 1. n.d. [1945–6.]

Contains 'Conon the critic on the six landscape painters of Greece'.

CREATIVE WRITING. Chicago. November 1938—March/ April 1941.

Begins as a mimeographed magazine.

Contributions?

THE CRITIC. Chicago. December 1966/January 1967.

Contains. 'Seraglios and Imbroglios.' Antrobus story.

CYPRUS REVIEW. Nicosia. Edited by Lawrence Durrell and later by George Wilkinson from X: 10, October 1954, until the end of 1955.

Contains contributions by Durrell; particuarly good is the number for July 1955, which contains 'Plus ça change, a Mental Excavation'—ancient figures from the museum with modern captions.
DAYLIGHT, I. London. 1941.
Contains Five Poems by George Seferis translated by Durrell and Katsimbalis.
DELTA. Paris. A continuation of THE BOOSTER with the same editors.
2ᵉ Année, No. 2. April 1938. 'Poem to Gerald'.
2ᵉ Année, No. 3. Xmas 1938. 'Hamlet Prince to China'.
No. 4. Easter 1939 [published in London]. 'The Sonnet of Hamlet'. Fourteen Sonnets.
DIOGENES, I: 3. Madison, Wisconsin. Autumn 1941.
Contains 'Letter to Seferis the Greek'.
DIRE 4 et 5. Montpellier. Printemps-Été 1963.
Contains 'Ode to a Lukewarm Eyebrow. "Mr Durrell and Miss Compton-Burnett meet with such praise in France as to raise many a lukewarm English eyebrow. . . . There is something in the English temper that loves a shortage, be it of words. . . ." Times Literary Supplement.'
'Picadilly'.
With translations into French of both poems by F.-J. Temple. Linocuts by de Bessil.
— 6. Automne 1963.
Contains 'Un Faust Irlandais (Scène Huit)'. Trans. F.-J. Temple.
THE ECONOMIST. London. 24th July 1954.
Contains 'The Cypriot's Dilemma'.
— 13th August 1954.
Contains 'Hush Over Cyprus'.
— 29th October 1954.
Contains 'Cypriots Watch and Wait'.
— 24th September 1955.
Contains 'Hellenism in Danger'.
'Mr Durrell made other contributions to The Economist in 1954 and 1955 but chiefly in the form of letters which were then used as a basis for editorials written in London.'

EGYPTIAN GAZETTE. Cairo. Numerous contributions by Durrell.

'Some time between April 1941 and the end of that year I ran a weekly funny column in the Egyptian Gazette. Pure rubbish in the Beachcomber vein. It earned me about ten pounds a month which as a refugee I needed. I didn't get taken on at the embassy until August of that year I think. Me and Rimbaud both! Searchers might look out for Aunt Norah who featured in this column. I also wrote numberless leaders (perhaps 15) on policy matters then deemed important. One, called "Quo Vadis" got a spate of telephone calls and fan letters. Why? It is a mystery. It was a stupendously banal piece—but on the party line!'—Note by Durrell.

ELLE. No. 1046. Paris. Janvier 1966 et seq.

Contains 'Judith, le nouveau roman de Lawrence Durrell'.

ENCOUNTER. No. 51. IX: 6. London. December 1957.

Contains 'The Shades of Dylan Thomas'.

— No. 96. XVII: 3. September 1961.

Contains 'Aphrodite' and 'A Persian Lady'.

— No. 121. XXI: 4. October 1963.

Contains 'Byzance'.

— January 1967.

Contains 'Blood count.'

— March 1967.

Contains 'Moonlight'.

ESQUIRE, LIII: 2, whole number 315. Chicago. February 1960.

Contains 'Clea'. [The first publication in America of a significant portion of Clea.]

THE EVENING STANDARD. London. 22nd November 1957.

Contains 'Letter in the Sofa' in the 'Did it Happen Series'.

Reprinted in The Glasgow Evening Citizen, 17th January 1959.

— 8th February 1958.

Contains 'The Disquieting American'.

Reprinted in The Evening Chonicle, Manchester, 12th May 1958; Nottingham Evening Post, 31st May 1958; The Evening Citizen, Glasgow, 15th October 1959; and as 'The Disquieting Yank' in The Hunts Post, 13th June 1963.

EXPERIMENTAL REVIEW. No. 2. Woodstock, New York. November 1940.
 Contains 'The Sermon'.
— No. 3. September 1941.
 Contains 'Hanged Man'; 'Three Carols'; 'In Crisis'; 'Father Nicolas'; 'Sermon of One'; 'Three Sons'; 'Fangbrand'. [These poems were all selected from the manuscript of A Private Country, then unpublished.]
FURIOSO, I: 4. New Haven, Connecticut. Summer 1941.
 Contains 'Carol in Corfu' and 'In Arcadia'.
GANGREL. London. n.d. [January 1945 or *post.*]
 Contains 'Conon in Alexandria'.
GAZEBO. Bath. Edited and published at Kingswood School as a contribution to the Freedom from Hunger Campaign. June 1963.
 Contains 'A Modern Troubadour'. Illustration by V. Webb.
GENTLEMEN'S QUARTERLY, 28: 5. New York. September 1959.
 Contains 'The Iron Hand'.
GEOGRAPHICAL MAGAZINE, VIII: 5. London. March 1939
 Contains 'Corfu: Isle of Legend'. Illustrated.
— XX: 6. October 1947.
 Contains 'The Island of the Rose' [Rhodes]. Illustrated.
GREEK HERITAGE. Athens. Edited by Kimon Firar. Winter 1963.
 Contains 'Grecian Olives', 'Scaffoldings' and 'Plaka'.
GREEK HORIZONS, I: 1. Athens. Summer 1946.
 Contains 'The Telephone'.
Note by Derek Patmore. In 1946 I was living in Athens, and as there were a number of gifted young English writers all working in Greece, I decided that it would be interesting to produce a literary quarterly called Greek Horizons. All my writer friends welcomed the idea, and Lawrence Durrell, who was then working as a British Information Officer, gave me a short story, The Telephone. Other contributors were Patrick Leigh Fermor, Osbert Lancaster, Steven Runciman, John Waller, and myself.

HARPER'S BAZAAR. London. January 1962.
Contains 'High Barbary', Antrobus Story.
HOLIDAY, 25: 1. Philadelphia. January 1959.
Contains 'The Worldly University of Grenoble'.
— 26: 5. November 1959.
Contains 'Ripe Living in Provence'.
— 27: 1. January 1960.
Contains 'Rhône'.
— 29: 1. January 1961.
Contains 'Geneva'.
— 29: 2. February 1961.
Contains 'Laura: a Portrait of Avignon'.
— 30: 8. August 1962.
Contains 'Postman's Palace—In Praise of Fanatics'.
— 31: 1. January 1963.
Contains 'The Gascony Touch'.
— October 1966.
Contains 'Oil for the Saint; piece about a return to Koloura in Corfu'.
HORIZON, XVII: 102. London. June 1948.
Contains 'Studies in Genius VI: Groddeck'.
— XX: 115. July 1949.
Contains 'Studies in Genius VIII: Henry Miller'.
INTERNATIONAL, I: 2. London. Spring 1965.
Contains 'The Most Remarkable Frenchwoman of Our Time'. [Alexandra David-Neel.] Illustrated. Translation into French appears in Elle, Paris, 17th Juillet 1964.
INTERNATIONAL POST. London. Durrell was appointed the drama critic for this weekly review of the arts and letters which was edited by Christopher Rowan Robinson and Tristram Pownall. The other weekly contributors included Swane Fox, Cyril Beaumont, John Gawsworth, and Eric Halfpenny. The magazine folded, however, and only the first number was put together. This issue was never published, but there is a paste-up of the magazine which does survive. First recorded by Anthony Knerr it later appeared in a bookseller's catalogue, House of Books, New York, n.d., No. 84. This number I: 1, 6th

April 1939, contains Durrell's reviews of two plays: 'Heaven and Charing Cross' by A. Danvers-Walker, and 'Family Reunion' by T. S. Eliot.

BULLETIN OF THE JOHN RYLANDS LIBRARY, 27: 1. Manchester. Winter 1942.

Contains 'Myth of Our History' [poem by George Seferis, translated by Durrell and G. Katsimbalis].

KINGDOM COME: The Magazine of War-Time Oxford. Edited by John Waller, etc. I: 4. Summer 1940.

Contains 'In Arcadia'.

KING'S SCHOOL REVIEW, I: 2. Canterbury. March 1960.

Contains 'The Moonlight of Your Smile'.

The Editorial states: "Two weeks ago a profile of Lawrence Durrell in The Observer stated, quite incorrectly, that he was educated at King's. On these grounds alone we wrote asking him for a contribution and were sent the excellent short story featured in this issue. Also enclosed was a letter:

'*I apologize for the nasty smear in The Observer. I wasn't responsible and indeed haven't seen it. I send you a short article as a form of apology. I hope you can mention in your notes that I was educated at St Edmund's or they may march on you. . . . I hope my name won't get you birched by the head.*' "

LILLIPUT. London. March 1958.

Contains 'La Valise'.

LISTENER. London. 27th October 1966.

Contains letter replying to Alexander Cockburn's review of Sauve Qui Peut.

LONDON MAGAZINE, I: 8. London. September 1954.

Contains 'Letters in Darkness'.

— III: 7. July 1956.

Contains 'A Cavafy Find'—three poems by C. P. Cavafy translated by Durrell.

— IV: 4. April 1957.

Contains review of books by Roy Fuller, D. J. Enright, and Philip Larkin.

— IV: 7. July 1957.

Contains 'How to Buy a House in Cyprus'.

— New Series, I: 11. February 1962.

Contains 'Context' [replies—together with other poets—to six questions on modern poetry].

— New Series, III: 9. December 1963.

Contains 'Stone Honey', 'Scaffoldings' and 'Strip Tease'.

— New Series, III: 10. January 1964.

Contains 'Bernard Spencer'. A Memoir, preface to Spencer's Last Poems.

— IV: 4. July 1965.

Contains '10', 'Troy', 'Leeches' and 'Geishas'.

— March 1967.

Contains 'Confederate'.

LUI. Paris and New York. June 1964.

Contains 'Lawrence du Midi'. (Reflections About Women.)

MADEMOISELLE, No. 50. New York. February 1960.

Contains 'Capital of Memory'.

— September 1961.

Contains 'High Barbary'. Antrobus story.

— September 1963.

Contains 'What Ho on The Rialto'. Antrobus story.

— 1964.

Contains 'In The Margin' and 'Poemandres'.

— November 1964.

Contains 'Scaffoldingings'.

— December 1966.

Contains 'Taking the Consequences.' Antrobus story.

MAN ABOUT TOWN, II: 1. London. January 1961.

Contains 'Mr Ought and Mrs Should'. (Anxieties of Our Time.)

NATION, 187: 2. New York. 19th July 1958.

Contains 'Cyprus: Personal Reflections'.

NEUROTICA, No. 3. U.S.A. Autumn 1948.

Contains 'Conon on Mnemons'.

NEW DIRECTIONS IN PROSE & POETRY, V. Norfolk, Connecticut. 1940.

Contains 'Poem in Space and Time', 'A Noctuary', 'Self' and 'At Corinth'.

THE NEW ENGLISH WEEKLY, X: 14. London. 11th
January 1937.
 Contains 'The Prince and Hamlet'.
— XIV: 11. 22nd December 1938.
 Contains 'Lines to Music'.
— XIV: 21. 2nd March 1939.
 Contains 'Logos'.
— XV: 14. 20th July 1939.
 Contains 'The Open Way'.
— XVI: 14. 25th January 1940.
 Contains 'Mysticism: the Yellow Peril'.
NEW POETRY. London. 1944—Edited by Nicholas Moore.
 Contributions?
NEW SALTIRE. No. I. Edinburgh. Summer 1961.
 Contains 'Sappho and After'.
THE NEW STATESMAN AND NATION, XL: 1017.
London. 2nd September 1950
 Contains 'Epitaph'.
— XL: 1019. 16th September 1950.
 Contains 'Water Colour of Venice'.
— XL: 1030. 2nd December 1950.
 Contains 'Education of a Cloud'.
— XLII: 1073. 29th September 1951,
 Contains 'Cradle Song'.
— XLII: 1078. 3rd November 1951.
 Contains 'Chanel'.
—XLV: 1154. 18th April 1953.
 Contains 'A Bowl of Roses'.
— L: 1282. 1st October 1955.
 Contains 'Nicosia'.
— LI: 1304. 10th March 1956.
 Contains 'Bitter Lemons'.
— LII: 1335. 13th October 1956.
 Contains 'Mythology'.
— LII: 1338. 3rd November 1956.
 Contains review 'Traveller's Tales'.
— LII: 1344. 15th December 1956.

Contains review 'Greece Interpreted'.
— LIII: 1348. 12th January 1957.
Contains 'The Moulder of Minds'.
— LIII: 1360. 6th April 1957.
Contains 'Cry Wolf'.
— LIII: 1364. 4th May 1957.
Contains review 'Poets' Kingdom'.
NEW YORK HERALD TRIBUNE BOOK REVIEW.
New York. 23rd August 1959.
Contains 'His Ship Came In and All Is Well'.
NEW YORK TIMES BOOK REVIEW. New York. 12th
June 1960.
Contains 'Landscape with Literary Figures'.
— 4th December 1960.
Contains 'These I've Read and Will Read Again' [answers to
questions about books he has read lately].
— 15th January 1961.
Contains 'A Traveller In Egypt' [review of 'Alexandria' by
E. M. Forster].
THE NEW YORKER. 6th November 1965.
Contains 'Delphi'.
— 20th November 1965.
Contains 'Salamis'.
NIGHT AND DAY. London. 9th September 1937.
Contains 'Obituary Notice'. A Tragedy by Charles Norden,
illustrated by Nancy Norden.
NOW, VIII. London. May–June [no year, post 1947].
Contains 'Elegy on the Closing of the French Brothels'.
THE OBSERVER. London. 22nd October 1961.
Contains 'Eleusis'.
—28th April 1963.
Contains 'Congenies'.
OLYMPIA, No. 1. Paris. 1962.
Contains 'Pursewarden's Incorrigibilia' and 'Frankie and
Johnny', (New Style). Portrait.
ORIENTATIONS. Vol. 1. No. 1. (A Forces Quarterly,
edited by G. S. Fraser). Cairo.

Contains 'A Landscape Gone' by Charles Norden.

PARIS REVIEW, No. 29, Paris. Winter-Spring 1963.

Contains six of the Durrell-Miller letters. Portrait.

PARNASSOS [Greek Cultural Society of New York], I: 2. New York. Autumn 1960.

Contains 'To Argos'. Printed with the Greek translation of the poem and with illustration by Ghika.

PARTISAN REVIEW, XIII: 5. New York. November–December 1946.

Contains 'Rodini' and 'Blind Homer'.

PENGUIN NEW WRITING, No. 29. London and New York. Autumn 1946.

Contains 'Eternal Contemporaries'.

— No. 32. 1947.

Contains 'From a Winter Journal'.

THE PEOPLE. London. 2nd February 1958.

Contains 'Did Emily Bronte live again in Dylan? . . . strange and mystic theory . . . put forward by Lawrence Durrell'.

PERSONAL LANDSCAPE. Cairo. A magazine of 'exile' edited by Robin Fedden, Lawrence Durrell and Bernard Spencer. Contributions by Durrell in all numbers. (For a selection of work drawn from this very rare magazine see PERSONAL LANDSCAPE, D. 11.)

— No. 1. January 1942.

Contains 'To Argos', 'To Ping-Kû, Asleep', 'Je est un autre', and 'Ideas about Poems'.

— No. 2. March 1942.

Contains 'Ideas about Poems: 2'.

— No. 3. June 1942.

Contains 'Conon in Exile'.

— I: 4. 1942.

Contains 'For a Nursery Mirror' and 'The Heraldic Universe'.

— II: 1. 1943.

Contains 'On First Looking Into Loeb's Horace' and 'Mythology'.

— II: 2. 1944.

Contains 'La Rochefoucauld' and 'The Poet Reviews Himself'.

— II: 3. 1944.
Contains 'Byron'.
— II: 4. 1945.
Contains 'Conon in Alexandria'.
See under Robin Fedden in section E for an account of this magazine.
PLAYBOY, 10: 12. Chicago. December 1963.
Contains 'A Corking Evening'. Antrobus story.
— 11: 12. December 1964.
Contains 'Sauve Qui Peut'. Antrobus story.
— September 1966.
Contains 'All to Scale'. Antrobus story.
POETRY (LONDON), I: 1. London. February 1939.
Contains 'Epitaph' and 'Island Fugue'.
— I: 2. April 1939.
Contains letter to Tambimuttu; theatre review of Eliot's Family Reunion.
— I: 3. November 1940.
Contains 'A Nocturary' and 'The Green Man'; also a review of Rilke's Duino Elegies.
— I: 4. January–February 1941.
Contains 'In a Time of Crisis'.
— I: 5. March–April 1941.
Contains 'Daphnis and Chloë'.
— I: 6. May–June 1941.
Contains 'Hero'.
— II: 7. October–November 1942.
Contains 'Epidaurus'.
— II: 10. 1944.
Contains a letter written to Tambimuttu 'Refugee Poets in Africa'.
— III: 11. September–October 1947.
Contains 'In the Garden of the Villa Cleobolus'.
— IV: 13. June–July 1948.
Contains 'Funchal', 'Teneriffe', and 'Sierra'.
— IV: 14. November–December 1948.
Contains 'Self to Not-Self'.

POETRY AND POVERTY. No. 2. London. n.d.

Contains 'Clouds of Glory'.

POETRY BOOK SOCIETY BULLETIN. No. 6. London.
June 1955.

Contains about twenty lines on poetry in general.

POETRY LONDON-NEW YORK. No. 1. New York.
March–April 1956.

Contains letter to Tambimuttu (dated 2nd February 1954)
about a proposed book of tributes to Dylan Thomas.

— No. 2. Winter 1956.

Contains 'At the Long Bar'.

— No. 3. Winter 1957.

Contains 'Eva Braun's Dream'.

POETRY REVIEW, XLI: 6. London. November–December 1950.

Contains 'Deus Loci'.

— XLIII: 1. January-February 1952.

Contains 'Constant Zarian, Triple Exile'.

POETRY WORLD, X: 12 and XI: 1. New York. July–
August 1939 [same issue].

Contains 'The Sonnet of Hamlet'.

POST. Philadelphia. 4th June 1966.

Contains 'The Little Affair in Paris'. Antrobus story.

PREUVES. No. 170. Paris. April 1965.

Contains 'Tse-lio-t'. French translation of the tribute which
appeared in The Atlantic monthly a month later.

PURPOSE, XI. London. April–June, 1939.

Contains 'The Simple Art of Truth: A First Study in Doctor
Graham Howe'. Review of Time and the Child by Graham
Howe.

QUEEN. London. 31st March 1959.

Contains 'Antrobus Commits a Felony'. [A Smircher
Smirched.]

RÉALITÉS. No. 120. Paris and New York. November 1960.

Contains 'I wish One Could Be More Like the Birds—to Sing
Unfaltering, at Peace'.

— June 1961.

Contains 'Women of the Mediterranean'.

Contains 'Delphi'. Afterwards published in Venture, New York.

RÉUNION PUBLICATION TRIMESTRAL, I: 1. Buenos Aires. Primavera de 1948.

Contains 'El Pensamiento de Groddeck'.

RHINOZeros. (An experimental typographic-calligraphic magazine.) Itzehoe, Germany. 1962.

Contains two pages reproducing Durrell's handwriting, the first in Greek the second in English (the latter with drawings), decorated with irregular lines of type.

— 1964.

One page in French and German.

RIGHT REVIEW. January 1939.

Contains 'A Letter from the Land of the Gods'.

SATURDAY EVENING POST. New York. 14th June 1966.

Contains 'The Little Affair in Paris.' Antrobus story.

SATURDAY REVIEW. New York. 5th December 1964.

Contains 'Portfolio'.

SCENE, VIII: 5. New York. October 1962.

Contains Trio 'Ballad of Psychoanalysis', 'At The Long Bar' and 'A Portrait of Theodora'.

SEVEN. No. 1. Taunton. Summer 1938.

Contains 'Ego'.

— No. 3. Winter 1938.

Contains 'Asylum in the Snow' and 'Carol in Corfu'.

— No. 4. Spring 1939.

Contains 'The Ego's Own Egg', 'The Hanged Man', 'Father Nicholas His Death', 'The Poet, I', 'A Small Scripture', and 'Adam'.

— No. 6. Fall 1939.

Contains 'Zero'.

— No. 7. Cambridge. Christmas 1939.

Contains translation of George Seferis's 'Message in a Bottle' and 'Untitled Poem' [with T. Stephanides and G. Katsimbalis].

SHOW. New York. December 1961.

Contains 'Acte' with an Introduction.

THE SPECTATOR, 190: 6, 513. London. 24th April 1953.

Contains 'Lesbos'.

THE SUNDAY TELEGRAPH. London. 26th March 1961.

Contains review of E. M. Forster, Alexandria: a History and a Guide.

THE SUNDAY TIMES. London. 23rd February 1958.

Contains 'If Garlic Be The Food of Love'. Antrobus story.

— 9th March 1958.

Contains 'Antrobus and the Bees in The Chancery'.

— 23rd March 1958.

Contains 'The Game's the Thing'. Antrobus story.

— 6th April 1958.

Contains 'The Unspeakable Attaché'. Antrobus story.

— 20th April 1958.

Contains 'The Iron Hand'. Antrobus story.

— 4th May 1958.

Contains 'Something À La Carte'. Antrobus story.

— 18th May 1958.

Contains 'The Old Training'. Antrobus story.

— 9th November 1958.

Contains 'Experts on Egypt'. Review of J. and S. Lacouture, Egypt in Transition.

— 27th September 1959.

Contains 'The Tassili Adventure'. Review of H. Lhote, The Search for the Tassili Frescoes.

—27th December 1959.

Contains 'The Complete Traveller's Handbook of Hazards'.

—3rd January 1960.

Contains 'A Traveller's Sorrows'.

— 1960.

Contains 'A Modern Troubador'.

— 1960.

Contains 'Cyprus'.

— 22nd December 1963.

Contains letter 'The Foundation', about African dancers

being provided with brassières when dancing before the Duke of Edinburgh.

3 ARTS QUARTERLY. No. 2. Summer 1960.

Contains 'First Steps'. [The first production of Sappho.]

— No. 3. 1960.

Contains 'Cavafy'.

ΤΑΧΥΔΡΟΜΟΣ. (Postman). Cairo. 15th August 1944.

Contains 'Tinos in August'. Poem by Durrell, dedicated to Theodore Stephanides and translated into Greek by E. Psara.

T'IEN HSIA MONTHLY, IX: 2. Shanghai. September 1939.

Contains 'Prospero's Isle'.

TIME AND TIDE. London. 31st September 1936 or 37.

Contains 'Ionian Profile', dedicated to Theodore Stephanides, by Charles Norden.

— 32: 49. 8th December 1951.

Contains 'Clouds of Glory'.

— 37: 48. 1st December 1956.

Contains 'Near Paphos'.

— 37: 49. 8th December 1956.

Contains review of books by Kingsley Amis, John Wain, K. Nott, W. Merwin, Siegfried Sassoon.

— 38: 11. 16th March 1957.

Contains 'Enigma Variations'. Review of Pound's Rock-Drill.

— 38: 16. 20th April 1957.

Contains review of Sargent's and Abse's Mavericks.

— 39: 49. 6th December 1958.

Contains 'Old Mathieu'.

THE TIMES. London. 22nd May 1964.

Contains letter on Cyprus.

THE TIMES LITERARY SUPPLEMENT. No. 2,467. London. 13th May 1949.

Contains 'Hellene & Philhellene'. Unsigned.

— No. 2,556. 26th January 1951.

Contains 'Sarajevo'.

— No. 2,578. 29th June 1951.

Contains 'The Sirens'.
— No. 2,589. 14th September 1951.
Contains 'River Water'.
— No. 2,720. Special Autumn Number. 6th August 1954.
Contains 'On Mirrors'.
— No. 2,813. 27th January 1956.
Contains 'The Octagon Room, National Gallery, '55'.
— No. 2,997. 7th August 1959.
Contains 'One Man's Meat'.
— No. 3,039. 27th May 1960.
Contains 'No Clue to Living. Limits of Control III'.
— No. 3,209. 30th August 1963.
Contains letter 'Ambiguous Gifts'.
— No. 3,275. 3rd December 1964.
Contains letter on Frank Harris.
— No. 3,295. 22nd April 1965.
Contains 'Vidourle'.
— No. 3,309. 29th July 1965.
Contains 'One Grey Greek Stone'.
— No. 3,318. 30th September 1965.
Contains 'Prix Blondel'.
— No. 3,345. 7th April 1966.
Contains letter 'Alexander's Tomb'.
TOWN. London. August 1966.
Contains 'The Little Affair in Paris'. Antrobus story.
TWO CITIES, I: 3. Paris. 15th December 1959.
Contains a lengthy extract from The Black Book with a revised version of the Introduction to the Olympia Press edition.
— I: 4. 15th May 1960.
Contains Introduction to Dylan Thomas's Letters to Lawrence Durrell.
— 7/8. Spring 1961.
Contains 'Down the Styx in an Air-conditioned Canoe'.
— 9. Autumn 1964.
Contains 'Letters to Jean Fanchette', and 'Ode to a lukewarm eyebrow'.
U. N. WORLD, VI. New York. August 1952.

Contains 'Family Portrait'.

VENTURE. New York. 1965.

Contains 'Durrell in Delphi'. Reprinted from Réalités.

VIEW, I. New York. February–March 1942. Edited Charles
H. Ford and Parkes Tyler.

Contains 'Daphnis and Chloë'.

— Series 3, No. 3. 1943.

Contains 'Mythology I' and 'Mythology II'.

VOGUE. New York and London. April 1956.

Contains 'Summer'.

— 131: 5. 1st March 1958.

Contains 'Family Portrait' and 'Cry Wolf' under the title of
'A Little Game'.

—21st September 1961.

Contains 'The Swami's Secret'. Antrobus story.

WEEKEND TELEGRAPH, Coloured Supplement. No. 14.
London. 23rd December 1964.

Contains 'A Corking Evening'. Antrobus story.

— No. 24. 5th March 1965.

Contains 'Sauve Qui Peut'. Antrobus story.

THE WINDMILL, II: 6. London. 1947.

Contains 'From a Writer's Journal'.

WOMAN'S OWN. London. 20th October 1962.

Contains 'Laura'. Fictionalized version of a Holiday article
on Avignon.

— 26th February—2nd April 1966.

Contains 'Judith'. In five parts.

ZEIT, DIE. Hamburg. 24th November 1961.

Contains Gründgens-Durrell: Briefwechsel über Actis. Illus.

— Nr. 30/17. 27th July 1962.

Contains 'Alle Uhren stehen.' Article on Rilke, translated into
German by von Dieter E. Zimmer. Later reprinted in The
Journal of German Studies.

G. GRAMOPHONE RECORDS & MUSICAL SETTINGS

1. JUPITER ANTHOLOGY OF 20TH CENTURY POETRY. Part II.

Contains 'Nemea'. Read by Pauline Letts.

Jupiter Recording. JUR ooA2.

2. SONGS ABOUT GREECE.

Contains 'Lesbos', music by Lennox Berkeley, and 'In Arcadia', music by T. W. Southam. Maureen Morelle (mezzo-soprano), Bryan Drake (baritone), Diana Wright (piano). With a printed sheet of words. The producer wrote: 'As this is not a very commercial recording—I doubt if we shall ever cover costs —Larry, with his usual kindness, has signed 50 numbered copies of the printed sheet of words.'

The picture on the sleeve is by Oscar Epfs (Lawrence Durrell) who used it for one of his Christmas cards, 1965.

Jupiter Recording. jep oC36.

3. POETS READING, No. 6. POEMS ON GREECE.

Text on sleeve by George Seferis.

Contains 'Nemea', 'To Argos', 'In Arcadia', 'Asphodels', 'Chalcidice', 'Aphrodite', 'Lesbos', 'Matapan'.

Jupiter Recording. jep oC28.

4. GRECIAN ECHOES. Selections from Bitter Lemons, Prospero's Cell and Reflections on a Marine Venus, chosen and read by Durrell.

LVA 1003–4. Lausanne, Switzerland.

5. AN IRISH FAUST, read by Durrell. The sleeve bears facsimiles of the handwriting of distinguished contributors to the series, including Durrell.

Les chefs-d'oeuvre du théâtre, de la littérature et de la poésie . . . lus par leurs auteurs.

LVA 201. Lausanne, Switzerland.

6. THE LOVE POEMS OF LAWRENCE DURRELL, read by Durrell at Montpellier. The sleeve bears an amusing account of the recording session.

New Rochelle, New York. Spoken Arts, Inc.

7. CONTEMPORARY POETS SET IN JAZZ. (With roneoed text.) Music by Wallace Southam, arranged by Ken Napper. Sung by Belle Gonzalez with jazz sextet.

Contains 'Lesbos'.

The picture on the sleeve by Lawrence Durrell was used for one of his Christmas cards, 1965.

Jupiter Recording. JUR OA11.

8. SOUND OF ELEVEN. The Peter Comton Big Band.

'. . . CLEA is one of three Peter Comton compositions on this LP which are named after novels by Lawrence Durrell. This 32-bar tune is largely devoted to Mike Carroll's trombone playing, but Colin Parnell is heard in a piano solo. The next track DJINN—another Peter Comton 'original'—also has a link with Lawrence Durrell, for the slow theme, played by just Ian Fenby, Ray Warleigh and bassist Peter Hughes, was originally entitled MELISSA, after one of the minor characters in the books. . . . The concluding track contains two other pieces—MOUNTOLIVE and BALTHAZAR—inspired by Durrell's novels. MOUNTOLIVE is constructed unusually, the eight-bar introduction being followed by a twelve-bar theme (not a blues), which resolves into the opening figure. This is succeeded by a second, and rather similar twelve-bar tune, but with a different chord sequence . . . the performance accelerates, culminating in the percussion solo which leads into BAL-THAZAR. This relatively conventional 32-bar tune—conventional by comparison with MOUNTOLIVE, anyway—has solos from Peter Ward (on tenor sax), Ian Fenby and Ray Warleigh.' From the sleeve by Charles Fox.

77 Records (Dobells). 77LEU12/14.

9. A RECITAL OF SONGS BY ENGLISH COMPOSERS.

Contains 'Nemea', music by T. W. Southam. Wilfred Brown (tenor), Margaret McNamee (piano).

Jupiter Recording. JUR 00A5.

WALKING IN MY SLEEP. Slow foxtrot, lyric by Larry Dell [Durrell], music by Tom Wallace [T. W. Southam]. Athens, Gaetanos. 1945.

NEMEA. Lyric by Durrell, music by T. W. Southam. London, Augener. 1950.

AUTUMN'S LEGACY: Op. 58 for High Voice and Pianoforte, by Lennox Berkeley. Commissioned by the Committee of the Cheltenham Festival 1962. First performance by Richard Lewis and Geoffrey Parsons. London, J. & W. Chester. 1963.
  Contains 'Lesbos'. .

NOTHING IS LOST, SWEET SELF. Lyric by Durrell, music by T. W. Southam. Facsimile of original score. Limited to 100 copies signed by author and composer. London, Turrett Books. 1967.

LESBOS. Lyric by Durrell, music by T. W. Southam. London, Oxford University Press. 1967.

H. SOUND RADIO

B.B.C. HS = Home Service   LP = Light Programme
        TP = Third Programme   Net. 3 = Network Three

N.B.—These dates accord to English practice thus: 25.12.68. = 25th December 1968.

Date	*Service*	*Programme*
9.9.47.	HS	Greek Peasant Superstitions. Talk by Lawrence Durrell.
17.9.47.	HS	China to Peru—Dreams & Divinations. Lawrence Durrell talks about ancient superstitions in modern Greece.
13.3.48.	LP	New Books and Old Books. *Cefalu* reviewed.
19.5.50.	TP	Poetry Now. Talk by Alan Ross with quotations from the poems of Lawrence Durrell and Norman Nicholson.
15.3.51. (repeated next day)	TP	Lawrence Durrell: Selected Poems. Arranged and produced by Terence Tiller.
31.7.52. (repeated 2.8.52.)	TP	New Soundings, No. 6. Edited and introduced by John Lehmann. 'Deus Loci' was read.

Date	Service	Programme
16.8.53. (repeated 17.8.53.)	HS	The Critics. Book: *Reflections on a Marine Venus* reviewed by Elspeth Huxley.
10.7.55.	TP	New Poetry. Introduced by Iain Fletcher. 'Letters in Darkness', 'Chanel' and 'Sarajevo' from *The Tree of Idleness*.
28.8.55 (repeated 30.8.55.)	HS	The Critics. Book: *The Tree of Idleness*, reviewed by G. S. Fraser.
13.11.55.	HS	The Plain Style. G. S. Fraser, the poet and critic, offers a selection of recently published poems that he has enjoyed. 'Style' by Lawrence Durrell.
4.10.56.	TP	*Freedom and Death* by Nikos Kazantzakis. Reviewed by Lawrence Durrell.
5.10.56.	TP	The Poet's Voice. Third Programme 10th Anniversary. An anthology of recent verse, with contributions from Lawrence Durrell.
9.12.56.	TP	New Poetry. Introduced by G. S. Fraser. *Selected Poems* by Lawrence Durrell.
3.3.57.	HS	Talking of Books. Arthur Calder-Marshall talks about the influence of the Mediterranean scene on some contemporary writers. He refers especially to Lawrence Durrell's *Justine*.
25.3.57.	TP	*Sappho*. Adapted and produced by Terence Tiller. Incidental music by Anthony Smith-Masters. Jill Balcon in title role.
23.4.57.	TP	The Heraldic Universe. *Justine* reviewed by Christopher Middleton.
4.5.57. (repeated 7.5.57.)	TP	Recent Novels. A discussion on *Justine* by Frank Kermode, Christopher Salmon and Angus Wilson.
30.11.57.	Net. 3	The World of Books. Introduced by Robin Holmes. Quotation: Extract from *Espirit de Corps* read by Norman Shelley.

Date	Service	Programme
.12.57.	TP	Poems by Seferis. Read in Greek and English by Elsa Verghis and Alan Wheatley. Translated by Lawrence Durrell and others.
28.12.57.	HS	The Ghost Train. An episode from *Esprit de Corps* read by Norman Shelley.
7.6.58.	Net. 3	The World of Books. Library List: Paul Ferris comments on some recently published books [*Balthazar*].
26.10.58. (repeated 30.10.58.)	HS	The Critics. Book: *Mountolive* reviewed by Elspeth Huxley.
21.12.58.	TP	Work in Progress. John Bowen talks about *Mountolive* and its place in the group of novels on which Lawrence Durrell is now working.
4.2.60.	TP	Comment. *Clea*.
6.2.60.	HS	The World of Books. Introduced by Robin Holmes. *Clea*.
19.4.60.	TP	Into the Forties. A literary miscellany. Compiled and introduced by John Lehmann. 'This Unimportant Morning'.
14.5.60.	HS	The World of Books. Introduced by Robin Holmes. *The Collected Poems of Lawrence Durrell*. 'Bitter Lemons' (poem).
23.7.60.	HS	The World of Books. William Sansom talks on a subject chosen by himself [*The Best of Henry Miller*].
21.3.61.	Net. 3	Talking of Films. Alexandria on Film. Lawrence Durrell, who is working on the script of Cleopatra, talks with Peter Duval Smith.
30.6.62.	HS	The World of Books. Introduced by Michael Vowden. Penguin Modern Poets, Vol. I (including John Heath-Stubbs), reviewed by Lawrence Durrell.
24.8.62.	HS	Readings on Record. Introduced by J.

Date	Service	Programme
		W. Lambert. 'Ballad of the Oedipus Complex' and 'La Rochefoucauld' read by Lawrence Durrell.
8.10.62.	TP	Discussion: Henry Miller and Lawrence Durrell discuss their writing with D. G. Bridson. A conversation recorded at Edinburgh during the Writers' Conference, August 1962.
21.1.63.	TP	Conversations with Lawrence Durrell, recorded in France by D. G. Bridson. (First of two programmes.) The subjects covered in this conversation include Lawrence Durrell's poetry, his books on Corfu, Rhodes, Cyprus and Alexandria, and his preference for life near the Mediterranean.
27.1.63.	TP	Conversations with Lawrence Durrell, recorded in France by D. G. Bridson. (Second of two programmes.) The subject of this conversation is mainly *The Alexandria Quartet*. The author explains the form of the work and his theories of construction.
29.1.63.	TP	Lawrence Durrell reading a selection of his own poetry. Introduced by D. G. Bridson.
5.2.63.	TP	Personal Anthology. Lawrence Durrell introduces and discusses poems of his own choice.
20.2.63.	TP	Extended version of Writers' Conference programme broadcast on 8.10.62.
16.9.63.	HS	For Schools: Prose and Verse. 'Night Fishing' from *Prospero's Cell*.
20.1.65.	TP	Islands. An examination of some of those islands—real or imaginary, geographical or symbolic—which have caught the im-

agination of poets from Spenser to Durrell. Programme compiled and introduced
by Terence Tiller. 'Delos'.

B.B.C. TELEVISION APPEARANCES

15.9.59 To-Night.
14.2.60 Monitor. The poet and novelist filmed at his home
in the Camargue, talking about his Alexandrian
novels [to Huw Wheldon].
2.6.60 To-Night. British Diplomats abroad.
7.8.60 Monitor. Summer Film Festival. Selection from first
three years of Monitor. Interview.
24.2.61 To-Night. Script for Cleopatra.
8.3.61 Wednesday Magazine.
4.4.61 Insight. The final programme in this series of exploration into our new understanding of nature.
THE VISION OF OUR AGE. Dr. Bronowski
discusses the characteristic expression of Insight and
Imagination in the twentieth century with Abdus
Salam, Eduardo Paolozzi, Eero Saarinen and Lawrence Durrell.
11.6.61 Book Stand. Alexandria Quartet.
22.8.61 To-Night.
19.10.65 Intimations. Interview with Malcolm Muggeridge.
Produced by Margaret McCall.
27.10.66 MIDDAY DIALOGUE. Lawrence Durrell in his
home in Provence comments on his own poetry and
engages in random reflections. Durrell's poetry read
by Marius Goring. Produced by Margaret McCall.

FRENCH RADIO

1.2.59 Etranger Mon Ami. By Dominique Arban. Paris.
5.5.62 Interview (About a session of signature) Montpellier-Languedoc.
5.12.59 Interview. Montpellier-Languedoc.

10.12.63   Un Corbeau de Toutes Couleurs. Play from novel by
           Claude Seignolle. Foreword by Durrell. Montpellier-
           Languedoc.
11.2.66   Roy Campbell et la Provence. Contribution by
           Durrell. Marseille-Provence.

FRENCH TELEVISION

31.1.64   Chez Lawrence Durrell. Script by F.–J. Temple.
           Radio-Télévision Française, Ière chaine.

C.B.S. TELEVISION

Colour Film, 'The Search for Ulysses'. Commentary.
A colour film of Durrell showing Sophia Loren
around places of interest in Israel was made for
American television. '*I acted her off her pretty little feet.*'

FILM

Durrell was commissioned to write a short story, on an Israeli
theme, as the basis of a film for Sophia Loren. The script itself
was arranged and expanded by other hands.

Durrell comments: '*. . . my first version did not please Miss Loren.
She was scared of playing an atomic physicist because she said, with endearing frankness, that nobody would ever believe in her as an intelligent
woman; she was a* fille du peuple *and had learned not to try and
operate outside her own natural limits, her* gamme. *I found her so worthy
of respect that I tore up the version and did another on the spot. In order to
please I accepted many ideas of which I did not approve from her literary
adviser and from Unger, the producer. . . . I haven't seen the result yet,
probably never will. I would have liked it to be good for Miss Loren's sake,
but film is film, and the wise man takes his money and runs for it; which
is what I did. No, I don't intend to publish in book form. Faulkner never
published his movie scripts, why should I?*'

See Section F. under Woman's Own.

INDEX

(The Bibliography is not included)

251